Keshav

Ancient Wisdom for Focused Living

Vinay Sutaria

Copyright © 2021 Vinay Sutaria

Vinay Sutaria has asserted his right under the Copyright, Design and Patents Act 1988 to be identified as the author of this work.

No part of this book may be reproduced by any mechanical, photographic or electronic process, or in the form of a phonographic recording; nor may it be stored in a retrieval system, transmitted or otherwise be copied for public or private use, other than for 'fair use' as brief quotations embodied in articles and reviews, without prior written permission of the publisher.

Every effort has been made to obtain the necessary permissions with reference to copyright material, both illustrative and quoted. We apologise for any omissions in this respect and will be pleased to make the appropriate acknowledgements in any future edition.

The information given in this book should not be used as a substitute for professional medical advice; you should always consult a medical practitioner. Any use of the information in this book is at the reader's discretion and risk. Neither the author nor the publisher can be held responsible for any loss, claim or damage arising out of the use, or misuse, of the suggestions made, the failure to seek medical advice or for any material on third-party websites.

Making or distributing electronic copies of this book constitutes copyright infringement and could subject the infringer to criminal and civil liability.

Cover design by Prime Graphics

All rights reserved.

First Edition: December 2021

A CIP catalogue record for this title is available from the British Library

Hardback ISBN: 978-1-8381985-6-5
Paperback ISBN: 978-1-8381985-7-2
eBook ISBN: 978-1-8381985-9-6

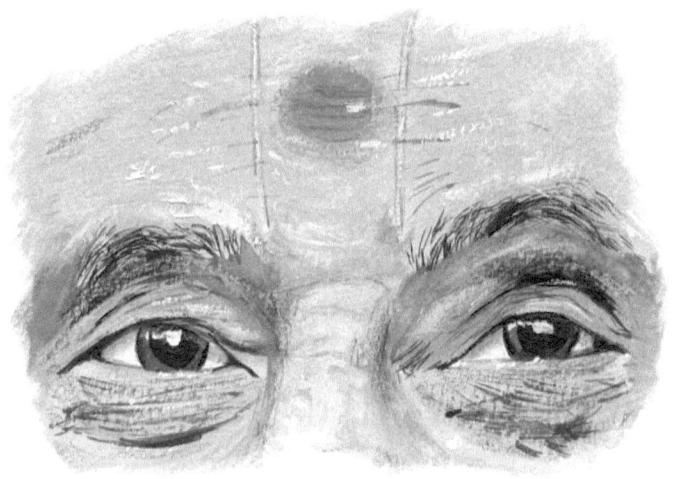

To my beloved, Pramukh Swami Maharaj,
the embodiment of transcendental bliss and joy,
on the occasion of his centennial birth celebrations.

ब्रह्मविद् आप्नोति परम्

Brahmavidāpnoti Param
One who knows Brahman, attains Parabrahman.
Taittiriya Upanishad 2.1

ब्रह्म वेद ब्रह्मैव भवति

Brahma Veda Brahmaiva Bhavati
One knows Brahman becomes like Brahman.
Mundaka Upanishad 3.2.9

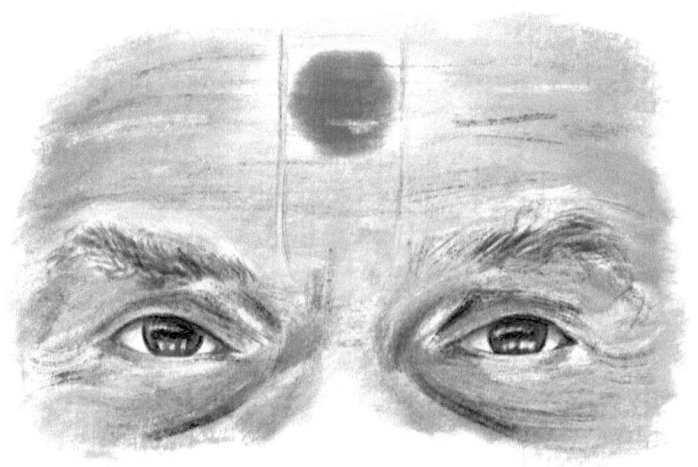

**To my guru, Mahant Swami Maharaj
for the constant inspiration, love and guidance
that he gives, gives and continues to give.**

त्वद्दासदासदासानां दासानां दासकिङ्करः ।
एवं विलसतां नित्यं दासत्ववैभवो मयि ॥

Tvad-dās-dās-dāsānām Dāsānām Dāsakim-karaha
Evam-vilasatām Nityām Dāsatva-vaibhavo Mayi

*I am the servant of your servant, five times over.
May such wealth of humility forever embellish me.*

योऽन्तःप्रविश्य मम वाचमिमां प्रसुप्तां
संजीवयत्यखिलशक्तिधरः स्वधाम्ना ।
अन्यांश्च हस्तचरणश्रवणत्वगादीन्
प्राणान् नमो भगवते पुरुषाय तुभ्यम् ॥

Yo'ntah pravishya mama vācham-imām prasuptām
Sanjīvayaty-akhila-shakti-dharah sva-dhāmnā
Anyānscha hasta-charana-shravana-tvag-ādin
Prānān namo bhagavate purushāya tubhyam

*I bow to Purushottam Nārāyan [the supreme being],
possessor of all powers, who, having entered my being,
has activated my dormant speech, and likewise empowered
the other organs such as the hands, feet, ears, skin
and all the vital forces, by virtue of his mere presence.*

Dhruvji's Prayer
Bhāgavata-Purāna 4.9.6

CONTENTS

Preface 3

The Mithila Matrix 9

The Kingdom of the Soul 13

Sarangpur 19

PART 1: BODY

Body 23

Exiting the Matrix 25

Prāna - The Life Force 31

Architecting the Kingdom 39

PART 2: MIND

Mind 67

The Commander and His Monkey 69

Ego: It's All About Me 81

Desire: The Source of Suffering 113

Anger: A Brief Insanity 135

The Fault of Fault-Finding 139

The Mind Games 143

The Modern Battles 157

Training the Monkey Mind 167

PART 3: SOUL

Soul 189

Hail The King 191

The Art of Dharma 193

The Art of Knowledge 209

The Art of Detachment 229

The Art of Bhakti 235

The Art of Ruling 247

Flourishing the Kingdom 279

A Final Message 283

Notes on Text and Translation

To accommodate for a wider audience I have tried to be reader-friendly in rendering Sanskrit and other non-English words into English. Traditionally, diacritical marks are used to distinguish between long and short vowels. I have tried to avoid this for the most part.

Sanskrit also employs three forms of 's' and in the interest of simplicity I have reduced them simply to 'sh' or 's'. Thus, I have rendered, for example, 'Kṛṣṅa' into 'Krishna'. I have not dropped the final short 'a' of Sanskrit as modern Indian languages tend to. For example, 'dharma' remains 'dharma' and not 'dharam'. The only exception to this is in names of individuals and key texts. For example, 'Arjuna' has become 'Arjun', and, 'Mahabharata' becomes 'Mahabharat'. Throughout the text, the diacritic 'ā', to indicate the long 'a' (as in c*a*r), has been used for better understanding of the words.

For uniformity, some non-English words have been standardised or simplified throughout the text. I have chosen not to italicise non-English words or titles of key sources. The sheer number of references would have made for cumbersome reading. For non-English names of people and places, I have used the common Anglicised spelling.

Preface

Screaming men and women were pulled out onto the streets to be publicly humiliated. Men with cut hair and shaved beards were paraded with their trousers cut off and signs hanging from their necks. They were made to drink dangerous quantities of castor oil. They were ordered to carry out pointless tasks, such as carrying mattresses back and forth, as well as the endless building and rebuilding of walls.

In Vienna, gangs of Jews, with jeering storm troopers standing over them, were forced onto their hands and knees to scrub anti-Nazi signs off the pavements. All sorts of reports of Nazi sadism were being seen. Jewish men *and* women were made to clean latrines. Hundreds of them were just picked at random off the streets to clean the toilets of the Nazi boys.

In occupied Eastern Europe, a seemingly joyful and musical crowd, watched as a group of Jews were forced to clean horse manure off a garage floor, all whilst being brutally beaten with rifles and crowbars. High-pressure hoses were forced into their mouths until their stomachs burst. When they were all dead, a second group of Jews were instructed to clean away the blood and bodies left over.

This is but a mere glimpse of Nazi Germany in the late 1930s. There seems to be a deep message in these nightmares. Do they tell us something real about who we truly are? How could such a cultured and brilliant people, like that of Germany, have voted a violent tyrant to be their leader? And then cheered him on hysterically, in squares crammed with thousands, as if he were a living god? By the end of this book, I hope you get the answer.

If you picked this book thinking that it will be another positive self-help book filled with tips and tricks to make you feel good, I apologise, but, you're in the wrong place. Over the past few years, I've read countless self-help books and I can tell you for sure, I have nothing new to add to the genre. If I'm being completely honest with you, I have come to a point where I end up shelving those books after reading the introductions because all the content sounds the same to me. So, yeah, we're turning the tables on that.

Two thousand years ago, Aristotle proposed that the pursuit of happiness was at the pinnacle of human desire. Two thousand years before him, the Bhāgavata-Purāṇa proposed that whatever one sets out do, in the end, all actions are for the sake of one's own happiness. Has anything really changed today? Are we really a selfish species that focuses on individual, self-entered happiness?

For at least 5,000 years, and probably much longer according to Vedic belief, people have been asking themselves what it means to live the 'focused life', or as some may simply call it the 'good life'. Five thousand years on, here we are, and still, we are searching for happiness. Deep down, to some extent, we are all dissatisfied. Let's put aside the fact that you may be good, spiritual, religious, noble, or moral. I'm guessing you wouldn't be reading this book unless you were carrying around a seed of unhappiness that doesn't seem to go away no matter what you do.

You may have read numerous self-help books, watched countless motivational videos on improving yourself, or even physically attended seminars to give you a boost of well-being, yet you keep seeing yourself going round on an endless loop. And, of course you would, because as great and wonderful as all this positivity may feel or sound, it is fleeting, and we know that this form of extrinsic motivation doesn't stick for long.

The astrophysicist and author Neil deGrasse Tyson once said, "It's easier to be told by others what to think and believe than it is to think for yourself." Well, I'm not here to tell you what to think. I am simply here to share with you lessons that have helped me, and that I hope can help you too. This is not just some personal development or self-help book, nor is it a manual or step-by-step guide to seeking happiness. Those books are located in the self-help category of Amazon or your nearest bookstore. Once you've bought one, read and done everything it prescribes, and you still find yourself feeling unsatisfied, come back here to understand why.

My own journey through the vast world of philosophy and psychology began with my own search for explanation and meaning. Having read scriptures and texts of my own faith and spiritual background, I sought affirmation, direction, confirmation, clarity, and insights into these beliefs, as well as those of others. I struggled initially. I really wanted to know why life seemed so easy for everyone else around me, yet so difficult for me.

Through this book, I aim to explore and unravel a puzzle that many thinkers and philosophers have pondered over for at least the last five millennia. I use their ideas (and some of mine too) to explain why we seem to know so little about our own self – our body, mind and soul. I weave together wisdom from ancient texts; facts, figures, and studies from psychology, sociology and neuroscience; philosophy and behavioural economics, and much more. I hope that this book serves its purpose in changing the way you think about the three layers to your being. Writing a book is of course rewarding, but reading a book is a commitment of time and money, and so I thank you for that. I've written this book in hope that I interest you to dive deeper into your own journey. I assure you that you don't need a degree in psychology or philosophy to understand or appreciate the content here. Nor do you need a library full of dusty, old books. All I ask of you is your willingness to try – your willingness to understand.

Over time, I have become convinced that there are certain individuals who have walked this earth, or are walking among us today, that have learnt how to truly live the focused life. As you read on, you may be able to attribute certain qualities to these types of individuals. For me, I found this in my gurus, Pramukh Swami Maharaj and Mahant Swami Maharaj, whose lives are the highest embodiment of fulfilment and wisdom. I have never witnessed this in anyone before. Superficially, anyone can say that they are blissful and at peace, but when situations crop up in life, our true nature oozes out. Yet, they are able to remain at their elevated states. I have included excerpts, teachings, and insights from their lives in this book too. I understand to some this may seem a bit biased, so I urge you to keep an open mind whilst you read. It's about experience over theory.

Each and every human on this planet has the sole objective in life to grow. Whether that is physically, socially, or spiritually. We all want to grow, but we struggle. We are trapped by the illusions of our own minds. In the end, it is not the obstacles that we face that we master, but ourselves.

How to Read This Book

If you are reading this book for the first time, I urge you to read it cover to cover. Most of the ideas shared in this book will be better understood if read in order. Once you have read the book in this way, feel free to delve into any section of your choice. I am certain that this reading experience will make you think and feel different. It will introduce you to ancient wisdom, scientific research and novel ideas – at times certain feelings and thoughts may arise which may be difficult to comprehend. If you find this to be the case, or, if you find the reading too challenging – stop. Put the book down for an hour or a few days. It'll be right there when you're ready to carry on.

Throughout the book, I may often switch between 'I' and 'we'. Although this may seem annoying, I have done so deliberately. The Vedic tradition teaches one to expand above 'I' to see 'I' in everything, thus becoming 'we'.

Please don't distribute this book as a free copy to anyone (unless gifted), as this taints the purpose of the book. This book is nominally priced and by encouraging others to purchase this book, they will be giving to a worthwhile cause.

I have tried my best to make this book, and the ideas within, as simple and straightforward as possible. The thoughts and ideas presented are clear. Self-help jargon or sugar-coated wisdom won't be spoon-fed to you. Some thoughts and ideas are left open-ended, leaving you to deal with some ambiguity and interpretation. Be prepared to think. Please keep an open mind. I hope that through this book, certain thoughts, feelings, reason and emotion that I feel are also evoked within you. Specific ideas and concepts may be repeated and emphasised more than once, and you might begin to wonder why this is the case. This too is done deliberately to reaffirm key ideas that are fundamental to understanding ourselves. Plenty of research supports the fact that the repetition of thoughts and ideas leads to neural patterns being formed within our brains, regardless of age.

As tempting as it may be, I request you to resist the urge to fly through the material. Allow yourself time to ponder, understand, and implement the concepts and ideas shared. It is by taking control of the things that control our behaviours that we create lasting change. We modify inputs to improve outputs. I am certain that even by reading and applying even one section will benefit those willing to practice. Be patient with yourself and me. Sustained growth requires patience and persistence. Take your time and enjoy the process, even when it seems demanding. Feel free to highlight, underline, and make notes wherever you want. This, to me, is a sign of a good reader.

The book is divided into three main parts, with further chapters and sections within them. Something I've personally started to outgrow, and that I'm no longer a fan of in books is when I see loads of references of where authors have heard or read something that they've decided to include as footnotes. I feel this often makes it difficult to read, and although I have done this myself in previous work, I now understand how distracting it can get. Whilst I will occasionally reference individuals throughout the text, the bulk of the credits and references have been included at the back of the book, along with a list of books and resources that I've consumed over the past few years. You can always go back and read these to dig deeper into any topic that we discuss here.

If any thoughts and ideas from this book resonate with you (or if you just generally wish to share your experiences and favourite parts), feel free to do so. Post pictures, stories and videos of your favourite pages, quotes, sections and experiences using the #**VinaySutaria** or #**TheKeshavWay**. This way I will also be able to see them and I would love to feature them on my social media pages.

I would like to apologise in advance for every instance in this book where you may feel offended. That was never my intention, but I understand that some of the things I believe, as well as how I see them, may not resonate with everybody. There are no ghost writers that have helped me. There is no one telling me what I should and shouldn't write. These are my views and my words alone. I also apologise in advance for the male-dominated 'subject' of some of the quotations and examples used in the book. This is merely indicative of the period in which they were written or spoken, and are not a reflection of any beliefs, intended target market, or any other underlying motive.

It's also worth noting a potential downside of the way that I communicate. I tend to bounce around from one place to another, linking thoughts and ideas as I go along. Whilst I've tried my best to limit jumping around, it's inevitable that it'll happen. Ideas when repeated can be reaffirmed. The only way to think properly is to force our minds to articulate our thoughts through the spoken or written word. I encourage you to make as many notes as possible – in the margins, in your notebooks, post-it notes, wherever – I promise I won't be offended by you doing this.

My knowledge may be broad, but it is also shallow. Most of the ideas covered in this book are also well documented in a wide range of books, academic papers, studies and periodicals which were some of the primary sources of my research. Most ideas are relatively uncontroversial. I do not declare that I am free of biases and afflictions, and I am certainly not immune to making mistakes in my writing. If any errors of fact are noted, or if any new findings supersede claims made in the book, I would be grateful to be notified via my social media or my website, vinaysutaria.com, so that future editions of this book can be corrected and updated.

Whatever advice you take away from here is all thanks to my gurus, authors and the teachers I have studied and learnt from. If any ideas or concepts relayed here go uncredited, it was never my intention to do so, but rather these ideas are integral in my thinking and ideology. I do not claim to know it all; I simply want to share with you what I have found in hope that it helps you too.

Peace, happiness, and freedom are not things to be sought in some distant land or reserved for the afterlife, for they exist within you – at this very moment – in fact, at every breath and step you take. I wrote this book with one fundamental question in mind: If the ancient philosophers and thinkers had taken it upon themselves to write a guidebook for twenty-first-century individuals, a book that would tell us how to live a focused life, what might that book have looked like? The pages that follow are my answer to this question.

Whilst recalling the prayer of Dhruvji, I truly hope you enjoy this book. May you discover and connect to Keshav.

With deepest gratitude and prayers.

Vinay Sutaria
16 November 2021
Sarangpur, India

The Mithila Matrix

In Vedic times, there lived a lineage of kings who ruled over the ancient region known as Mithila (also known as Videha). It is located in the Eastern part of the South-Asian Peninsula. In the royal tradition at the time, the entire lineage of kings were known as Janak, which literally means 'father'.

One such King Janak was known to hold regular assemblies of scholars and philosophers to discuss spiritual and philosophical topics. He had a deep desire within his heart to discern the real from the unreal. In Hinduism, this notion is known as vivek (discretion).

After a long day filled with discussions and lavish meals, Janak retired to bed. Half way through the night he awoke to the sound of horns and the beatings of drum. His attendants ran into the room shouting, "Your majesty! The kingdom of Mithila is under attack!"

Janak shot up, put on his battle attire, prepared his horse and weapons, and rode into battle under the night sky. He was captured by the invaders, forced to surrender his kingdom and go into exile in order to protect the people of his kingdom. He obliged, walking away with nothing left to his name. He felt humiliated and weak, travelling around and begging food from one and all. Everyone rejected him. No one wanted anything to do with a begging man. Ravaging with hunger, he eventually came to a shelter which provided food for the poor. When it was his turn to get something to satisfy his hunger, there were only a few scraps of food left. He accepted it. He couldn't go another day without food. Just as he was about to put a morsel of food into his mouth, it was knocked out of his hands into a small hole. He cried in agony at his own condition. Then he woke up. Janak looked around and saw himself on his bed, in his chambers, within his palace. The lanterns were burning and the crickets were chirping.

"Is *this* real or was *that* real?" He muttered to himself.

Awoken by the noise from his quarters, his attendants ran into his room and asked the king what had just happened. "Is this real or was that real?" Janak asked his attendants. His guards were confused as to what their king was talking about. From that day on, whoever he met or spoke to, he asked one question: Is this real or was that real?

He asked this same question to his queens, his ministers, and the scholars and philosophers of his kingdom. Word quickly spread throughout the kingdom that the king had gone mad. One young scholar named Ashtavakra came to hear about this, and he made his way towards the palace. Ashtavakra literally means 'eight bends', and described him perfectly. He suffered deformities from birth, resulting in physical handicaps. Despite being one of the youngest scholars in the kingdom, he was wise, and so Janak often confided in him and saw him as a teacher.

"King Janak! I shall answer your question" Ashtavakra said staring Janak straight in the eyes, "If *this* is real, then *that* was real. If *that* was real, then *this* is real. If *this* is false, then *that* was false. But you should know Janak, if *that* is false, then *this* is false too."

Ashtavakra didn't need any context. He very well knew what Janak was talking about. "Janak, look around you. Here, you are surrounded by jewels, luxuries, women, wealth, comfort and respect. Tell me, did any of this exist in your dreams?"

Janak, confused, shook his head.

"What you experienced in your dream, is any of that currently present?"

"No, it isn't," responded Janak.

"Janak, no objects or feelings are real, whether they be in your dream state or woken state. One dream finishes when your eyes open, and the other dream ends when your eyes close."

"If it is all false, should I to believe that nothing is real?" Janak asked curiously.

Ashtavakra smiled and then revealed, "The experience itself is not real, but *you* experienced it. You are the common unchanging element in both states. *You are real*. You are on a level deeper than the physical and subtle bodies. You are the ātmā."

Janak soon grasped the fundamental meaning to human existence.

He ignored the false credo that 'ignorance is bliss' (in this context). Janak realised the path to the focused life. Alexander the Great was enveloped by this very ignorance. Howard Hughes, Napoleon, Stalin, and Hitler too. The list can go on. Probably all of us are affected by this ignorance to some greater or lesser extent. When we fail to adopt vivek in our lives, we fall prey to ignorance in all of its deceptive forms.

In a world enveloped by ignorance, we are immersed deep within that very ignorance that we fail to realise the discretion between pleasure and pain, joy and sorrow, failure and success. Along with many other truths of life, Janak realised this, and that was what set him free.

This book is a small attempt at unveilling the ignorance that stops us from distinguishing between the truth and untruth. I am not some elevated individual who has reached the highest truth and wishes to reveal it to you. I am very much on the same path as you. But I can say that I have personally witnessed those who live the truth. I have interacted with those who have risen above the ignorance that surrounds us all – living in an elevated state of joy and peace – living the ultimate focused life. We will be exploring three domains: the body (the physical), the mind (the mental), and the soul (the spiritual).

No one will tell you this stuff because most people don't benefit from doing so. But I aim to share some with you, unconventional truths that afflict our minds and show you practical, ancient and scientifically-supported ways to enable you to live a more focused life. Experience is more important than theory.

In my previous book I wrote about happiness in a very broad sense. In which I sometimes referred to happiness as a mood that fluctuates in our daily lives and at other times I referred to the state of bliss and fulfilment. In this book, when we discuss happiness, it's about an internal state – a feeling of peace and fulfilment. It follows that, happiness isn't merely a fleeting mood, but a state of being. You can be amidst the turmoils of modern life and still remain fulfilled. You can be frustrated (a fleeting mood), yet still be happy (content from within).

Socrates admonished one to know thyself. To know oneself is to know one's body, mind, and soul. This book takes you on the first steps to doing just that. It aims to map out a path that everyone, of any background, can follow, offering a framework at a level that even a newcomer into the world of spirituality and philosophy may grasp. So, now that Janak has woken up and seen his kingdom, it's time for us to see ours.

The Kingdom of the Soul

The Monkey, the Tesla, and the Passenger. You may have heard of this analogy before. The Monkey is your mind, the Tesla is your body, and the Passenger is your true self. Well, this *was* the analogy I originally came up with to describe who we are as individuals. I'd like to revamp this whole analogy now. In his primary teachings collated in the Vachanāmrut, Bhagwan Shri Swaminarayan (referred to simply as 'Swaminarayan' hereafter) uses a unique metaphor to describe who we are[1]. We'll call this metaphor, 'The Kingdom of the Soul'.

Janak had a kingdom. It's obvious, he was a king. You too, are a king. You too, have a kingdom. You probably think I've lost it, but for a moment try to visualise this. There's a kingdom and that's your body. How beautiful and well-maintained that kingdom remains, is down to the king himself and the subjects. You are the king. When I say 'you' I specifically mean your true self. In Vedic teachings, the true self is denoted by many terms such as, ātmā, jiva, jivātmā, etc.

I am normally not fond of translating Sanskrit words into English equivalents due to the loss of it's original sentiment, but we can loosely translate the word to mean the soul. Throughout our journey, we will use the word 'jiva', 'ātmā', and 'jivātmā' interchangeably. You are not the body – the kingdom isn't you. You live within the kingdom. And as for the subjects... well that's where it starts to get a bit tricky. Nevertheless, we cannot forget them. The subjects of the kingdom are the forms of ignorance.

The People

The king's commander is the mind. The subjects are the senses. Normally, the mind is seen as a whole, but in Swaminarayan's teachings, rooted in Vedic philosophy, it is understood broadly to be made up of four inner faculties, each carrying out a different function.

What we normally refer to as the mind, is known as manas (pronounced 'mun'), which is 'basic awareness'. It's what we use to think and feel. Then there is buddhi, or 'intellect', whose job is to determine, analyse, judge, and reason. At a more subtle level is the chitta. This is the equivalent of the 'subconscious', or, the 'memory bank'. The chitta also has the job of contemplating. At the most subtle level, we have ahamkāra, literally meaning 'I-maker'. When we refer to the word ahamkāra in this context, it doesn't mean the general Hindi equivalent of the ego. This ahamkāra affirms identity – it gives us a sense of existence and individuality. Simply put, manas, buddhi, chitta and ahamkara, are that by which a person can think and feel, reason, contemplate and affirm identity, respectively. These four make up what we call the antahkarana, or the 'inner faculties', which describe the Vedic mind as a whole. In general, they are all collectively referred to as the manas, or mind, which is one but functions in the four different ways. For ease of reading, we will refer to the antahkarana as 'mind', unless we are specifically discussing an individual function of it. The mind (or its four faculties) can be seen as the ministers of the kingdom.

The senses are that through which we 'know' and perform actions. They are known as the indriyas and there are ten of them in total. We can understand these as groups of five. Firstly, we have the five gnān-indriyas (cognitive senses) – sight, hearing, touch, taste and smell. These should not be confused with their corresponding sense organs, but instead should be understood as that which allows the sense organs to function, i.e. sight allows the eyes to see, hearing allows the ears to hear, etc. The other five indriyas are known as the karma-indriyas (action senses) – speech, dexterity, locomotion, excretion and generation (or reproduction). These too, are not physical organs but they operate through their respective external organs, i.e. the mouth, hands, feet, anus and genitals. All ten of the indriyas can be collectively known as the 'ten senses', or simply, 'senses'.

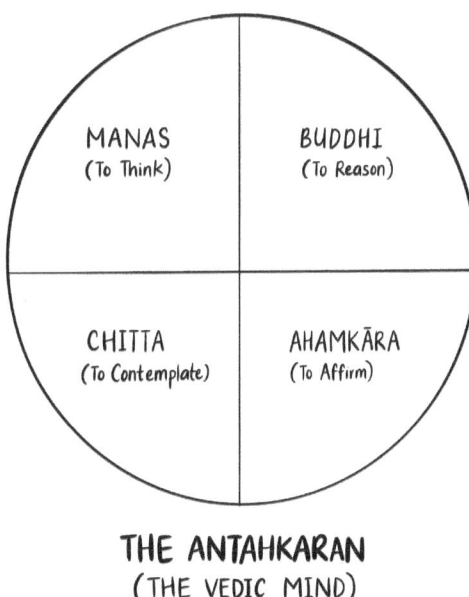

THE ANTAHKARAN
(THE VEDIC MIND)

This analogy, as well as the description of the human mind as a whole, is shared by Swaminarayan in his teachings. I think this is the perfect starting point for us to delve deeper into our being, as we begin to understand who we truly are, and how we can live a focused life.

The Kingdom

Swaminarayan refers to the three bodies doctrine.[2] This is that, there are three layers to our bodies. To make this easier to understand, and to put it into the context of our kingdom, I share with you another metaphor.

First is the 'gross (sthul) body' composed of the five material elements, i.e. earth, water, light, air and space. This is the body that we see physically, and it is what supports the senses, mind, etc. of the next body. Understand this physical body to be the kingdom that is seen by all. Second is the 'subtle (sukshma) body', sometimes also referred to as the 'astral/mental body'. The ten senses and the mind (comprising of the four inner faculties) that we just explored, along with the functioning of the senses through sound, touch, sight, taste, and smell, form this body. This can be understood as the palace. Along with the king, the ministers and certain subjects reside within the palace. Their job is to ensure the functioning of the kingdom, and the maintenance of the palace. The third body is the most important and unique. It is known as the 'causal (kāran) body' which, according to Vedic theology, stores the karmas of every life and is also the very root of ignorance that causes the jiva to remain in the cycle of rebirth. Understand this to be the garden of the palace. The king is immensely attached to this garden hence, the reason it is the hardest to break through.

The three bodies should be understood as mere instruments for the jiva (the king) but, it is the misidentification with these three bodies (or their components, such as the mind and senses) that are the cause of ignorance. It's important that we distinguish the king from the kingdom and subjects. That is, to distinguish the jiva from the body, mind and senses. How would it sound if I told you that the king was being thrown around by his subjects? That is exactly what is happening within your kingdom (and mine too). The jiva has seemingly lost its true inherent power. It has been enveloped by ignorance, failing to realise its own individuality and nature.

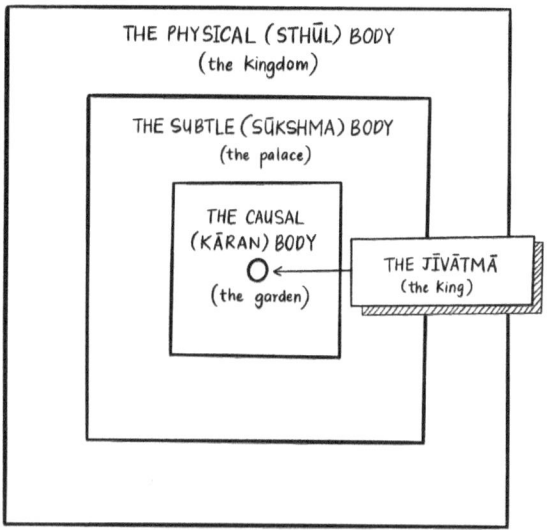

THE THREE BODIES

THE KINGDOM OF THE SOUL

The Art of Ruling

We want the king to be free to rule his kingdom and subjects properly. This is in fact what we all seek. During our rule of this kingdom, most of us will encounter hardship and difficulty, many of us will be plagued by physical and emotional pain, stress, sadness, loneliness, and anxiety. While we often equate these problems as a by-product of the demands of modern life, human life has always been difficult and the same challenges have been faced for centuries.

Most kings want their kingdom to prosper, so that the king can be at peace. The Hindus calls this state samatvam, or, stithpragna – 'evenness' and 'equilibrium'. The Greeks, *euthymia* and *hesychia*. The Christians call it *aequanimitas*. I simply like to call it, Keshav.

We all wants good physical and mental health. We want wisdom, understanding, peace, and freedom. The problem lies in our means of pursuing these basic human needs. We're treading the wrong roads. It's almost as though we're being pulled by the different, and often competing, demands of human life. The state of Keshav itself personifies not being battered by the dualities of life, its ups and downs, its pleasures and its suffering. It implies equanimity, and ultimately, the serene, inner peace that is at the core of one's true being.

The aim of this book is to provide an essential backdrop to the kingdom, the people, and the king, that is the body, the mind, and the soul, respectively. We will explore each of these areas in turn, beginning at the outermost layer, the body.

Everyday we wake up and see ourselves in the mirror, but who is really staring back at us? What about all the people we see when we walk down the street? What about the friends and family that we interact with on a daily basis? What is the significance of us inheriting this kingdom, and how must we nurture it so that we don't treat it as a mere commodity?

We will understand the working of our mind and its components. Why are the subjects of our kingdom so unruly? Why is it that sometimes the people of the kingdom are good, and at other times they seem to run wild? Are humans selfish by nature? Why do we favour those close to us, and shun those who do not agree with our views and opinions? What is the root cause of all misery, and then, what is the solution to this misery?

Finally, we will meet the king – the true ruler of this kingdom and its subjects – the eternal ātmā. Is there really an eternal entity within us? How do we unlock and experience the inherent happiness associated with, and stemming from, the ātmā? Take a deep breath and hold tight, there are going to be many bumps along the road in this journey. But, if you're ready, let's begin.

Sarangpur

Sat, Aug 13 2016, 6:15 PM

Bapa has reverted to Akshardham at around 6pm.

On 13 August 2016, at around 6.15 p.m. IST, everyone's phones started firing up. No one expected this day to come soon. Pramukh Swami Maharaj had renounced his mortal body. He had been suffering from a chest infection for the past week, from which he was gradually recovering, but this… this was unexpected. The one who gave his all to the world had left this world in a silent, yet divine way. Hundreds and thousands flocked to the small and serene village of Sarangpur to catch one last glimpse of this magnificent personality, who had influenced the lives of millions – old and young, rich and poor, urban-dwellers and villagers. He was a guru, a father, and a brother to one and all.

It is only right that I begin with remembering those to whom I owe everything. Pramukh Swami was the embodiment of bliss. A peaceful, humble, simple and spiritual personality. A rare soul who always lived for others, whilst constantly remaining focused on God. He was an advocate for world peace, and was revered as one of the most influential spiritual leaders of the world. Pramukh Swami lived by his maxim, 'In the joy of others, lies our own', and dedicated his life to selfless service for the spiritual and social uplift of society. For seven decades, he inspired countless individuals. He visited over 17,000 villages, towns and cities, for the betterment of humankind. In addition to the renowned Swaminarayan Akshardham complexes, he has gifted the world with over 1,100 mandirs. These mandirs and cultural complexes have become hallmarks in preserving Vedic culture and performing social services.

Pramukh Swami (1921-2016) was the fifth spiritual successor in Bhagwan Shri Swaminarayan's succession of Gunātit gurus, and he uplifted and inspired spirituality in the lives of millions of people. In his presence, the highest levels of bliss and peace were experienced, and today, many others continue to tread this path.

Before his passing, he appointed his successor – my current guru – Mahant Swami (b. 1933) to helm the worldwide socio-spiritual activities that he had put into fruition. Today, Mahant Swami presides as the spiritual guru to millions of individuals around the world. He serves as a constant inspiration and guide to living a pure life. Mahant Swami is the epitome of all virtues. A peaceful, humble, simple, and spiritual personality. A rare soul who lives and breathes among us, whilst always remaining focused on God.

On the seventeenth of August, the final rites of Pramukh Swami were conducted. It was a day that we all knew, at the back of our minds, would come, but one that we prayed we would never have to witness. Over the course of the past few days, millions had passed through this tiny village to catch one last glimpse of Pramukh Swami. Today, in that very same village with a mere population of 5,000, around 70,000 individuals had gathered for the final rites. Before his demise, Pramukh Swami had specified that when he passes, his final rites be conducted at such a spot, that even after his demise, he could constantly have the darshan of the murti[s] of God, and where he could be blessed with being in the vicinity of his guru's vision – forever. Who could say such a thing? Only one who had lived their entire life so purely could utter such words.

At around 5.11 p.m., Pramukh Swami was placed on the funeral pyre, comprising of neatly arranged logs and neem wood, as dignitaries and well-wishers shared their experiences with Pramukh Swami. Amidst Vedic chanting, at exactly 5.36 p.m., Mahant Swami lit the funeral pyre. With a loud and concurrent echo of 'Jay Swaminarayan!' (Hail Swaminarayan!), the entire village dropped to a complete silence. Tears filled the eyes of those physically present, as well as millions witnessing this event live on television across the globe. There was an eruption of cries from all corners of the assembly. The life and breath of Sarangpur had been snatched away. The life and breath of this millions across the world had been taken away. This is when it struck me that today, here I was breathing, and there he was not. I had only met Pramukh Swami a few times in my early years, and that too, for some short moments. Yet, the impact that he had on my life is unfathomable. Here I am trying to put words onto paper and I struggle to hold back my emotions.

> Two years had passed and I was in that very village of Sarangpur. It was a place that only seemed to be sprawling during festivals or special occasions, otherwise it was a silent and majestic village. It took me close to two years to realise that Pramukh Swami had not left us. He was here. He was there. In fact, he was everywhere. Why? Because, he was everything. Over time I have become convinced that both Pramukh Swami and Mahant Swami live every moment of their lives centred at the highest levels of bliss and serenity, that which I have never witnessed before.
> "Vinay?" Spoke the swami (ordained monk), "Are you even listening to what I am saying, or is your mind somewhere else?"
> I was daydreaming. I hadn't even caught a word of what he had just said. He had placed his hand on my shoulder and shook me, bringing me back into the moment. The clock had just struck midday, as the sun beamed down, filling every inch of this beautiful land with light.
> "I was telling you the story of King Janak. It seems like your body is here, but your mind is in a world of it's own!" He joked.
> "No, seriously. You're right. Sometimes it honestly feels like that." I replied.
> "Listen," he said, "Go and have your lunch now. We can talk in the afternoon. You're meeting Mahant Swami later, right?"
> I nodded with excitement. After a year apart, I was finally going to meet face-to-face with my guru once again.

The passing of Pramukh Swami had hit me like a ton of bricks. Although I believe, and have also experienced first-hand, that he truly was a divine being much incomprehensible to our minds, nevertheless, his demise was soul-shattering. I remember the first time I heard his voice. I can still remember how soothing it was; how calming it was. Today, there is silence. I remember his soft touch and loving pats on my head. Today, I cherish those moments. Pramukh Swami was home. Sarangpur became his home. It was the place that countless like me chose to return to over and over again. He made me who I am today. He showed me real, genuine love and compassion, despite me feeling I was unworthy of it. His love was unconditional and unmatched. Above all, he was beautiful, majestic and divine. He embodied bliss, and that's what kept me at his door. But this was it. This was the last time I would see Pramukh Swami's physical form. As the flames of the pyre soared into the sky, here we were, our physical bodies breathing and walking, and he was no more.

Pramukh Swami blessed the land of this earth with his divine presence for ninety-five years. You and I – we may not be here for that long, or we might be – we simply don't know. Hence, the premise of this book is not only how to live well, but how to die well too. The art of living is also the art of dying. When you live well, you can die well too. What happens when we close our eyes for the last time may seem like a mystery, but we are here now, that we know for sure. In order to live a focused life, our body, mind, and our soul must all be in harmony. That in itself is the experience of Keshav.

Keshav is beyond us, within us, and amidst us. Keshav isn't any one particular object, place, or person. In this journey, I want you to create your own Keshav. For some, it may be their inspiration – the source of all courage, hope and faith – in the form of a true guru, or, even God himself. For others, Keshav may be taken as a heightened state of bliss and tranquility – the state of stillness. One thing is certain, a part of you *is* Keshav. As we unravel this seemingly elusive mystery, I will leave it to you to decide what you want your Keshav to be – your true self, your God, your guru, the final state of stillness – you decide.

As the sun began to set, I felt the cool wind blow through the window. I put my pen down and closed my screen. I swiftly made my way down the staircase and through the courtyard towards the back quarters. There again, waiting at the door, I met the swami I had been conversing and learning from for the past two days.

"Are you ready?" He asked in his gentle voice.

I nodded. He smiled and slowly opened the door. The commotion around us on the campus seemed to stop. There was a subtle silence and coolness to that moment. As the door opened, there he was, seated with a letter in his hand, and a pen in his right. He looked up to me and smiled. I made my way in…

BODY

Exiting the Matrix

> **I see it now – this world is swiftly passing.**
> *Karna in the Mahabharat*

One day, you and everyone you love, will die. And probably beyond a small group of people for an extremely brief period of time, little of what you say or do will ever matter. Everything that you or I think or do is but an elaborate avoidance of this most profound truth. This fundamental truth hit me hardest when the most important person in my life passed. It made me realise that in this grand cosmic game, we are nothing. It's time to exit the matrix.

The Greatest Wonder

The Vana Parva (Book of the Forest) of the Mahābhārat shares a very insightful story into the true nature of death. Towards the end of their exile, the Pāndava brothers along with their mother Kunti and wife Drapaudi were on the outskirts of a dense forest. Their mother was thirsty. As there was no water within range, Arjun immediately climbed a tree and at a distance he saw a lake. Yudhishthir, the eldest of the brothers, instructed one of the twins, Nakul, to go and fetch some water from the lake. Upon approaching the crystal clear water, he went up to scoop some of the water but immediately he heard a voice: "Don't you dare take any water without answering my questions, otherwise you will meet your death!" Nakul ignored these words and went to scoop up the water. He fell unconscious there and then. When Nakul didn't return, Yudhishthir sent the other twin brother, Sahadev, who also met with the same fate without listening to the words. The same thing happened with Arjun and Bhim. Yudhishthir began to worry and went to investigate what was going on. He was shocked to see all his brothers unconscious on the banks of the lake. He began to cry and scream, for his brothers seemed dead to him. That is when a yaksha (celestial being) in the form of a crane approached Yudhishthir, who spoke: "I am a yaksha in the form of a crane, eating fish and water plants. Because of me, all of your brothers are dead. I asked them not to take any water from this lake without answering my questions. If you dare do the same, you will meet the same fate."

A question-answer dialogue commenced, with the yaksha asking Yudhishthir a total of 114 questions. At the end of answering all of the questions to the satisfaction of the yaksha, the brothers were revived and allowed to take the water. One such question asked was, "What is the greatest wonder of the world?" Yudhishthir could have easily spoken about the kingdom that they used to rule, or the kingdom of Hastinapur itself, but his answer was more profound. He said:

ahani ahani bhūtāni gacchantīha yamālayam
seshāh sthāvaram icchanti kim āscharyam atah param[1]

Although one sees hundreds and thousands
of beings dying at every moment before his very eyes,
he never for once seems to believe that
he too will meet the same fate and prepare accordingly.
What can be more astonishing than this?

This seems like nothing but the truth. When people come close to their end and death is staring them in the face, that is when they really open their eyes, and then regret begins to swamp their minds.

Whilst on his deathbed at the age of 88, the Italian sculptor, painter, architect and poet, Michelangelo said: "I regret that I have not done enough for the salvation of my soul." The same sort of regrets were shared by Alexander the Great, even after conquering half the world. King Solomon and Napoleon too. All successful and great in their own capacity, but they all died in misery. One died with regret, one after trying to commit suicide four times, and one was so close to telling his soldiers to take his life. Napoleon said: "I have not known six happy days in my life." Solomon declared: "I have seen all the things that are to be seen under the sun, all of them are meaningless, I have simply been chasing after wind."

So what is the point? Why does humankind chase thing after thing, seeking pleasure, gratification, fame, and success, if at the end it will all be of no use?

In her book *The Top Five Regrets of the Dying*, Bronnie Ware reveals that the most common and consistent regret her patients expressed was, "I wish I had the courage to live a life true to myself, not the life others expected of me." [2] Of all the things a dying person regrets about their life, this is it: living a life that is extrinsically motivated – a life dictated by social norms and those around you. This is the very reason death scares us. In fact, it terrifies us. And because of that, we avoid thinking about it, talking about it, sometimes even accepting it – even when it is happening to someone close to us. That is why confronting the reality of our own mortality is so important.

Going back to the characters we just talked about, Napoleon, just like Alexander, died a miserable death. He also said, "Men of great ambition have sought happiness and have found fame." What he means is that behind every goal is the drive to be happy and fulfilled. But, when egotism and our base nature take hold, we lose track of our goal and end up somewhere we never intended. And then, it hits us at the last moment, when it is probably too late. Even Aurangzeb said, "I came a stranger to this world and a stranger I depart."

Howard Hughes (despite his current reputation as some kind of ingenious rebel) was not a happy man – no matter how amazing and cool his life might seem from the movies or history books. When he was near death, one of his aides sought to reassure him during his suffering. "What an incredible life you have led!" The aide said to him. Hughes shook his head and replied with the sad, regretful, yet empathic honesty of someone close to their end, "If you had ever swapped places in life with me, I would be willing to bet that you would have demanded to swap back before the passing of the first week."[3]

Leonardo Da Vinci said, "As a well-spent day brings a happy sleep, so a well-employed life brings a happy death." We want to avoid what the business strategist Jim Collins calls the 'undisciplined pursuit of more'. For that very reason, we're going to limit our conversation about the pursuit of happiness in this book. Instead, we're going to talk about a disciplined lifestyle – a focused life. We're going to learn about synchronising the mind, body and soul – that is where true peace, freedom, and bliss lie. None of us are long for this world. Death hangs over us all – whether we notice it or not – whether we believe it or not. There's no escaping the tragedy of life, which is that we are all ageing from the day we are born. Our reluctancy to honestly examine the experience of ageing and dying has increased the harm we inflict on others and denied them the basic comforts they most need. There is always a final proximate cause that gets written down on the death certificate – respiratory failure, cardiac arrest, or something. But in truth, no single disease will lead you to your end; the culprit is just the accumulated crumbling of the bodily systems while medicine carries out its maintenance measures and patch jobs. We do not like thinking about this eventuality. As a result, most of us are unprepared for it. Nevertheless, history has shown us time and time again that as people become aware of the finitude of their life, they do not ask for much. They do not seek more riches. They do not seek more power. They seek stillness. They seek solitude. They seek freedom.

Medicine can only keep us going for so long. Death *is* an enemy, and it's one with superior forces. Eventually, it *will* win. The art of focused living is a skill. In fact, the art of life is a skill in itself. One that necessitates you to accept the fundamental truth of death. That is why, we must always begin with the end in mind.

Memento Mori

Reminding ourselves each day that we will die helps us treat our time as a gift. The Romans would remind themselves every day, 'memento mori', remember you are mortal. Marcus Antonius, the secret lover of Cleopatra, said, "All individual things pass away. Seek your liberation with diligence." This was around 2,000 years ago. Go back another 2,000 years, and this truth was echoed in the East. Whether that be the ancient rishis (seers) who composed the Vedic texts, or Buddha, they too realised the need to liberate oneself.

A wandering monk once visited the kingdom ruled by King Janak. After roaming the kingdom, he asked people, "Who is the best spiritual guide here?" To his surprise, almost every person in the kingdom referred to him the name of King Janak. The monk was confused and irritated. After all, how can a king living in an affluent palace, surrounded by a luxurious and lavish lifestyle, be at a heightened spiritual state? He thought that maybe these subjects are scared of the king, either that or, they don't understand the true meaning behind spirituality. Still, he chose to visit the king and upon seeing him, he asked, "Oh King Janak! The learned and lay all speak highly of you in this kingdom? Tell me, how can you – a worldly man of pleasures – be more spiritual than those who have given up everything for the sake of knowing the highest truth?"

Janak replied, "Dear one, you have come from a distant place to this kingdom. I'm sure you must be very tired from the long journey. You should eat and rest, we can discuss this tomorrow."

The king instructed his servants to feed the monk at the royal dinner table with a variety of dishes that would please his palates. Extending his royal hospitality, the king personally took the monk to a spacious room, surrounded with plenty of comforts, advising him to relax and sleep in this room. The monk was elated. However, when he entered the room and looked up, to his surprise there was a huge sword hanging from the ceiling, directly above the bed. "Why is this sword hanging here, just above the bed?" Asked the perplexed monk.

"Oh! Please don't be worried about that. It is just a tradition and old custom of the Videhis. It has been here for several generations. You just rest well, sleep, and we will meet in the morning."

King Janak left the monk to rest after his tired journey. But, the monk was restless all night, worried that the sword might fall on him and kill him. He couldn't close his eyes, even though he was tired. This fear and worry kept him awake all night. The next morning, when Janak met him, he asked, "Dear one, did you sleep well last night?"

"Oh King! How could I have slept! There was a huge sword hanging right at my neck!" The monk explained his predicament.

That is when King Janak smiled and said, "When one knows death is certain, how can the pleasures of the world sway him away? How can the worldly duties ever limit his eyes from the supreme goal? The knowledge of the sword kept you awake the whole night. Similarly, the awareness of the fragility of life, and the true nature of life, does not allow me to indulge in the worldly pleasures. Even whilst I live in this palace carrying out my duties, I remain detached. Death is always in front of me."

Death doesn't make life pointless, but rather purposeful. Our fear of death is a looming obstacle in our lives. It shapes our decisions, our outlook, and our actions. Shakespeare himself, writes in *The Tempest*, "Every third thought shall be my grave." Part of the reason we have so much trouble with this acceptance is because our relationship with our own existence is totally messed up. We may not say it, but deep down we act and behave like we're immortal. We truly forget how light our grip on life really is. It's a cliché question to ask but, "What would you change about your life if the doctor told you that you had cancer?" After our answer, we inevitably comfort ourselves with the same insidious lie: "Well, thank God I don't have cancer." But we do. The diagnosis is terminal for all of us. A death sentence already has been decreed and looms over us. Tomorrow, we could discover we have cancer. Two weeks from now, a heavy branch could fall from a tree and take us with it. Death is certain from the moment we are born. Our heart will beat without fail for an uncertain period of time, and then one day, it will stop. That is a guarantee. The question then is, will you be ready for when that day comes?

The denial of this simple, yet humbling reality is the sole reason we attempt to build monuments to our own greatness. It is why we worry and argue so much. It is why we chase after pleasure, and money, yet we still don't feel that peace we seek whilst we are alive.

Isn't it ironic that we spend so much of our precious time on earth either impotently fighting death or futilely attempting to ignore the thought of it? That day is not the end of us, it is the true beginning.

Much of this book will be about how to live well. But in doing so, it is also about how to die well. Death is where all three domains come together – body, mind, and soul. We must treat this vessel that we inhabit for the duration of our stay on this planet well, or we will be forced to abandon it early. We must learn to work with our mind, in order to think rationally and clearly about our own fate. We must find spiritual meaning, purpose, and goodness during this lifetime itself. And so, as we proceed on, just remember this: You too are going to die, and that is because you too were fortunate enough to have lived.

Prāna – The Life Force

If you travelled back in time some 5,000 years to the borders of now-modern-day Afghanistan, Pakistan, and north-west India, you would see sand, Rocky Mountains, dusty trees, red soil, and wide-open plains – the same landscape that today covers most of the Middle East. But if you looked a little more, you would also find something else. You would find five-million people living in cities of baked-brick tract houses, roads that were meticulously constructed with geometric patterns, and even children playing with copper, bronze, and tin toys. On every street you would see public bathing pools with fresh, running water, and toilets piped to complex sanitation systems. Amidst the marketplace, you would find tradesmen measuring goods with weights and standardised rulers and sculptors carving elaborate figures into stone, among many others.

This was the Indus-Saraswati civilisation, named after the two rivers that flowed through the valley. I prefer to call this civilisation by the land it belonged to, Bhārat. It was the largest geographical civilisation, totalling some 300,000 square miles, and was also one of the most advanced of ancient human civilisations. The people of this civilisation believed in the magnificent and transformative power of prāna – 'life force', 'breath', or, 'life'.

A seal engraving unearthed in this area in the late 1920s depicts an individual (believed by many to be a depiction of the Hindu deity Shiva) in a clear pose. He sits upright with his arms outstretched and his hands with thumbs in front placed on his knees. His legs are crossed and the soles of his feet are joined, with his toes pointing down. His abdomen filled with air, as he consciously inhales. Many such artefacts have been found documenting such 'yogic' postures. Bhārat was the birthplace of yoga. In two texts based of Vedic literature known as the Upanishads, namely the Brihadāranyaka and Chāndogya, the earliest lessons of breathing and prāna are mentioned. By around 500 BCE, these techniques had been further filtered and synthesised into Patanjali Yogasutra. Slow breathing, holding of the breath, deep breathing with the diaphragm, and extended exhalations all first appear in this ancient text. Here's an example passage from the text:

> *When a wave comes, it washes over your and runs up the beach.*
> *Then, it turns around. And recedes over you, going back into the ocean.*
> *This is like the breath, which exhales, transitions, inhales, transitions,*
> *and then starts the process again.*
> **Patanjali Yogasutra 2.51**

In the Yogasutra, there is no mention of moving between, or even repeating, poses. This is a modernised and construed concept. In fact, the Sanskrit word āsana originally means 'to sit', or, 'posture'.

It referred to both, the act of sitting and that on which you sit. The earliest yoga was the science and wisdom of holding still and building prāna (life force/vital energy) through breathing, a concept that was documented around 3,000 years ago. Changing how you breathe will change how you live. It is the most important thing we need to do properly in order to keep the kingdom running smoothly.

Nose or Mouth?

Back then, the Hindus (that's what they've been called since 500 BCE) considered breath (prāna) and spirit to be the same thing. In fact, even today, Hindus consider prāna to be linked directly with the soul, spirit, or life. It is believed that there were even sages and monks who used breathing not only to lengthen their lifespan, but also to reach higher levels of consciousness. Breathing was a trained art – it was medicine. Have you noticed how the modern-day human being is the only species with chronically crooked teeth? This is to do with the way we breathe. By the law of averages, you will take approximately 670 million breaths in your lifetime. For all we know, we might have already taken half of those.

Today, around forty per cent of the population suffer from chronic nasal obstruction, and about half of us habitually breathe using our mouth instead of our nose. Females and children are most victims.

In the late 1970s and early 80s, Egil P. Harvold carried out some disturbing experiments. From a lab in San Francisco, he gathered a troop of rhesus monkeys. He split them into two groups, stuffing one group's nasal cavities with silicone plugs, and leaving another half as they were. The ones with silicone plugs couldn't remove them, nor were they able to breathe through their noses at all. They were forced to adapt to constant breathing through their mouths.[1]

Over the next six months, Harvold measured different aspects of the monkeys' face structure. He measured their dental arches, the angles of their chins, the lengths of their faces, and more. He came to find that the monkeys who had silicone plugs put up their noses, developed a downward growth pattern, narrowing of dental arches, crooked teeth, and gaping mouths. He repeated the experiments, keeping animals obstructed for two years. They came out even worse.

It turns out that breathing through your mouth changes the physical body and transforms airways, all for the worse. Inhaling air through the mouth decreases pressure, causing soft tissues in the back of the mouth to loosen and flex inwards, creating less overall space and making breathing more difficult. Inhaling through the nose is how we should be breathing. It has the opposite effect. By inhaling through the nose, air is forced against the back of the throat, making the airways wider and breathing easier. In Harvold's monkey studies, after two years of forced breathing through the mouth, he removed the silicone plugs. Slowly, but surely, the monkeys relearned how to breathe through their noses. And with time, their faces and airways remodelled. Their jaws moved forward and their facial structures and airways morphed back into their wide and natural state. It can work for us too.

The nose is crucial because it not only clears the air entering our lungs, but it also heats it and moistens it for easier absorption. Your mouth won't do this. You might already know this, but what you may not know is that proper breathing can also trigger a variety of hormones and chemicals that lower blood pressure and aid digestion. It also responds to the stages of a woman's menstrual cycle, and regulates heart rate. Have you ever considered how the nostrils of every living human pulse to their own rhythm? Start breathing through your nose. I'm sure your body will thank you for it.

The ancient Vedic texts mentioned earlier also describe particular methods of breathing using each nostril. Latest research has confirmed this. Breathing through your right nostril is like accelerating a car. Circulation speeds up, your body gets hotter, and cortisol levels, blood pressure and heart rate all increase. Why? Simply because the right side of the nose activates the sympathetic nervous system, the 'fight-or-flight' mechanism. It also feeds more blood to the opposite hemisphere of the brain, specifically to the prefrontal cortex, which is the part of the brain associated with logical decisions, language and computing.

Inhaling through the left nostril has the opposite effect. It works like a car's braking system. The left nostril is more deeply connected to the parasympathetic nervous system, the 'rest-and-relax' side that lowers temperature and blood pressure, cools the body, and reduces anxiety. Left-nostril breathing shifts blood flow to the opposite side of the prefrontal cortex, the right area that plays a role in creative thought, emotions, formation of mental abstractions, and negative emotions.

It's all about balance. It's not one or the other. In Vedic scriptures, the manipulation of bodily functions through forced breathing via the nostrils is called nādi shodhana. In Sanskrit, 'nādi' means 'channel' and 'shodhana' means 'purification'.

Why Breath is Everything

Breathing correctly is essential, simply because so many of us do it in the wrong way. Dr. Mark Burhenne, who has been studying the links between breathing and sleep for decades, says that breathing through the mouth contributes to periodontal disease and bad breath. It was also the number one cause of cavities, even more than sugar consumption, bad diet, or poor hygiene. It is all to do with regular use. Whatever input you give in, defines the output you get out. If you deny the regular use of your nose, it will atrophy. The opposite is true too. Keeping the nose constantly in use will train the tissues in the naval cavity and throat to flex and stay open.[2]

According to researchers of the Framingham Study, a longitudinal research program spanning 70 years focusing on heart disease, our ability to breathe full breaths was 'literally a measure of living capacity'.[3]

The late yoga teacher B. K. S. Iyengar said, "The yogi's life is not measured by the number of his days, but the number of his breaths." Some researchers also suspect that the industrialisation of food could be one of the reasons that our mouths have shrunk and our breathing is being destroyed. Ninety-five per cent of modern, processed food is soft. This means we don't chew enough. Our ancient ancestors chewed for ages. Ayurveda also encourages more time in chewing. The more we gnaw, the more stem cells release, the more bone density and growth we will trigger, the younger we will look and the better we will breathe. These are not just false assumptions or ideas – it's ancient wisdom backed up by modern science.

From the moment we are born, our bodies automatically execute this most essential function for immediate survival. Improper breathing creates unnecessary suffering and a lower feeling for human potential. It caps how well we are able to perform, and forces us to get by on limited oxygen, reduced blood flow, and diminished brainpower. I don't think I even need to get into the profound ways that breathing helps with stress. It affects our blood flow, heart rate, and it also affects your pH (the body's acidity level), which influences almost every process within your body.

Contrary to popular belief, it's not about taking big breaths. By doing this, we actually become more tired from over-breathing and even reduce the amount of oxygen we take in. Basically, we should breathe through our noses all day, every day. The list of advantages to nose breathing are (excuse me) breathtaking. Now, you may be wondering what to do if you have a clogged nose, right? Well, I have good news for you. Unless you have a skeletal problem, a tissue obstruction, or silicone plugs stuck up there, the very act of using your nose will help in opening up those cavities. If you can't move any air through a congested nose, then obviously, your mouth will be needed until you are healthy enough to start using your nose again.

Meditation – Breath in Practice

Today, the word 'meditation' is often misunderstood, poorly represented, or mixed up in a slurry of many other buzzwords. Most modern Westerners see meditation simply as a form of relaxation. You put on some yoga pants or leggings, sit in a warm, comfy room for ten minutes, you close your eyes and listen to a soothing voice on your phone telling you that everything's okay, everything's going great, follow your heart, blah, blah, blah. But real meditation is far more intense than simply trying to de-stress yourself using some fancy apps. Proper meditation requires you to sit quietly and critically observe yourself. Every thought, every judgement, every inclination, every little fidget or flake of emotion must be observed, captured, acknowledged and then released. Meditation is difficult to define because it varies throughout different cultures, religions and traditions. For the purpose of this book, these are my definitions, based on what we have discussed so far.

First we have mindfulness, this is where we focus our attention and be present in the current moment. It involves being conscious and aware of something, maybe everything, maybe one thing. It requires you to be 'in the now' and to direct your focus towards a specific thing. To some, this may sound like some jargon, but we can simplify it. Some may choose to make their God or Guru their focus point during meditation, but I understand that many may not be comfortable or adept at this to begin with. They can simply focus on their breathing. We've just talked about breathing through the nose, and this is the perfect time to do it – through mindful meditation. Many Hindus throughout the world start their day with a form of meditation called prāṇāyāma, or, 'the control of breath'.

A simple breathing exercise that anyone can start with is called anulom-vilom, which is, 'alternate nostril breathing'. This form of breathing aims to balance the left and right hemispheres of the brain (as mentioned earlier), by giving them an equal amount of oxygen. It has a calming effect on the mind, breath and heartbeat by stimulating the parasympathetic nervous system. It is best performed after bathing in the morning, but you can perform it at any time of the day.

To begin with, sit in a comfortable cross-legged position on the floor, and keep your back upright. Exhale completely. Closing your right nostril with your right thumb, breathe in through your left nostril for a count of four. Then, close both nostrils. Use either the little finger or ring finger of the same right hand to do this. Aim to hold your breath for eight or sixteen counts. Take off your thumb from your right nostril and breathe out through your right nostril for eight counts. You then repeat this with breathing in through your right nostril, holding your breath, then exhaling through your left nostril. Whilst performing this exercise, ensure you always use your right thumb for the right nostril. Some choose to perform this exercise for a couple of minutes, whilst others perform it for ten minutes or more. Start for a short period of time, and as you get used to it, try perform it for longer.

Another form of meditation is contemplation. This is kind of like thinking about thinking. It is a process of training the mind to interpret and process thoughts differently. It requires time, courage, and honesty. It also involves sitting with our beliefs and emotions, deciphering which ones do not serve us, which ones are beneficial, and which ones need modification or repair. Most people avoid meditation because they realise what it truly is: it's confronting your pain, it's observing the interior workings of the commander (the mind) and subjects (the senses). As opposed to mindful meditation, which is a totally passive process, contemplation is an active process. It is vitally important that we introspect and contemplate too. We will come back to the topic of meditation a little later.

Architecting the Kingdom

> If a person puts even one measure of effort
> into following ritual and the standards of righteousness,
> he will get back twice as much.
> *Xunzi*

The majority of the problems that manifest in our body are driven entirely by our lifestyle. From the moment we open our eyes, it's go, go, go. We keep going until we're finally in bed, and then, we're straight into our emails or social media. I am as much of a victim to this as you are. We struggle to give time to ourselves. Everything that we do throughout the day is for someone else. Our lack of routine and relaxation is probably one of the most pressing issues in this modern society.

In this fast-paced world, humankind is struggling. There is so much going on around us, that our body struggles to cope with, yet our mind to tell us keep on going, and going, and going. We repeat cycles five times a week, waiting for the weekend to approach. And when Friday arrives, we receive calls and messages, dragging us into further commitments that we struggle to say 'no' to.

That is why there are certain foundations we must put in place to architect our kingdom and allow for it to prosper. We will explore certain habits and lifestyle practices in turn, to help with our physical body. We need to balance both the internal and external, and that is why we work our way inwards.

Sleep

Research has shown that as we approach twenty or so hours without sleep, we are as cognitively impaired as a drunk person.[1] Our brain responds more slowly and our judgement is significantly impaired. Some say, "I'll sleep when I'm dead," as they speed up that very death, both literally and figuratively. They trade their health for a few more working hours. They trade the long-term viability of their business or their career before the urgency of some tempered crisis. If we treat sleep as a luxury, it is the first to go when we get busy. If sleep is what happens only when everything is done, work and others will constantly be invading your personal space. Arthur Schopenhauer said, "Sleep is the source of all health and energy." Sleep is critical for the smooth functioning of the body and mind. It was only about a century ago that people would easily clock in ten to eleven hours of sleep every night. But then, 1869 happened. Thomas Edison invented the light bulb and eliminated the darkness and mystery of night. Very soon, with the introduction of cheaper electricity, lights blazed from every city, town, and over time, even to the smallest of villages. The early 1900s saw sleep dropping to nine hours each night. By the 1950s, television reduced it to eight hours, and now with 24-hour programming, Netflix, the internet, as well as all the other distractions in the past 70 years alone, the average human being sleeps six and a half hours or less.

A recent study also found that lack of sleep increases negative repetitive thinking. Abusing the body leads the mind to abuse itself. Now, it's time to see why sleep is built into our biology. Why is it so important for us to switch off?[2]

The NHS tells us that if you suffer from prolonged periods of poor sleep, you can be at risk of developing more long-term and rather serious health conditions, such as respiratory problems, heart disease and diabetes. The NHS advice also states that 'people who sleep less than seven hours a day tend to gain more weight and have a higher risk of becoming obese than those who get the recommended seven hours'. This is primarily believed to be because sleep-deprived people have reduced levels of leptin (the chemical that makes you feel full) and increased levels of ghrelin (the hunger stimulating hormone). Data also suggests a heightened risk of anxiety and depression. Presumably, even life expectancy can be shortened. Aside from these long-term issues, there is further evidence to show that poor sleep compromises your immune system. It is possible that if you always seem to get a cough or cold, then poor sleep could at least be partly to blame. A lack of sleep impacts on almost every area of life. It might be the most dangerous thing we still refuse to take seriously. Lack of sleep is connected most obviously to irritability, mood instability, and poor decision making. If the kingdom is not in a stable condition, the commander and subjects are obviously going to be furious. Chronic sleep deprivation can also lead to young people being misdiagnosed as suffering from ADHD or depression, when in fact it's the lack of quality rest that's preventing them from functioning properly. Eating too late also seems to be commonly associated with disturbing sleep efficiency as your digestive system will still be too active when you are trying to fall asleep. Making sure your bedroom is free of all light and noise is always a good idea and a simple measure you can put in place to stack the odds in your favour.

Sleep deprivation is a major issue. There is a high probability that the Chernobyl disaster could be related to lack of sleep. The engineers on site had been working for at least thirteen hours.[3] The Challenger space shuttle, which exploded within seconds after lift-off in 1986, killed all seven members on board. A few of the managers who were part of the launch had only slept for two hours, before reporting to work at 1 a.m.[4] Sleep deprivation seriously does kill. An astounding thirty-one per cent of drivers worldwide, fall asleep at the wheel at least once in their lives. In the UK, one in every five employees has missed work or arrived late due to fatigue. Ariana Huffington talks about a dinner date she went on. Her date bragged on about how he'd slept for only four hours the previous night. Whilst he moaned on and on, she said that she wanted to tell him that if he'd gotten five hours instead, the dinner would have been 'a lot more interesting'. She says that the simplest way to lead a more productive, inspired, and joyful life is to sleep.

Today's society attempts to give us a badge of honour for the amount of hours we are able to stay awake. Edison himself said that sleep was 'a criminal waste of time, inherited from our cave days'. He died from complications related to diabetes. I mean, isn't the allure to stay awake so huge? There's just so much more you can do – watch another episode of Friends, read another book or blog post, slide into DMs, fire up the group chats. Some say it is only children that need so much sleep, but science shows that, it takes seven to nine hours of quality sleep to maximise health and well-being. One thing I came across time and time again during my research was that people who have more and better quality of sleep, report higher levels of life satisfaction and happiness. Those who have less and poorer sleep are several times more likely to develop depression.

Modern science has discovered 'sleep cycles', of which there are four. Stage one is the light sleep stage. You can be woken easily at this point, but within minutes of dropping off, your eye movement slows down; stage two is still fairly light, but your brain waves begin to slow down; stage three is when deeper sleep commences, with slower brain waves, no eye movement or muscle activity. It is harder for you to be woken by anything going on in the outside world. The final fourth stage is the so-called rapid eye movement sleep (REM). It is believed that we enter this stage around 90 minutes after falling asleep. Each REM phase lasts around an hour, with the average adult experiencing around five or six REM cycles each night.

Whilst science focuses on the duration of sleep, the Vedic texts focus on the quality of sleep, coupled with rest and peaceful activities before and after sleep. But one thing that they do mention, which even I struggle with most of the time, is waking before sunrise or during brahma muharat (generally around 90 minutes before sunrise). We hate doing it, we don't even see ourselves doing this, and it is largely due to the fact that we sleep too late, so we aren't getting enough quality rest. To ensure that we get quality sleep, we need to pay close attention to what we do before we shut our eyes, and what we do as soon as we open our eyes. An optimal way to get quality sleep is to divide your sleep into 90-minute chunks.

- 10.00 p.m. to 11.30 p.m.
- 11.30 p.m. to 1.00 a.m.
- 1.00 a.m. to 2.30 a.m.
- 2.30 a.m. to 4.00 a.m.
- 4.00 a.m. to 5.30 a.m.
- 5.30 a.m. to 7.00 a.m.

Depending on the time you are trying to sleep, and if you can't wake up naturally, set your alarm to the half-hour of the end of any one of the chunks. For example, if I am in bed at 11.00 p.m., aiming to sleep by 11.30 p.m., and I want to wake up by 7.00 a.m., I would set my alarm between 6.30 a.m. and 7.00 a.m. This accounts for REM cycles too, so I shouldn't wake up tired and fatigued. Here are a few more tips to ensure you get the best rest.

1. **No caffeine after 3.00 p.m.**
   Caffeine doesn't boost our energy in the way that we assume. It cheats the body into believing that we aren't as tired as we think, but what's going on inside, well, only the inside knows. As soon as you wake up, uour brain produces a neurotransmitter called adenosine. Our nervous system constantly tracks its quantity in our body. Caffeine also stimulates the production of adrenaline. Caffeine has a half-life of around five to eight hours. A cup of coffee has around 200mg of caffeine. If you consume this cup at around 8 a.m. in the morning, the caffeine will float around in your blood at full power until around 4 p.m. It takes around 24 hours for all the caffeine to get flushed out of your system. That's why – no caffeine after 3.00 p.m. if you want good sleep. I know of people that seem to be able to drink coffees before bed and still sleep like babies for the recommended eight hours. But, the quality of their sleep, and their ability to go into the deeper stages of sleep are damaged. If you feel the need, drink water instead.

2. **Ban blue and white light ASAP.**
   There are an entire set of organisms and electrochemical reactions in the brain that work furiously to keep us awake. There are also another bunch, striving equally hard to make us sleep. Each group becomes weaker and weaker, depending on which one you support. This back-and-forth game between sleep and wakefulness is known as the circadian rhythm.
   A few hours after sunset, the circadian rhythm begins to wind down and the adenosine-induced sleep pressure builds up. The army that is responsible for sleep becomes stronger, and that is when the secretion of the sleep hormone – melatonin – begins. There are specialised light receptors in our eyes called rods and cones. As daylight fades away and darkness creeps in, these signal to the brain to start letting the sleep army have a winning position. For millions of years, human eyes were exposed to red-orange-yellow glows of fire, or the gentle

cooling light of the stars and moon at night. This light ambience would signal the brain about the onset of night and the need to prepare for sleep. The mechanism is so fine-tuned that even white-blue light of a full moon can make people sleep five minutes later and wake up twenty minutes earlier than normal.

Now, stop and imagine what the full-spectrum light that you stare into at night is doing to this delicate system within your brain. The illumination from the screen of your TV, laptop or phone isn't a mellow amber signalling you to fall asleep. Studies have shown that the use of back-lit screens (television, computers, and mobile phones) at night, can lead to sleep disorders. A 2016 study found of around 3,000 students found that some were waking up ten times a night to just check their phone. Research shows that even people who manage to clock eight hours of sleep after being exposed to blue-white light, wake up tired and far from refreshed. Their quality of sleep is highly compromised. I can personally vouch for this. To aid this (but not to allow your mindless scrolling) use the Night Shift mode (if you have an iPhone), there are similar functions or apps available on Android. Replace the light fixtures in your home with ambient lighting, such as amber-yellow illumination. Minimise the blue and white light, at least when you are in bed.

3. **Create a Safe Haven and Ritual**

    We are creatures of habit and habitat. Remove all unnecessary clutter from your bedroom and keep the zone spotlessly clean. Believe me, this will completely transform the quality of your sleep. For the ritual part, try to go to sleep, and wake up, at the same time every day. If you can't sleep, don't stay in bed. Read. Meditate. Journal. Don't oversleep either. If you're sleeping more than ten hours in one go, you may have a condition called hypersomnia.

One final note, according to an ancient Vedic text called the Vāstu Shāstra, try and sleep with your head facing south or east. This is believed to have many benefits, including increased concentration, memory, and quality sleep that makes you feel refreshed. It works. And remember, it's not how long you sleep, it's how well you sleep.

Routines

Routines are truly under-appreciated by most people. A good routine is not only a source of great comfort and stability, but it is also the platform from which stimulating and fulfilling work is possible. Great sages and philosophers know that complete freedom is a nightmare. As human beings we need routines in order to function properly. I am not saying we're machines, but routines really do root us. Routines are prerequisites of excellence, and particularly in an unpredictable world, good habits are a haven of certainty. Freedom, power, success, or peace all require self-discipline. Discipline comes from routines – it is how we maintain that freedom. When our thoughts are empty and our body is in movement, we perform at our best.

Routines start from the moment we wake up. Founder and CEO of Twitter, Jack Dorsey, gets up at 5 a.m., the poet John Milton was up at 4 a.m. to read and contemplate, so that by 7 a.m. he could be well into his writing. Mahant Swami wakes up daily between 3 a.m. and 4.30 a.m. to begin his meditation and reading. I'm sure you've heard many other examples of early birds. It all goes back to sleep. When we sleep and how well we sleep determines how and when we wake up. In Sarangpur, swamis are in the mandir sanctum by 5.45 a.m. for the morning rituals. When your body becomes busy with the familiar, the mind is able to relax. Most of us wake up to face the day with an endless number of bewildering and overwhelming choices, one after another. *What do I wear? What should I eat? What time do I need to be in the office? Should I leave now or in a while?* I don't even need to say, but this is exhausting. The psychologist William James talked about making habits our ally instead of our enemy. He said, "There is no more miserable human being than one in whom nothing is habitual but indecision." We must get our day scheduled. We must limit interruptions. We must limit the number of choices we make.

> *I was sat reading in the library and it was around 12.30 p.m. when a bell rang in the distance. There was commotion outside in the courtyard of the ashram. As I looked out of the window I saw groups of swamis chattering and walking with notepads and pens in their hands. It was amazing to see how they were so rooted in their routines. Could this be one of the primary reasons they are able to maintain their inner calm and composure?*

The daily routine for the swamis living in the training centre here in Sarangpur itself is extraordinary. The day commences at 4.00 a.m., as they bathe and perform their personal prayers. At around 5.45 a.m. they attend the morning rituals in the mandir sanctum. From 6.00 a.m. they are all engaged in various forms of service such as: cleaning the mandir compound and complex, making flower garlands for the deities, cutting vegetables for the daily meals, preparing meals, performing pujas, adorning the deities, cleaning the ashram, etc. At 7.15 a.m. they all attend the adorning ritual and singing known as the shangār ārti. They then head for breakfast before the morning discourses are held at 8.00 a.m. In these discourses, senior swamis discourse based on the teachings of Swaminarayan, giving guidance and inspiration to the training swamis. Between 9.00 a.m. and 12.00 noon they all study, based on a set syllabus, within the ashram. At 12.00 noon they have their lunch, which they eat in a small wooden bowl, mixing all their food with water. At 12.30 p.m., further discourses are held in the assembly hall, thereafter, they rest or engage in personal study. At 4.00 p.m., they all gather for collective meditation and scriptural readings. From 4.30 p.m. to 6.30 p.m., study classes are held. At 7.30 p.m., the evening rituals are performed, followed by dinner at 8.00 p.m., and another assembly at 8.45 p.m., in which devotional songs are sung by all. They then return to their communal rooms where they spend an hour in personal study before they retire for the night.

They use an extremely thin mattress for bedding, and they sleep in the common dormitories or on the terrace (depending on the weather). Nobody has separate rooms. Despite hailing from different countries, regions, socio-economic and educational backgrounds, they blend with one another in perfect harmony. They regularly observe between five to seven waterless fasts every month, regardless of the heat, and many take only one meal a day. They also undertake many other difficult austerities. After spending a total of five to ten years in the training centre in Sarangpur, Mahant Swami assigns them to mandirs across the world to engage in a variety of services. At over 1,000 mandirs, the swamis actively manage over 160 humanitarian services, including social, educational, moral, cultural and spiritual activities. This cadre of learned and dedicated swamis seek to attain spiritual liberation and serve society, following the credo of Pramukh Swami, 'In the joy of others, lies our own'.

I know how overwhelming this all sounds, but they manage it. It's a personal choice that they make to detach from all of their relations and possessions, to lead a new life, and serve society. Yet, what shocks me even more is that despite having such a hectic and seemingly monotonous routine, they remained fulfilled and at peace.

Whatever we do, whether it be eating, working, reading, exercising, or meditating, we must try to do these things at the same time each day. This way our body learns the patterns. Eat meals at consistent times daily and refrain from eating large meals too close to bedtime. If your routine is such that it doesn't allow for three or four regular meals on a steady schedule, try eating smaller portions regularly every few hours to keep your metabolism going. Settings workouts at a consistent time too each day helps establish a better circadian rhythm.

According to Dr. Barbara Oakley, professor at Oakland University, the human brain uses two modes of learning – focused and diffused. The former is when you actively learn things from the external stimuli around you, which results in the creation of neural circuits. Typically, the brain cannot sustain this mode for more than 30 minutes. Basically, any form of focused activity is tiring (if we spend too long on it).

The diffused mode is when you are more or less on autopilot. This mode is active in routines such as bathing, driving, walking, and so on. You aren't thinking about the activity as you're doing it, and thoughts in the brain are drifting from one to the next. Simply staring out of a window is diffused mode. Looking for something as you stare out is focused mode. Meditation is an excellent practice to encourage diffused brain activity.

Whatever activity or work you set out to do, try not to spend more than 45 minutes on it in one go. Your brain struggles to hold attention for longer than this time period. It differs from person to person, but you will know how long you can engage in focused work. To switch from focused mode to diffused mode, get up from your desk or whatever you're doing, stretch, get a change of scene and relax for about fifteen to twenty minutes. This gives your brain some time off. Then you can return to what you were doing or tackle something new. The key is not to overwork yourself.

Let's also briefly talk about multitasking. Study after study has shown that there is no such thing as multitasking. The bottom line is that there is a very real chemical, electrical and physical change that occurs in the brain when we are performing a particular task. If we continuously switch and hop between tasks, it triggers a full-on change. Our brain cannot and does not know how to jump between such changes effectively. Research has shown that people who think they can multitask actually can't and don't. They have poor recall, hazy understanding, slumped productivity, and so on. Their cognitive ability is also compromised.

When in focused mode, ensure you shield yourself from distractions. One of the worst attackers at this point will be your mobile phone, or in the latest updates, desktop notifications. One of the best things you can do is to switch off your Internet, or put your phone on 'Do Not Disturb' mode. You can check your messages and emails after you're done with the work at hand. Use this little trick and watch your productivity soar to unbelievable heights. Your brain will definitely love you for doing this.

Work

The modern culture puts so much emphasis on work. The more work you do, the more successful you become. The more work you do, the more people look up to you. The more work you do, the more this and the more that. But is any of this true?

During the Industrial Revolution, it was common for labourers to work sixteen-hour shifts, six days per week. For several decades, the typical and legal workday was reduced to ten hours, then eventually eight. In 1926, Henry Ford shrunk the expected work-week for his staff from six days to five, dropping weekly work hours from forty-eight to forty. This change produced notably higher productivity, and so many other sectors followed Ford's lead. In 1938, a law was passed stating that staff working over forty-four hours would earn overtime pay. That law was then amended two years later, making the legal work-week forty hours long.

Today, only eight per cent of full-time workers work less than forty hours per week. The average work-week for hourly workers is forty-seven. Salaried employees average forty-nine hours per week. Those numbers struggle to factor in the work that occurs from home or during the commute. So, what happened? Where did we go wrong?

Without a contrarian approach, we automatically gravitate to the middle (why this is the case will come later on in the read). It's now 'normal' to work forty-nine hours per week. People agree to this schedule simply because the majority of others have accepted it. So here again, we risk falling into a common trap, where average working people are exhausted, unfulfilled, unhappy and anxious. And, I can almost guarantee that you feel this way too – at least at times.

In most cases, eight hours a day, five days per week should be plenty of time to do great work. Okay, people like Elon Musk or Jeff Bezos may work sixteen to twenty hours per day, but the rest of us aren't building a car company and space rockets, whilst simultaneously boring tunnels under busy cities. Nor are we trying to conquer the world. If we aren't doing those things, but we still brag about our insanely busy and hectic work schedules, that's probably not heroism, it's pure stupidity.

Some people may make £100k per year working twelve-hour days, seven days a week. But someone else is making £100k working only twelve hours a week. Both may be respectable, in fact, some may even look up to the first and shun the other, but who is the real genius?

Recent reports show that the average American checks their smartphone over fifty times per day.[5] That's multiple opportunities per hour to lose flow. If it takes thirty minutes of focused work to get into a solid flow state, that means the average worker never reaches it. But, it's not just the electronic notifications and texts that get in the way. It's also people, the environment, noise, mistakes, calls, emails, failing systems, and more. You must know how dropping in to deliver one quick message can quickly turn into a ten-minute chat, derailing our focus for another forty minutes.

We need to learn to get the job done and get out. Raise your standards. This also means asking yourself whether the current job you're at is where you need to be in order to become the best version of yourself? If your focus is growth and promotion, make sure you define the steps needed to accomplish that mission. Rewards reflect effort and competency. Past mistakes are bruises too, not tattoos.

It's not always about the hustle. Remember that slowing down makes us do most things better. Don't run around aimlessly just because everyone around you is, hoping to get lucky. Assess the results as you go, modify systems, and implement improvements. Don't delay all the gratification from your work either. Life is always hard, but our work should continuously progress alongside the growth of our capabilities and character. There is no path to peace that does not require diligent patience and accurate execution. Regardless of who you are, you deserve that much at least.

Boundaries

Man is *not* a beast of burden. Yes, we all have important duties – to our country, to our faith, to our coworkers, to provide for our families. But, we're not going to be able to do that if we're not taking care of ourselves, or if we have stretched ourselves to the breaking point. "Burn out or fade away?" – that was the question in Kurt Cobain's suicide note. How is that even a dilemma? Boundaries are key.

A recent study found that subjects would rather give themselves an electric shock than experience boredom for even a few minutes.[6] And we wonder why people do so many dumb things? Our best and most lasting work comes from the things we do patiently and with care. We should look fearfully, even sympathetically, at the people who become slaves to their calendars, scheduling in every little thing. Of those who require a staff of ten to handle all their ongoing projects, whose lives seem to resemble some fugitive fleeingß one scene for the next. That's not work, that's servitude. We all need to get better at saying no. If doctors, firemen and police officers get to use being 'on call' as their personal shield, are we not on call in our own lives? Are our own bodies not on call for our families, relationships, for our self-improvement, for our own self? When we learn what to say no to, we can say yes to the things that truly matter.

We feel overwhelmed. We feel resentment towards people asking for our help. We avoid phone calls and interactions with people that we feel will ask us for something. We make comments about helping people and then getting nothing in return. We feel burnt out. We have no time to ourselves. The number one reason that we avoid saying no and setting boundaries is because we fear the reaction of others. Fear is not rooted in fact. It is rooted in negative thoughts and the stories that the monkey tells the commander (we tell ourselves). People don't know what you want, and you can't expect them to either. It's your responsibility to make that clear from the get-go. Clarity will save you in every relationship.

Studies show that anxiety is rising – it's clearly obvious. Complicated relationships are among the leading causes of increased rates of anxiety. Depression and anxiety are the two most common reasons people pursue therapy or drugs. Boundaries are expectations and needs that help us to feel safe and comfortable in our relationships and personal lives. They help us to stay mentally and emotionally well.

They allow for our kingdom to flourish. Learning when to say no and when to say yes is an essential part of feeling comfortable when interacting with others. It's important to note that we don't want to avoid people or situations. That is a passive-aggressive way of expression – it is based on fear. We must verbally communicate our boundaries to others: "Hey, that sounds great and I respect the plan that's been set. If anything changes, please let me know a few hours before." Your time is important too. People benefit from you not having limits. Make your boundaries clear – look after yourself too – no excuses. You don't want to burn yourself out. An article published by the Harvard Gazette found that doctor burnout costs the healthcare system $4.6 billion a year. As a result, doctors make critical medical mistakes, misdiagnosing illnesses, prescribing wrong medication, and not paying attention to essential details. There are a number of areas where boundaries play a key role.

When it comes to family, it is important that we share our issues with our partner but you will need to set boundaries. We may all have a past we're not comfortable digging up, or anything for that matter. Both parties must agree with this, especially when it comes to bringing up children. When it comes to intimate relationships, you must assess why you're in a relationship with a certain person. How do you engage with them? Does it feel right to you? Can you make peace with differing opinions and commitments? Poor communication is the leading cause of divorce and breakups.

Some people chronically complain to us. We must empathise where possible. Lead by example and don't complain. We never know what's truly going on inside someone's head. Ask before offering an opinion. Be mindful of whether the person can handle the truth. Never be dismissive (e.g., 'It could be worse', or, 'You'll get over it'). If you're not sure how to help, make it clear, tell them to seek alternate help. Every conversation that we have with others, we must consciously consider the purpose behind it.

I believe our work life is the place where most of us will be struggling to set boundaries and say no. Especially in a toxic work environment, your emotional and mental health is put on the line. When your work environment is toxic, it reflects in your home life and personal relationships. A toxic environment could include: working long hours, gossiping, unpaid hours, being given more work in a limited time frame, a narcissistic boss, bullying, being sexually harassed, being mistreated based on race, physical ability, background or personal choices. If any of these are the case, write them down. Raise them with the relevant people. Talk to them about the office culture. Find support outside the office to manage the stress. Here's some things you must do, regardless of what you do. Use up all your vacation time. Don't allow for one day to go unused. This is an opportunity for you to recharge and reset. You are not a machine. Take advantage of this when you have an employer that offers paid time off. According to the US Travel Association, in 2018, American workers failed to use 768 million days of paid time off – a nine per cent increase from 2017. Don't check work emails on the weekend, and don't work whilst on vacation unless it's an emergency. Find hobbies and activities that have nothing to do with work. Just relax.

Social media is another key area that boundaries are prudent. Something we will come to later. The email you think you need so desperately to respond to can wait. All those WhatsApp groups that are pinging on your phone can wait. It's okay to say no too. It's okay to opt out of that phone call or that last-minute work get-together. In Japan, they have a word, karōshi, which translates to 'death from overwork'. Remember that the main cause of injury for elite athletes is not tripping and falling. It's not collisions or accidents either. It's overuse. Work does not set you free. It will kill you if you're not careful. We're a human being, not a human doing for a reason. The body that each of us have is a gift. The kingdom must be architected properly. Don't work to death. Don't burn out. Protect your gift.

Move

An investigation by the World Health Organisation (WHO) found that, in Europe and the USA, fifty per cent of women and forty per cent of men are insufficiently active, compared with South-East Asia where the figures are fifteen per cent and nineteen per cent.[7] Another recent study involving the US army showed that extreme levels of exercise can contribute to an increase in leaky gut.[8] So, what do we do?

I'm sure that I am not the one whose social media feed is flooded with people, including many fitness coaches, professionals and doctors documenting their 5 a.m. workouts despite obvious exhaustion. Whilst their intentions may be good, their message is misplaced and causing a huge amount of damage. If the life you live is already making you exhausted, can you justify putting in more work in the gym?

A 2010 study that examined sitting as an emerging health risk found that many adults spend seventy per cent of their day in a seat, whilst the other thirty per cent involved doing only light activity.[9] Physical inactivity is one of the biggest causes of premature death, and according to WHO, accounts for fifteen per cent of all deaths in the world. It's a greater health risk than being overweight or obese. Other studies have suggested that it can be as bad for us as smoking, and yet, we continue to take it lightly.[10]

Start walking. We've all got to do it. Aim for between 5,000 to 10,000 steps per day. Just like breathing, walking is a fundamental process. It's one of the core activities that the brain does without the need for conscious control. Make it a rule to never sit down for more than an hour at a time either. Put a reminder or an alarm on your computer, phone, or watch to alert you every hour, and if you haven't stood up, get up and go get a drink, snack, or some fresh air. A recent study found that exposure to bright morning light correlates with a lower body weight. This makes sense, as it fits what we know about the body's natural circadian rhythms.

Nikola Tesla discovered the rotating magnetic field, one of the most important scientific discoveries of all time, on a walk through a city park in Budapest in 1882. Charles Darwin's daily schedule included several walks, as did those of Steve Jobs and the groundbreaking psychologist Daniel Kahneman, who himself said, "It was the physical activity in the body that got my brain going." Mahant Swami, for the past three to four decades at the least, has made his daily walks a ritual. We are in motion when we walk, but it isn't conscious or forced motion – it is repetitive, ritualised motion. It is deliberate. It is an exercise in peace.

A study at New Mexico Highlands University found that the force from our footsteps can increase the supply of blood to the brain.[11] Researchers at Stanford have found that walkers perform better on tests that measure 'creative divergent thinking' during and after walks.[12] A study from Duke University found that walking could be as an effective of a treatment for major depression in some patients as medicine.[13] The key to a good walk is to be aware. You must be present and open to the experience, not distracted by your mobile phone. If you can, keep your phone at home. If not, then put it away. Walking is an affordable luxury available to each and every one of us, regardless of our background.

Drink

You truly are what you eat and drink. You may have heard of the phrase: garbage in, garbage out. Good in, good out. Every day, on an average, around 2kg of food goes through that opening in your body that you call your mouth. This works out at around 60kg a month, which is a little short of a tonne a year. That's equal to the weight of a giraffe. If you keep eating like this for 50 years, you'll have consumed the weight of ten adult African elephants! Socrates set a wonderful example: Rather than living to eat – rather than spending our life pursuing the pleasure to be derived from food – we should eat to live. But we don't. I don't and you probably don't either. So many of us obsess over obscure, fringe items while ignoring basic standards for eating and drinking that carry massive weight.

Starting with water, we all know how essential it is to life. In the human body, the vast majority of metabolic processes and biochemical reactions occur in a watery solution. Without enough water for each reaction, those processes struggle, and our systems and functions suffer. It is estimated that seventy per cent of Americans are dehydrated, despite living in a country of clean, cheap, running water. I myself never considered dehydration as a potential cause of my health issues, but I now realise that my body was persistently crying out for this one thing.

When we are dehydrated, our bodies go into distress mode, leading to our brain having to steal the water it needs to survive from our body. It then leaves the other organs to wrestle with the deficit. Our muscular function and blood circulation are restricted. We suffer from memory loss and a lack of concentration. Our pH becomes acidic. Anxiety levels rise, and we become more irritable. Inflammation increases, and our bodies become stiff and tired. Our immune system is compromised, making us more susceptible to illness. We take much longer to heal and recover, and our system is unable to clear toxic substances and other waste products. Through dehydration, proper digestion is also inhibited. Try to go until the afternoon without fluids and you will notice headaches and brain fog starting to set in. Our skin and oral cavities become dry. Energy levels drop, endurance diminishes, and we age faster.

The Mayo Clinic recommends 2.7 litres of water per day for women and 3.7 litres for men. Other sources say that the correct amount of daily water in ounces is equal to forty per cent to sixty per cent of your body weight in pounds. I myself, didn't have time for all these measurements and calculations, and I'm sure you don't want to spend too much time on them either. Here's a simpler way to know if you are drinking enough water. Check the colour of your urine. If it's pale and clear, you are sufficiently hydrated, if it's yellow or darker, your slacking. This is the best indicator for hydration on an individual level. Five glasses of water a day reduces the risk of a heart attack by 41 per cent. Why do you think that when we have the flu or a fever, we are told to drink plenty of fluids? What if we just stay hydrated and avoided sickness altogether?

Hydration has also been proven to impact mood. Even mild dehydration negatively affects our attitude and energy. When lacking adequate water, our body is under stress and perceives the occurrence as a threat (as it should). Stress hormones and neurotransmitters are released, heightening our anxiety and tension. Fatigue and confusion set in, making it harder for us to carry out the tasks in front of us, which only elevate our stress levels even more. If you want to maintain a positive mood, manage your water. Many of the fluids we drink actually force us to become more dehydrated, even though they are mostly made up of water. Drinks like coffee, tea, sodas, and energy drinks send us to the bathroom to urinate more often. Simply put, the more chemicals, flavours, additives, caffeine, sugars, and whatever else is in our drinks, the more water we will require to flush them out from our system. Water washes out waste and toxins faster than other drinks, without adding more waste products. If you dislike drinking water, use some natural flavourings or infusions such as cucumber, mint leaves or lemon. Steady, consistent replenishment throughout the day is best.

Āyurveda is an ancient Vedic lifestyle practice. The word āyurveda is made up two root words, 'āyus' meaning 'life', and 'veda' meaning 'knowledge'. Unfortunately, in the modern world, it is often misinterpreted as an 'alternate pseudoscience' or diluted down to 'medicine', but it is truly more than that. Āyurveda favours hot or warm water over cold or iced water, which can slow down metabolism. Warm water has increased therapeutic benefits. It has the capacity to stimulate hunger, aid digestion, soothe the throat, cleanse the body channels, including the bladder, and relieve hiccups too. It also advises us to sip warm water throughout the day, but to minimise drinking before, during, and just after mealtimes. Just drink enough water, plain and simple.

Eat

The Greek physician Hippocrates said, "Let food be thy medicine and medicine be thy food." Every year there are new fads, diets, packages, and programs aimed at helping people lose weight, gain weight, detox, or feel better. Not only that, but many aspects of our food system are unhealthy and corrupt. Many food items are intentionally designed to create dependency and addictions, not optimal health. Unfortunately, our healthcare system seems to be complicit in many ways. As a society, we have strayed from healthy living in almost every area of life because of trends, marketing, profits, and consumer behaviour. As individuals, we must be willing to be the one percent and lead the focused life in whatever way necessary.

Just look around. The results from following the masses are painfully apparent. Perhaps, for the first time in human history, entire nations of people are dying of malnutrition in the presence of excess food. What is going on? A lack of adequate nutrition is contributing to the further breakdown of bodily systems and resulting in more pain, anxiety, depression, and poor performance.

The human body has an incredibly ability to heal and meet our daily needs simply by us putting the right food into it. Proper eating is a lifestyle, not a one-time appointment. If we stop eating manufactured, overly-processed 'food', and begin to eat real food, we will surely notice a difference. By real food, I mean food solely derived from ingredients that the earth naturally provides.

Not only is much of what we eat today devoid of any nutritional value, but it's loaded with potentially harmful things. So many of the ingredients in our food products have no business being in our body. Our systems are not equipped to process many of the lab-created chemicals present in our food in the modern world today. I am not here to preach a diet to you. Nor am I here to tell you to be vegetarian, or vegan, or whatever. That is a conscious decision for you to make. Only you alone can decide which diet you think is best for you, as well as for the betterment of the planet at large. I am a vegetarian, but I have made that decision not solely based on cultural or religious grounds, but on an ethical and scientific understanding. Nevertheless, there are certain alarming facts that apply to us all, where research is continuously being aimed at today, and so that is what we will focus on here.

The Microbiome

There are trillions of microscopic organisms that reside in and on our bodies making up what we call the microbiome. More specifically, I want to talk about the gut microbiome. There are ten times the number of microbial cells in the human gut alone, than in the entire human body. In their normal state, the gut microbiome has a myriad of positive functions, including protection from invasion and the modulation of the immune system. When we eat, we are feeding all those trillions of bacteria that make up our microbiome.

Research in this area is still growing, but picking up. The best guess at the moment is that an ideal microbiome is a diverse one, capable of adaption and job sharing. These bugs have evolved with us over millions of years and live off the food we take in and, in return, provide a huge array of services to the human body. For example, one species makes serotonin, which is the hormone linked with mood. Others manufacture vitamins. Think of your own gut bug community as the staff in a factory that are producing products that you need to stay alive.

Numerous scientific studies show that seventy per cent of our immune system activity takes place in and around our gut. According to one study, there are actually more immune reactions in your gut, over the course of one day, than in the rest of your body in your entire lifetime. Over the years our gut population have been decimated by modern industrial living, food additives, unnecessary ingredients, high levels of stress, the overuse of antibiotics, and much more. We know this because studies have been carried on individuals that are still living life as we once did thousands of years ago. When you start eating differently, your microbiome will begin to change within two to three days. Simply getting five different vegetables into your diet daily can accelerate the process of optimising your microbiome. Our systems thrive from biodiversity in our diet, it simply cannot stick to eating the same thing day-in and day-out. Overeating the same things over time can cause damage and imbalance. If we think about evolutionary history, we should assume that our bodies are not meant to eat avocados or chips for 52 weeks straight or toast for breakfast every single day. I can only share what has worked for me, and ayurveda has worked tremendously for my gut microbiome. Good health starts with a healthy gut, so, I want to take you on a small diversion to the world of ayurvedic health.

An Ayurvedic Diet
Āyurveda teaches that the main source of energy for your body and mind comes from the food that you eat. In fact, the ancient Vedic teachings perceive all human experiences as 'food'. This includes your thoughts and what you digest through your five senses. Your brain is in a continuous dialogue with your digestive system, and so, mental, emotional, as well as sensory disturbances, can put a serious strain on your digestion. Taking just one example, in the West, we are used to eating with a spoon, fork, or knife; in the East, food is eaten with the hands. Hold on though, there are practical reasons for this too. It is believed that our five fingers represent the five elements, namely, earth, water, fire, air, and space (ether). Using our hands enables us to infuse this collective energy into every morsel. Ayurveda also promotes other habits and techniques to optimise our diet. Let's look at some of the most popular ones.

First there is the consumption of mung beans, a form of legumes, often referred to as 'the queen of legumes'. They are highly nutritious and wholesome, making them suitable for everybody. It is a great source of protein, carbohydrates, and fibre. It is a complete food source, that nourishes the body tissues, yet it is still light in quality, which is rare. Particularly in the West, mung is not widely known or used, yet it is easily available. That is a real shame. Mung beans are considered an alkaline food, since they are rich in minerals such as calcium, magnesium, and potassium, They also have a low glycaemic index (GI), which means they provide a slow release of energy to the bloodstream from their breakdown during digestion. Mahant Swami's diet consisted of only mung for many years, as he realised the clear benefit of this superfood. Even today, he includes mung in his regular diet.

Focusing on mindful eating practices can also be hugely beneficial. This means giving a hundred per cent focus on being nourished by your meal. It means avoiding eating meals if you feel nervous, anxious, worried, or distracted. To eat mindfully means to be present and give your full attention to your meal, engaging all your senses in the process of eating. Regulating mealtimes and portions is also helpful. Increased frequency of meals is fine, as long there is a genuine hunger and the previous meal has digested, which is usually within two to three hours. Slowing down the time you take to eat your meal and chew your food will help you digest better and prevent the formation of abdominal discomfort and gas. Thrive on a simple, well-cooked, and easy-to-digest diet. It is recommended to have vegetables lightly cooked, baked, or steamed, and eaten while hot as opposed to consuming raw vegetables and salads. Salads are okay occasionally, but if you are opting for salads regularly, go for a cooked salad – roast your vegetables and eat them with lettuce leaves at room temperatures. Try to eat minimal cold foods, and yes, this includes frozen items, iced or carbonated drinks, foods straight out of the fridge and lunchtime classics like sandwiches. Stimulate warmth in the body by drinking plenty of warm water and herbal teas, such as ginger, lemon, cardamon, tulsi (holy basil) or fennel. Ensure that you have three regulated and satisfying meals a day, but avoid late-night binge eating. Eat a light, balanced breakfast the following morning, and aim to have your main meal of the day at lunchtime if possible. Always take time to sit down and eat; do not eat whilst standing, driving, or walking. Sitting down to eat ensures that your stomach is in a relaxed state. Many Eastern cultures choose to sit on the floor, cross-legged (sukhāsana), which helps the blood flow to the abdomen. The slight bend forward and back, to eat from the plate on the floor, increases the secretion of stomach acids and engages the abdominal muscles, which results in improved digestion. This way of eating, helps to control overconsumption of food, as the upper part of the stomach naturally gets compressed, reducing the capacity to overeat. Eating in a hurry is also known to trigger indigestion, bloating, and possibly abdominal pain. Chew your food well – barely any of us do this – we eat as though it is a chore or a race. According to self-proclaimed diet expert, Horace Fletcher, in the 1800s, we should chew our food thirty-two times before swallowing it. Stop eating when you feel satisfied. Portion control is key. Avoid drinking too much water before, during, and immediately after your meal, as this can weaken your digestive fire. Drinks at mealtime are fine, but they should be just enough to moisten your food and not completely douse your digestive fire. I could go on about the three doshas and agni, but this book isn't here to serve as an ayurvedic guide. This is merely an overview of some mindful eating practices that have worked for me and many others. Maybe you could give them a try too.

Ghee and Buttermilk
Ghee (clarified butter) and buttermilk (chās) are both potions for health. Ghee is a nourishing tonic to the nervous system and the brain. It is known to improve perception, clarity, and memory. It also

nourishes, supports and improves the functions of the eyes. By clarifying butter, most of the milk proteins are removed, leaving you with a virtually lactose-free cooking fat, free from hydrogenated fats and trans-fatty acids, protecting against free radical damage. It is easy to digest, stimulating stomach acid secretion and aiding absorption of nutrients. Ghee also plays a key role in the promotion of immunity, fertility, intelligence, vision, liver, kidney and brain function, and enzyme function in the intestines. I must point out now that ghee should be used with caution in cases of obesity and high cholesterol. Buttermilk, commonly known as chās in India also improves digestion, reduces fatigue, cleanses channels and increases appetite for food. It is greatly beneficial for restoring intestinal bacteria.

Chās (Buttermilk)
Ingredients *(Serves 1)*:
1/4 cup natural set yoghurt (if possible, homemade)
3/4 cup purified cold water
1/4 tsp ground cumin
Pinch or two rock salt
Fresh coriander leaves (chopped – optional)

Method:
Simply blend or churn the yoghurt and water with a hand whisk or blender for 1-2 minutes.
Remove the froth that foams at the top.
Whisk again if the foam is not fully extracted (it should look like opaque, cloudy water).
Add the cumin and salt.
Add finely chopped coriander leaves and stir (optional).
Serve at room temperature.

Sugar

The war for and against sugar is still being fought today. We have outsourced our food choices to massive global corporations. They're the ones deciding what goes into their products and, therefore, what goes on in our bodies. In this way, decisions made in faraway corporate boardrooms are causing cascades of biological changes to happen inside us – changes that could cause pain, stress, infirmity, and even shorten our lives. If you're eating processed or pre-packed food there's a very good chance that your intake of the sticky white stuff is through the roof. The only way to get any real idea about the amount you're consuming is to get into the habit of looking at labels. I started this years ago and I'm still shocked by how many seemingly 'healthy' foods contain sugar as a prominent ingredient.

These retailers are playing fast and loose with our health – and our National Health Service – simply to gain the very tiniest imagined advantage over their rivals. Sugar is finding its way into more and more of our foodstuffs, and it's we who end up paying, not only at the tills but also with our health. Type 2 diabetes is now at genuine crisis levels in the UK. Since 1996, the number of Britons diagnosed with the condition has more than doubled, from 1.4 million to nearly 3.5 million. On top of that, there's an estimated further 1.1 million currently living with it, undiagnosed. Even the food we give our children is spiked with sugar. The recommended daily intake for children is five cubes, and the average British child consumes three cubes at breakfast alone. Did you know that just a few centuries ago, sugar was seen as a luxury commodity? Today, refined white sugar has become a highly addictive substance, and it is considered to be nothing more than 'empty calories', giving the body energy without any nutritional value. With the abundance of processed and packaged foods available in the supermarkets, most of the time we have very little awareness of how much sugar the food we eat contains.

This refined white sugar gets absorbed directly into the bloodstream, bringing instant energy to the body, which can be helpful in emergency cases, where immediate energy is needed. If continuous consumption of sugar persists, however, it puts pressure on the digestive organs to constantly regulate levels of glucose; the body starts to lose its functionality. Natural sugars (simple carbohydrates) found in fruits and sweet vegetables do provide nutrients on the other hand, as well as essential digestible fibre. Complex carbohydrates, found in grains, nuts, seeds, legumes and vegetables, are always favoured, as they release a steady flow of energy as well as providing the body with essential nutrients – proteins, vitamins, minerals, fats and vital nutrients. Excessive sugar intake has been linked to diabetes, anxiety, depression, adrenal dysfunction, hyperactivity and more. As a society, we are addicted to sugar, and the food companies know it. They are happy to make you dependent on their products by adding copious amounts of sugar. Shopping the perimeter of the store, you will notice how it is generally much healthier than the centre aisles where the highly processed food sits.

The main part of the problem is that the overconsumption of sugar seems to alter our taste buds. As they become used to it, our bodies crave more and more. We're biologically hardwired to crave sugar. One of the world's leading experts in evolutionary biology, Harvard's Professor Daniel Lieberman, says that sugar is a 'deep, ancient craving' that probably evolved to help us survive. But modern food technology has allowed ultra-sweet flavours to proliferate. A once useful survival adaption has now become problematic. Because there's so much sugar in our diets, we regularly find our blood sugar levels soaring. Studies into the effects of these sudden sugar spikes on the brain have found they trigger intense activation in a region called the nucleus accumbent, an area that's involved with reward, pleasure, addiction and saliency (how drawn you are to a stimulus that causes these effects, such as a chocolate bar or a milkshake). Remarkably, this is the same area that lights up in people who have addictions to drugs such as cocaine, heroin and nicotine.

Summing Up
I'm sorry to stretch this part of the book out, but I seriously think a good diet is key to the well-being of our bodies. Particularly as it directly affects our thoughts and feelings. Approximately twenty-five per cent of your meal should be good proteins. You may increase this by about five per cent if you are actively exercising.

Over the past few years, it has become substantially easier to find healthier foods because the industry is waking up to the issues, and consumers are demanding better options. I don't want you to rant about not being able to afford organic foods or smarter options either. Others talk about how inconvenient it is to cook and spend extra time preparing real food. Let me remind you that taking four prescription drugs, giving yourself daily injections, and having triple bypass surgery is expensive and rather inconvenient too. How much does it cost to miss a week of work due to getting sick? I guarantee that you can find an organic, or at least natural, version of almost everything that you like to eat. It may cost a bit more to get a healthier version, but it must become a way of life. Nature provides food in seasons, which is how we should consume them. Overexposure to certain foods can produce a harmful sensitivity to them. It may cost a bit more to get a healthier version, but it must become a way of life. Take charge of your health and wellbeing, because no one else can do that for you. Begin with your diet.

Relax

When it comes to relaxing, a surprising number of people don't get any. It's important that we have a little switch-off time in our routine. For at least fifteen to thirty minutes each day, and more if possible, stop everything and be selfish. *Choose* to relax. *Choose* to give yourself some time. It must be something for you and you alone. Do something, but don't use your phone, tablet, or computer. And also, don't feel guilty for giving yourself time.

I suffered intensely from ulcerative colitis and Crohn's disease – I still do, but it's under better control with small lifestyle changes. It's a nasty bowel complaint where you get painful stomach cramps, straining headaches, and having to keep visiting the bathroom. What did the doctors do? They said the leading cause will probably be stress, and they handed me over prescription after prescription. Even after this, the symptoms settled for a while, and then showed up again. I knew I had to take matters into my own hands. After being on and off with my Ayurvedic diet, I began thirty minute walks intermittently throughout the week. As well as this, I found time to relax, at least four times a week. I did things that I love and that were solely for me. I felt my symptoms reduce by up to fifty per cent. I'm not saying this will work for every colitis or Crohn's patient. There's no way to prove even that – everyone is different. The important fact is that I gave some time to myself in my daily routine. By making space for yourself for up to thirty minutes per day can help normalise cortisol levels within your body. Cortisol has been identified as one of our principal stress-response hormones. Hormone levels spike and fall at different times throughout the day, in natural cycles, and they also rise and fall in response to things that are happening to us. It's obvious that cortisol levels surge significantly when we're stressed.

Contrary to popular belief, stress isn't necessarily bad. We've evolved to experience stress for many good reasons. After all, we're a resilient species. Cortisol works by activating what is known as our sympathetic nervous system – your fight-or-flight response. In the modern world, we are *constantly* in fight-or-flight mode. We spend our days with our cortisol levels continuously ramped right up, and our sympathetic nervous systems activated. We're no longer being chased by lions like the hunter-gatherers thousands of years ago, but we're being attacked by life.

> **The Automatic Nervous System (ANS)**
>
> Our nervous system has two parts. The first is the sympathetic nervous system, which causes the body to release stress-response hormones such as noradrenaline and cortisol. It causes heart rate to quicken, lung tubes to widen, muscles to contract, pupils to dilate, and switches off digestion. In the short term, the sympathetic nervous system helps us to deal with stress, but if it's continuously activated… well, then it's clear how that can be problematic.
>
> In modern society, this fight-or-flight system activates when we're rushing to hand in an assignment or meet a deadline, when we're getting stressed on our commute to work, when we are late for the school run, or when we are putting our body through a tough workout. This automatic response can be managed, as long as we take the right steps to balance it out with rest and relaxation.
>
> The other part is the parasympathetic system, which allows for the body to rest and relax. It works at a much slower rate than the sympathetic part. When it is activated, our saliva production increases, digestive enzymes are released, our heart rate drops, and our muscles relax. It allows for us to digest food appropriately, de-stress, and sleep soundly.
>
> To help us manage the stress of modern life, we should encourage the activation of the parasympathetic nervous system as much as we possibly can.

Every hormone in your body is made up from the same basic stuff – LDL cholesterol. Your body naturally has a limited supply of this and, when things are working well, it portions it off nicely, so there's enough to go around. There's enough to make oestrogen, progesterone, testosterone – and also cortisol. But what happens when we're in one of these long-term states of stress? In these states, cortisol, thinking that it is under attack, snatches LDL cholesterol from the other hormones. Your body then prioritises the generation of cortisol. It thinks you need it to cope with the drama and keeps making more and more of it. This upsets the finely-tuned balance of hormones within your marvellous body.

When we're constantly stressed, our bodies respond as if we're under attack. You will have noticed this. We go into a kind of emergency mode and divert resources to the processes most necessary for our survival. If this is simply short-term, then great, but in the long term this can create huge problems. It can lead to weight gain and sleep disruption. It can also exhaust the immune system. The thing is, your body can't tell the difference between emotional, physical and nutritional stress. It can't tell the difference between the stress of not meeting a deadline or mortgage payment, or the stress you feel when your Instagram post gets negative comments on it. To your system, it's the same as a lion chasing you, and so it reacts in the same way, each and every time.

There is a clear link between stress and your body. When your body thinks it's under attack, it puts your immune system into an emergency state. We call this heightened immune response 'inflammation' and, again, we're not supposed to be in this state for an extended period of time. Inflammation is the leading, visible symptom of both colitis and Crohn's too. Chronic inflammation (in medical terms, any bad condition that stays around for too long is known as 'chronic') underpins pretty much every single degenerative disease that we can have, including heart attacks, strokes, and even Alzheimer's disease.

A 2016 paper published by researchers from King's College, London, highlighted just one of the ways inflammation can have a surprising impact on the connected body. They showed a remarkable link between inflammation and depression. The scientists suggested that it can be predicted which patients suffering from depression will respond to conventional antidepressants by giving them blood tests that show levels of inflammation. They found that patients with heightened levels of inflammation do not respond to conventional antidepressants. The results confirm what other scientific research has been suggesting for years – depression itself can be a symptom of biological changes in the body, driven by inflammation. Depression is simply a name we give to a broad group of symptoms, but the word itself doesn't tell us anything about the root cause of the problem.

Simply by making space for yourself, whether that be to relax by meditating, walking, exercising, or the like, you can normalise cortisol levels in your body. Don't simply go by my word, science proves it too. Your body will be reminded what it's like not to feel under attack all of the time. I strongly believe that modern life, even if it's simply checking all your WhatsApp messages, is stressful. I find it stressful myself. So, what do we have to lose by properly architecting our kingdom? Nothing whatsoever. Ironically, it's the people who say they don't have enough time for themselves who need it the most.

The Mind-Body Connection

We've covered the topics of death, life through breath, sleep, routines, work, boundaries, movement, drinking, eating, and relaxing. If you've reached this far into the read, then you're probably wondering why we have spent so much time discussing the body. Well, let me tell you.

There is a clear and obvious connection between the mind and body, and we could even say that this is due to the fact that the mind is part of the subtle body. In the last few decades, modern medical science has begun to acknowledge the mind-body connection. A powerful example of this is the placebo effect.

A harmless substance, like a sugar pill, is given to patients instead of prescription drugs. However, patients are told they are being given medicine for their illness. The consequence of consuming the placebo is that patients mentally believe they will now get well, and their mind induces them to recuperate, even without taking real medicine.

Whatever you do, don't become inactive, remain active until your body physically allows. If our body is finely tuned, we can begin to work on the mind. Until we architect the kingdom to a high standard, the ministers and subjects won't live with peace and understanding. They will constantly try to overrule the king. In other words, if the body is taken care of, we can start to focus on understanding and taming the workings of the mind, and then we can look at allowing the soul to flourish. And with that, I now introduce you to the commander of the kingdom – the mind.

MIND

The Commander and His Monkey

> Except for the uncontrolled and misguided mind,
> no greater enemy lurks within this world.
> *Bhakta Prahlad*

The commander (the mind) is the closest aide to the king. Unfortunately, the commander carries around a pet monkey. This pet monkey distracts the commander from carrying out his duties towards the king and the kingdom, and so it diverts its attention to the subjects. The commander is the head of the ministers (the senses).

The mind is *not* the brain. The brain is a physical, tangible organ within your body, whereas the mind is intangible. The location of the mind within the body can be debated, but for simplicity and the purpose of reading, we will assume it's within your head. But still, the mind is part of your body, namely the subtle body. Hence, there is a direct link between your mind and body.

Each and every single thing that we think or do in our lives comes down to the mind. Every thought, feeling, experience, or action passes through the mind. Yet, you are distinct. The failure to have this discretion in our lives, and thus manage our minds, is the sole cause of all suffering. John Milton wrote: "The mind is its own place, and in itself can make a heaven of hell, a hell of heaven."[1] Krishna also says to Arjun, "For him who has conquered the mind, the mind is the best of friends; but for the one who has failed do so, his very mind will be the greatest enemy."[2]

The Mind

We often equate the mind with the brain, which isn't wrong in general, but this limits the ideas associated with the mind. In Vedic teachings, the mind is responsible for thinking and feeling (through manas – the thinker), reasoning (through buddhi – the reasoner), contemplating (through chitta – the contemplator), and affirming (through ahamkāra – the I-maker). For the ātmā to process any information it receives through the senses (the subjects), it uses the faculty of the mind (the commander, or ministers if we break the mind down into its four faculties). Subjects of the kingdom don't interact with the king directly, they do so only through the ministers. The eyes might see a yellow flower, and through the optic nerve, electrical impulses travel to the brain and produce an image for the 'seer'. It is then the mind who responds to the flower, recognising it, giving it the colour 'red' and identifying it as 'flower'. Sometimes, it responds with emotion. Again for emphasis, the brain is the physical organ in the physical body, that links the physical body to the intangible mind. It does this through the senses.

For millennia, thinkers and philosophers have wrestled with ideas of whether the mind, with its responses to sensory stimuli and inputs, determine who we are. Five hundred years ago, Western philosopher-mathematician René Descartes proposed that it is by the actions of the mind that we know we exist. That is why he famously proclaimed: *cogito ergo sum*, "I think, therefore I am." The Vedic teachings turn this idea on its head and proclaim, 'I am, therefore I think'. Swaminarayan mentions that it is solely due to the presence and power of the atma that the mind (and the body) can even function. It is clear that the brain is part of the physical (gross) body and the mind is part of the subtle (astral) body. Nevertheless, putting everything else about the physical or subtle body aside, both bodies are still material.

The four inner faculties are generally informed by the stimuli that they receive from the senses. Similar to a computer's hard drive, the mind can be understood as a repository of facts, stories and memories. The mind doesn't necessarily understand the significance of the information that it receives and processes, but placing sensations into two broad categories, namely pleasure and pain, it responds accordingly. How these sensations are categorised is largely based on previous associations with similar sensations.

Every single experience that we have, whether it comes from the eyes, ears, nose, tongue, or skin, leaves a lasting impression on the mind. The software of the mind is updated constantly through our daily experiences and interactions. To give another example, say you're crossing a street and you notice a car coming towards you, depending on how fast the car is moving and your previous experiences with cars moving at similar speeds, the mind will produce an almost instinctive response. If you have associated vehicles with accidents, injury and death, you may feel a sense of fear. On the other hand, if you associate cars with prestige, luxury and glamour, you may feel jealousy. Research even shows that phobias are heightened responses to past sensory inputs that have left strong, negative impressions on the mind.

The mind is constantly changing based on our constantly changing experiences. As a child, we may have been afraid of climbing up a mountain and looking over the edge of the mountain cliff, but by the time you're an adult, that very same view can be exhilarating. What happened? Your mind adapted and changed. Similarly, any thoughts and feelings you experience can also be changed to help you live a more focused and blissful life. Even the things that invoke little emotion in us can become objects of passion or pain within moments. By identifying with our mind, we subject ourselves to these shifting emotional states. By disidentifying with our mind, we rise above these emotional states. They are still present, they don't disappear, but they become insignificant. We are separate from our thoughts, feelings and our mind. If we weren't, how could we direct the mind away from them?

The mind is an amazing and powerful tool, but only if controlled and used to one's advantage. Objectively, it can be seen as a brilliant creation. Subjectively, it can make one's life unbearable. As we will explore, the mind functions very much like a troublemaking monkey. Whether it be in the Upanishads and other Vedic scriptures, or whether it be Buddha in his teachings, this has been emphasised throughout all Eastern philosophy. Gunatitanand Swami, the first spiritual successor of Swaminarayan, extensively talked of the mind as a monkey. In one such talk he says, "The mind is like a mischievous monkey; it keeps on flitting."[3] We notice this in our day-to-day lives as well. We fail to concentrate on any one thing properly for a good amount of time. We are constantly distracted by things around us. What is important to us at one moment is dropped as soon as something else comes along. The mind really is like a monkey. I don't like giving negative connotations to the mind, and so, to help explain how the mind can be controlled and tamed, let's recall the commander (the mind) has a pet monkey that often distracts him. Either you can go with this, or you can assume that the mind of the commander is the monkey, but this may unnecessarily complicate things, hence I prefer the former. Like a monkey with a banana, when we give the mind a more fulfilling and beneficial focus through control, we can easily overcome its negative tendencies and distractions. Only when the mind is in focus can we truly begin to nourish the needs of our ātmā. I am a firm believer that it is extremely difficult (but not impossible) to control the mind with meditation, mindfulness, or such activities alone. Instead, we need to give the mind a much higher engagement – constantly. Swaminarayan says that one should continuously keep the mind engaged and never let it run idle. I'm sure you've heard the phrase, "An idle mind is the devil's workshop." The mind is a tool to be used by the ātmā for a higher purpose, not the other way round.

The Role of Intelligence

The power to decide what we value and how we should strive to achieve what we value, is beyond the scope of the mind (manas). The power to discern and discriminate lies with the intelligence (buddhi). In the classic metaphor of the Katha Upanishad, known as the Ratha Kalpanā, it is the intelligence that holds the reigns of the body-chariot. [4] In the adaption of our analogy, we can assume the intellect to be the 'controlled' commander, who not being distracted by the monkey, ministers and subjects, governs them and works in synchronisation with (and for) the king. The intellect is the faculty that guides the mind, distinguishing the right from the wrong, the moral from the immoral, the truth from the illusion, and the positive from the negative. It is through the intelligence that we can develop discretion (vivek). If I walk past the cake shop and the scent tempts me, my mind will likely interpret the aroma as being pleasurable. It will then think, "I want it." But if I have diabetes, or I'm not feeling well, my intelligence will (hopefully) stop me from actually going in and getting myself a slice. However, if the intelligence is not controlled, or properly trained, it will give in to the mind's demand and I might well suffer the consequences.

THE RATHA KALPANA

In this metaphor, the ātmā is a passenger, seated on a chariot, pulled by five horses. The chariot depicts the body, and the five horses are the senses. The reins are the mind, and they are held by the intelligence, the charioteer. All of these are directed by the ātmā, or at least, that's the plan. Ideally, it should the ātmā that disciplines the intelligence to control the mind, which in turn controls the senses. When self-awareness is absent, the passenger is not in charge. Rather, the ātmā gets overpowered, unable to direct the intelligence, so it is easily pulled this way, and that too, by a restless mind and uncontrolled senses. Transformation can begin when we use our intelligence to take control of the reigns of the mind and senses.

The Role of Ego

From a Vedic perspective, all self-conceptions stem from the I-maker (ahamkāra). For ease of reading, we will refer to the I-maker as the ego. It's important to note that the ego referred to here doesn't directly refer to the negative trait of the ego in the sense of narcissistic pride and vanity. The ego in this context refers to self-identity. In our general social interactions, the ego may well refer to our sense of self-esteem, and someone who expresses their self-esteem at the expense of others is known as 'egotistical'.

Almost every school of thought has depicted the ego in different ways. The German philosopher Immanuel Kant wrote, "The transcendental ego is the thinker of our thoughts, the subject of our experiences, the willer of our actions, and the agent of the various activities of synthesis that help to constitute the world we experience."

The Vedic texts differentiate between the true ego and the false ego in a similar manner. The true ego can often be misunderstood, and it has a negative touch to it, hence the term 'ātmā', 'self', or, 'soul' are more applicable. To overcome the illusion of the mind and body, and to identify with the true essence of our being – the ātmā – is at the core of all spiritual endeavour on this earth. The ātmā is the conscious living force within each of us. It is the pure self. It is true and existent (sat), conscious (chitta) and the embodiment of bliss (ānanda). In Swaminarayan theology, the aim of the human life is defined as becoming one with (or realising) Brahman [Akshar], and to be situated with Parabrahman [Purushottam]. The denial or negation of this truth is what leads to identification with the mind and its illusions. The ego we use to define ourselves in the modern world: British or Indian, black or white, male or female, are all false in comparison to the ātmā. This is the reason that we all think, "I am this body, and everything in relation to this body is mine." Living in today's world, it is so easy to pin our identity on social labels – man, woman, young, old, fat, slim, Indian, British, black, white, Hindu, Muslim – or to base it on what we have, know, or feel. But it is the excessive identification with these external labels, the body, and the mind, that is at the root of suffering. The most dangerous effect of the false ego is the toll it takes on the ātmā. If we allow the ego to take charge, the ātmā becomes almost weak and frail, or so it seems. The ego, which allows the misidentification to the body and mind to flourish, is also the cause of rebirth according to Vedic philosophy.

Your True Identity

Now that we've touched upon the key faculties of the mind, it is fitting to discuss our true identity. This will set the scene for what is to come in the following pages and the remainder of this book. When we are engrossed in physical and mental identities, we simply have no time, energy or need to ponder on our true nature. With so many distractions just a hand's reach away, this question is more relevant now than ever before. We *must* find deeper meaning in our life. The ancient spiritual texts of India have always emphasised the necessity to know one's true identity. In fact, the Upanishads and Bhagavad-Gitā both begin with a thorough analysis of our identity in all of its layers. The ātmā is one's true identity. It is ever-existing, eternal, and indestructible. It has a conscious essence, the nature of which is blissful awareness. Since the ātmā experiences the notions of time, space, and the physical world through the body, understanding who and what we are begins by understanding who and what we are not. We are not the body that we inhabit. We are not the mind that plays us about either. We live in the body. We use the mind as a tool. But we are the ātmā.

No matter how impressive a car may be, it cannot function without its driver, but the driver can always function without the car. That's how we can distinguish the material body and mind from the atma. We identify with the body and mind because of the direct experiences they provide, along with our attachment to those very sensations. In fact, we spend so much time seeking out these sensations through our physical and mental bodies that we feel as if we are those bodies. This in itself is an illusion too. The ātmā is not one with the body, it merely inhabits the body. The ātmā is the observer living inside the body; it is the 'I' who is experiencing. The gross, subtle and even the causal body have no power without the ātmā. Perception and the prāna stop the moment the ātmā leaves the body – the phenomenon that we call death.

I would also like to briefly mention suffering at this point too. Suffering is a universal experience. We all suffer physically, mentally, and emotionally. But as we develop a deeper level of self-awareness, we learn to acknowledge suffering, and accept it without identifying ourselves with it. Eventually, we hope to even transcend it.

Before we begin to explore the bumpy terrains of the mind, I want to take you on a small detour into the relationship between the mind and the brain, and how both can often trick us. It's time for you to meet the pet monkey.

Higher than the gross body are the senses.
Higher than the senses is the mind.
Higher than the mind is the intelligence.
Higher than the intelligence is the ātmā.
Bhagavad-Gitā 3.42

Who Rules the World?

The mind can also be simplified into two parts: the Thinker (the commander) and the Feeler (the monkey), who often diverts the attention of the commander to do what the other ministers and subjects want. The Thinker represents all our conscious thoughts, as well as our ability to make calculations, reason through various options, and express ideas through language. It makes up ninety-eight per cent of all our thinking. The Feeler represents our emotions, impulses, intuition, and instincts. While the Thinker may be calculating payment schedules on your credit card statement, the Feeler is the one who wants to just let it go and run away to Barbados. The Feeler makes up two per cent of all our thinking. The Feeler is not necessary bad. Likewise, the Thinker is not necessarily good either. Each have their own strengths and weaknesses.

The Thinker is conscientious, accurate, and impartial. It is methodical and rational, but it's a bit slow. It requires a lot of effort and energy, and like a muscle, it must be built up over time and can become fatigued if overexerted. Understand this to be like a tired aide to the king, frantically running around with tasks at hand all day and night. The Feeler, however, arrives at its conclusions quite quickly and effortlessly. Understand this to be like the monkey drawing conclusions from what the other ministers and subjects talk about. The problem lies in the fact that the Feeler is often inaccurate and irrational. I mean, not everything that goes around is true, right? And, how can we even trust the untamed monkey? The monkey is also a bit dramatic; it has a bad habit of overreacting and going crazy.

Looking at the bigger picture, when we normally think of ourselves and the decisions that we make, we generally like to assume that the commander is driving our decisions, and the monkey is tamed and only distracts the commander at times. The kingdom is functioning well, the subjects are under control and the ministers align themselves with the commander and king, accomplishing our goals and figuring how to make the kingdom prosper. That is, until the royal court step out of the kingdom and see the royal members of other kingdoms. That is when the monkey goes full-on crazy. That is when the real games begin.

The unfortunate truth is that it is often the monkey shaping most of our thoughts and decisions. It doesn't matter whether you're Alexander the Great, Elon Musk, or just a normal person, everyone is controlled by the monkey (at least initially). The reason for this is simple: *we are ultimately moved to action only by emotion*. That's because action is itself emotion. Emotion is the biological hydraulic system that is pushing our bodies into movement. Think about it, everything that you do is powered by emotion. You work to provide for your family, why? Because the emotion of love is there. Your ancestor hunter-gatherers, thousands of years ago, ran away when they saw a lion. Why? The emotion of fear was there. Emotion inspires action, and action inspires emotion. Neither can be separated. Emotions are a part and parcel of life in this world, and we must learn to acknowledge and work with them, not merely shun them.

If you take a moment to think about it, most problems in this world are rooted in emotion. Emotion comes from the mind and ego, and so, it can also be said that every problem in this world stems from the mind and ego of an individual. Self-control is an emotional problem; laziness is an emotional problem; lust is an emotional problem; anger is an emotional problem; procrastination is an emotional problem; impulsiveness an emotional one. Every problem comes down to our emotions.

Relying on intellect alone to understand how we can change our behaviour doesn't serve us in any way. Someone smoking cigarettes already *knows* they need to stop. Someone who is having symptoms of diabetes already *knows* they need to cut down on sugar. The same principle can be applied to negative people and situations, we *know* the damage it will do us at some point. And it's not only because we don't know better, it's also because we don't *feel* better. Emotional feelings can only be solved through emotional solutions. The only way to solve the negative tendencies thrown towards us by the monkey is by taming the monkey itself. The commander *must* take back control over the monkey. As Daniel Kahneman once put it, the Thinker is 'the supporting character who imagines herself to be the lead actor'.[5]

It is the Feeler that generates the emotions that cause us to move into action, and it is the Thinker that suggests where to direct that action. The monkey begs for attention, the commander gives it. Moral psychologist Jonathan Haidt compares these two to an elephant and its rider.[6] The rider can gently steer and pull the elephant in a particular direction, but ultimately the elephant is going to go where it wants to go. Likewise, the monkey sometimes has a mind of its own too.

Know the Monkey

You may have noticed, you might not have, but you have a constant dialogue running inside your head that never seems to stop. It just keeps going and going. This is the monkey inside your head. The monkey hates being told what to do. It will try to do anything it can to make the life of everyone else in the kingdom miserable. Despite being closest to the commander, its best friends are in fact the subjects of the kingdom. It seems like the monkey and the commander have developed a really unhealthy and unstable relationship over time. The commander is easily influenced by the monkey, falling into traps again and again. This is known as the 'self-serving bias', and it is pretty much the basis of everything bad about humanity and the world. This self-serving bias is a direct manifestation of the ego. Simply put, it is what makes us prejudiced and a little bit self-centred. We assume that what *feels* right to us *is* right. We make snap judgements about almost all people, places, groups, ideas, and beliefs, most of which are unfair or even a little bit bigoted.

In its worst form, the self-serving bias can become outright delusion. This causes us to believe in a reality of our own, which is not real – the ultimate illusion. This smudges memories and exaggerates facts, all in service of the monkey's never-ending craving to create narratives. We'll be looking at such biases and fallacies in a short while.

For some, the untamed monkey drives them towards attention and money. For others, it drives them towards power. These are the most dangerous monkeys. They set to work justifying their abuse and subjugation of others through intellectual-sounding theories about economics, politics, race, genetics, gender, biology, history, philosophy, and so on. Sir John Dalberg-Action said, "Power tends to corrupt, but absolute power corrupts absolutely." I can say with pride and joy that this fact has not held true for my gurus. Pramukh Swami had absolute power of the socio-spiritual organisation, yet it never corrupted him. Never in the forty-five years of his leadership. But, when we take a look at the rest of history, we see how this fact holds true. Only those who have full control over their emotions and mind can live a life where power does not corrupt. It means nothing to them. They live a life of higher values and purpose.

The untamed monkey bullies the commander, and so the commander develops a sort of Stockholm syndrome – it can't imagine a life of service towards the king, its only focus now is on pleasing and justifying the monkey. The untamed monkey is what inspired ancient philosophers to warn us against the overindulgence, precedence and worship of feelings. For most of human history, people who have let their feelings and emotions control them have been brutal, superstitious, and inhumane. The overindulgence of emotion leads to destruction, and likewise, so does the repression of emotion. Those who deny their feelings and emotions numb themselves from the world around them. By rejecting emotions, we reject making valued and unbiased judgements, that is, deciding that one thing is better than another. As a result, one becomes indifferent to life and the results of their decisions. They struggle to engage with others. Their relationships suffer. They live a life filled with crisis. Ultimately, they end up living an unfocused life.

Tame the Monkey

The only language the monkey really understands is empathy. Instead of bombarding the monkey with facts and reason, we need to start asking it how it feels. We need to have conversations with the monkey. How will the monkey respond? Not with words, but with feelings.

We underestimate the importance of having conversations with the monkey and allowing it to let out its feelings. Sometimes we just need to let our feelings out into the air, in the right way of course, because the more they breathe, the weaker their grip on the commander and the kingdom. To tame the monkey, we must continuously bargain with it too. The monkey needs to feel it is striking a good bargain with the commander.

The best way to do this is by offering the monkey something easy with a fitting emotional benefit. For example, feeling good after a walk or workout, pursuing a career that feels significant and aligns with your purpose, or being admired and respected by others for your values. When we begin to do this, the monkey will respond with another emotion, either positive or negative. If the emotional response is positive, the monkey is willing to work with the commander – but only a bit. Remember that feelings never last. They are always fleeting. That is why we must start small. If the monkey's response is negative, you simply acknowledge the negative emotion and offer another compromise. Rinse and repeat. But whatever you do, you must never confront the monkey directly.

The only means by which we will succeed in taming the monkey is by having conversations with it. The best method of doing this is through constant contemplation. Again, here too, you cannot jump straight into the deep end. Start small and introspect at the start and end of your day. What do I need to do today? What have I done today? This form of dialogue needs to take place continuously in order for us to begin taming the mind. Others may have the opposite problem: They will have to train their commander to be adamant against the monkey. They will have to force it to propose an independent thought – a new direction – which is unique from the monkey's feelings. They will have to ask themselves, what if the monkey is wrong to feel this way? And then, they must consider the alternatives. In psychology, this is referred to as 'emotional regulation'. It's not an easy job, for sure, but it's the best job you will carry out.

You may be able to tame the mind. You may be able to understand and work with your feelings. You may even be able to get a hold on your emotions. But what about the enemies that affect all of us on a daily basis? The enemies that we struggle to maintain a grip over. These enemies are not just within us; they are like a swarm throughout all of society. There are times when we all feel victim to the world around us, or worse, to our own minds.

Sometimes, regardless of what we do – or set out to do – these inner enemies get the better of us. We have no idea how to move forward. The greatest enemies are those that have infiltrated into the kingdom. They live within the kingdom. They plan to destroy you from within the kingdom. They hide among the subjects. There will be times where we will have to prepare for fierce battles with these enemies. I encourage everyone to read the rest of this part of the book in order first, as I will be, then you are welcome to visit any topic of your choice, whenever you feel like doing so.

> Here I was, in the serene and divine village of Sarangpur, and here in front of me was an individual, who had not only mastered his mind, but had disassociated with it. In front of me was a truly great personality who believed himself to be distinct not only from the body, but also the mind.
> I had heard many stories of his greatness, but until now I had rarely seen it first-hand. I had heard, how, despite many obstacles and issues in his life, he remained at joy and peace – ever content and blissful. I wanted to know, if any, what were his secrets to this joy?

Ego: It's All About Me

> The first principle is that you must not fool yourself,
> And you are the easiest person to fool.
> *Richard Feynman*

We buy expensive homes with loans far beyond our ability to pay. The same goes for cars and luxury goods. We strive to create a 'personal brand' (also known as 'self-branding'), packaging ourselves like a product to be sold. When our unhealthy ego becomes almost obsessive, everything we do becomes tailored around 'me, me me'. This is what we call narcissism. It's the belief in an inflated sense of one's own importance.

Wherever you are, whoever you are, and whatever you do, your worst enemy is already within you – your ego. The ego that we refer to here goes by the more casual definition that we see. It's the unhealthy belief in one's own importance and significance. Arrogance. Conceit. Vanity. Grandiosity. Self-centred ambition. I switch between using the words 'ego' and 'narcissism'. It's when the notion of ourselves and the world grows so inflated that it begins to distort the reality that surrounds us.

I was very indecisive on whether to include an extensive chapter on this topic, but with the prevailing culture in the modern world, and to live the focused life, I think it is of great importance, now more than ever before. So, here we go.

In data from 37,000 college students, narcissistic personality traits rose just as fast as obesity from the 1980s to present day, with the shift especially pronounced for women.¹ Narcissism isn't simply a confident attitude or a healthy feeling of self-worth; in fact, there's nothing wrong with that. Narcissists are *over*confident, and unlike most people high in self-esteem, they place little value on emotionally close relationships. With the rise of the Internet, people can now present an inflated and self-focused view of themselves to the world, and it encourages us to spend hours each day contemplating our own images. If this isn't narcissistic, what else is it?

Adolf Hitler's narcissism caused the humiliation and inhumane massacre of over sixty million people. His arrogance and narcissism thinking killed three per cent of the world's population at the time. Ego.

Jim Jones, born to parents who thought their child was a messiah turned out to amass nearly 1,000 followers and establish a small community of his own in South America.² Through his delusional, narcissistic mindset of manipulation, he led over 900 people, including 304 children, to kill themselves by consuming a grape-flavoured drink laced with cyanide. It's where the phrase 'Don't drink the Kool-Aid' comes from. Ego.

Saddam Hussein rounded up over 800 men, women, and children after a failed assassination attempt and detained them for over two years.³ At the same time, he tortured and executed 148 of the men for taking part in the assassination attempt. Ego.

The engineers of the Titanic believed so strongly that the ship was unsinkable that they only equipped it with the legal minimum safety precautions, despite the fact that the safety regulations at the time were not designed for boats this big of a size.⁴ There was nowhere near enough crew to sail the ship safely through the Antarctic, and there was nowhere near enough life boats to prepare for any kind of disaster. The ship itself didn't have a great design for the time, with flood compartments not being watertight, allowing all of the compartments to fill once the boat sank to a certain point. The materials used were also shoddy. Low-quality iron was used for the rivers which became easily brittle in cold conditions. 1,500 people died. Ego.

The cause of every war, invasion and dispute throughout the history of humankind can be narrowed down to one common enemy – the ego. Swaminarayan even went as far to say, "Ego is the greatest of all sins and biggest of all blemishes."⁵ Many faiths believe that pride, same as the ego here, is a sin because it is a lie. One that convinces people that they are better than they are, or even better than the God that made them. The Vedic texts share numerous stories of those whose pride has engulfed them and who have then become delusional. Pride leads to arrogance, and then away from humility and connection with those around us. As the famous conqueror and warrior Genghis Khan groomed his sons and generals to succeed him later in life, he would repeatedly warn them, "If you can't swallow your pride, you can't lead." We must prepare for pride and get rid of it as soon as we notice it. American novelist Flannery O'Connor said, "The first product of self-knowledge is humility."

The (un)Joys of Admiring Yourself

I get it. Admiring yourself feels good and makes you happy. If we believe in ourselves, we are more likely to keep trying when we don't succeed the first time. Maybe you agree that self-admiration has certainly been successful in raising individual's opinions of themselves. We're not here to get into the nitty-gritty of this topic, but we will focus on self-admiration as modern culture promotes it, as a general feeling of self-love that doesn't distinguish between a healthy sense of self-worth and the unhealthy ego that can instead result.

You may have heard of Joel Osteen – the man with a contagious smile – and, he is also the pastor of the largest church in the United States. He goes to the extent of saying: "God wants us to have healthy, positive self-images. He wants us to feel good about ourselves." Self-esteem is considered, as one author put it, America's 'national wonder drug'. I don't think it's limited to America though, not even the Western world either, it's infecting the whole of modern culture.

If you went onto Google in 2010 and searched 'how to love yourself', you would get around 191,000 hits; in 2021, it revealed over 2 million results. With such tips as 'Make a note every time someone says something nice about you', 'Stop all criticism', and 'Look at yourself in the mirror and say, "You look great!"' Many self-help books also maintain the notion that loving yourself is a cure-all. If we just believe in ourselves, the advice goes, anything is possible. A 2009 well-known bestseller even goes to the extent of promising that you can get anything you want (especially material things) simply by visualising them, "If you just visualise it, it will become yours."

We have taken the desire for self-admiration a bit too far – so far that our culture has blurred the distinction between self-esteem and the ego in an extremely self-destructive way. The modern world has overdosed on self-admiration, and this 'wonder drug' comes with some serious side effects such as arrogance and self-centredness.

Some people may ask, "So should we just hate ourselves instead?" Of course not. Saying that hating yourself is the only alternative to loving yourself is ignorant and silly. Obesity researchers don't tell everyone they should become anorexic. I'm not suggesting self-hatred. You can like yourself just fine without loving yourself in excess. In fact, it would be better for all of society not to concentrate on self-feelings – positive or negative – quite so much. Instead, we should focus on life: our relationships with others, our work, our spiritual practices, or the beauty of the natural world. Take a moment to think about the deepest joy you experience in life and I can almost guarantee it won't come from thinking about how great you are.

In a 2009 US poll of more than 1,000 college students, two out of three individuals agreed with the statement, "My generation of young people is more self-promoting, narcissistic, overconfident, and attention-seeking than previous generations."[6]

A question that I've been asked online many times: Isn't a little narcissism needed in a competitive world? Think about it this way: if self-admiration caused success, why do the countries with presumably the highest self-esteem in the world not have the most successful individuals? In a 2006 study, thirty-nine per cent of American eighth-graders were confident of their maths skills, compared to only six per cent of Korean eighth-graders. The Koreans, however, far exceeded the American students' actual performance on maths tests.[7]

I also want to be clear that I am not arguing against a passion for a career and 'doing what you love'. But, there is a big difference between 'doing what you love' and 'loving yourself'. Being passionate about what you do can actually counter egotism. This is the idea of 'flow' – people who can do this, and that draw joy from doing something they love, are less defensive in the face of criticism, perhaps because they don't feel the need to defend their ego anymore.[8]

The Roots of Discontent

Whether we believe in the theory of evolution or not, one thing is certain, the ego seems to have been part of creation for millennia. Biologists and anthropologists have said how animals like chimpanzees and other mammals, share the seemingly innate, tribal trait of ego. We humans are tribal too. We're preoccupied with status and hierarchy; we're biased towards our own groups and prejudiced against others. It's almost automatic. It's almost how we think. It's who we are. To live a human life is to live tribally. Children as young as six, when shown pictures of people from other races in ambiguous situations, will tend to assume they're up to no good. It's also been observed that babies universally prefer faces of their own race.[9] We are blatantly aware of how dangerous this type of thinking can be, yet our minds helplessly make us tribal, dividing the world between 'my group' and 'your group'.

We also care so much about what others think of us that it is believed to be one of humanity's strongest preoccupations. Children begin to manage their reputations and status at around the age of five.[10] A core aspect of the human mind is maintaining a deep interest in, and trying to control, what others think of us. Our monkey is our PR agent. Our reputations fluctuate with gossip. The delicious tales we tell each other often radically change how others view us, and how we view others. We can't help but gossip. Studies that measure how much of a human conversation gossip constitutes put the mark at between sixty-five and ninety per cent.[11] Despite the gendered stereotype, men are no less prone to gossip than women – they just tend to do it less when women are around to hear them.[12] But so what? Does it do us any harm? It's fun, right? One team of researchers found that negative gossip can affect our vision, causing us to automatically attend more to its subject.[13]

But what am I trying to get at? It seems that the deepest causes of our modern feelings of perfectionism could well be rooted within our minds. History shows us how great kings and emperors throughout the lands tried their best to fight, conquer, and rise to the top. They didn't just crave a good reputation in order to stay safe; they wanted to rise to the very top of the tribe. The child psychologist Professor Paul Bloom explains that these aspects are not acquired through learning. They do not come from the mother, or from school, or church; they are instead the products of biological evolution.[14] Humans are self-conscious creatures. We're constantly watching ourselves, judging ourselves, just as other people are judging us.

The ego is what makes us experience life as a story. Because of the way our minds function, our sense of 'me' naturally run in narrative mode: we feel as if we're the heroes of the plot of our lives, one complete with friends, enemies, fortune, fate, and quests for happiness and success. Our minds cast haloes around our friends and plant horns on the heads of our enemies. We're constantly moving on, pursuing goals and aspirations, on an active quest to make our lives somewhat better. This form of ego is to feel as if we are, in the words of neuroscientist Professor Chris Frith, the 'invisible actor at the centre of the world'. A recent study examining various forms of biases found that 'virtually all individuals irrationally inflate their moral qualities'.[15]

Work by psychologists including Professor Nicholas Epley has shown an especially unpleasant bias in which we tend to cast ourselves as heroes, whilst throwing shade on others around us.[16] The human mind is not merely a storyteller, it is also a hero-maker – and the hero it makes is you. The surprising thing is that it's only during our teenage years that we start to understand our lives as a 'grand narrative'. The stories that we tell ourselves and others give our life meaning and purpose. It distracts us from the real chaos and hopelessness of the truth – the truth that we are not inherently unique and special – we just *are*.

We must always remain alert, as modern culture fuels our ego more than ever before. You can follow the idolised celebrities you look up to on Instagram, you can find and watch TED Talks on almost any topic, feasting upon inspiration and validation that would never have been comprehendible twenty years ago. You can become a director of an only-on-paper company. You can announce your engagement, the birth of your child, your new job role in your dream company on social media, and then let all the congratulations and praises roll in. All of us are victims to this. I am as much as you are. It's only a matter of degree. Despite the changes in technology, we are told to believe in our own uniqueness above everything else. We are told that whatever we do is best. This is manipulative and misleading. With the growth of numerous self-help and motivational books, you can find almost any 'secret' to feed your ego and seek the validation that this enemy so deeply desires. Take a dive into the history books and you will find that most famous men and women were notoriously egotistical. But so were many of its greatest failures. In fact, many more.

Today's society almost makes us dependent on validation and entitlement. It seems to us that we cannot progress without it. For almost a generation, parents, teachers and mentors have emphasised on building up everyone's *self-esteem*. It was from there that public figures and motivational speakers began exclusively aiming to inspire, encourage and assure us that we can do whatever we set our minds to. In reality, this does nothing but make us weak. It leads us to doubt our capabilities, exposes us to our greatest insecurities, and leaves us with a false sense of hope. You may argue that the ability to evaluate one's own capabilities is the most important skill of all, and that without it, improvement is impossible. And you're right, it *is* more pleasurable to focus on our talents, strengths and capabilities, but where will that get you? Arrogance, vanity and self-absorption all inhibit growth.

We live in a world that tells us to keep and promote our 'personal brand'. We're expected to tell stories in order to sell our work, our talents, and our skills. After enough time, we forget where the line is that separates fiction from truth. Everyone is susceptible to being stuck in their own head. Take a walk through the streets and look at the people around you. We plug in our headphones and play a soundtrack. We don't make eye contact, and if we do it's briefly, because we're too cool to talk to anyone. We replay the successful interview or meeting we're heading *towards* in our head. We don't just see this on walks, but everywhere. At dinners, at parties, at social gatherings – we stay stuck inside our heads instead of engaging with the world around us. This is an obsession of the mind that we're all susceptible to. Whether you run a software startup, or you're working your way up the ranks of a corporate hierarchy, we have all fallen madly in love with the idea of 'I' and 'me'.

With the rise of social media in the past decade, everyone, everywhere is able to fuel their ego. There are no exceptions to this. *Any* individual on social media is able to satisfy their ego in some way or another. I use social media too, so I'm not trying to say I am exempt, but I know how it works and what it does to your brain. I will tell you. But not now, later. Social media and the rise of technology fuels what is often known as the 'Paris Hilton Effect'. Because we're wired to direct our attention towards the people who are already the subject of attention, we'll sometimes be drawn to people in the media without really knowing why. But our being drawn to them makes the media want to focus on them even more. We then attend to them more, then the media attends to them more, and the constant feedback loop continues. We copy people. We're helplessly drawn to them. We identify the ones who seem to know best how to get ahead of the game, we watch them, we listen to them, we open ourselves to their influence, and we try to become them. We internalise the things they teach us. They become a part of us. This is how a culture, predominantly focused on fuelling the ego, spreads.

The constant bombardment of 'expressing yourself' might make a simple yet effective advertising slogan, and it has been used to sell everything from customised t-shirts to Botox. Over the past two decades, technology has allowed us to take self-expression to a whole new level with our own personal websites, social media accounts, videos, and blogging. The media has also shifted towards self-expression because, of course, opinion is a lot cheaper to obtain than actual information. All this self-expression would probably be fine if what was expressed held some value, but that is often not the case. We all know people who, in person or online, talk because they want to, and not because they actually have something meaningful to contribute.

The ego is further fuelled with our obsession with wanting to be in control of all events in life. We want to assure ourselves that we are the cause of the effects in our life. Psychologists describe the 'effectance motive' – the drive to manipulate and control elements in the world – as almost a basic a need as food and water. We just can't be left alone; we don't want to be. When people are left floating in darkened salt-water tanks with their eyes covered, they experience what is known as 'stimulus-action hunger', which they'll seek to soothe by rubbing their fingers together, or by making waves in the water, as an example. A study saw 409 individuals stripped of their phones and put in a room alone, for up to fifteen minutes, with nothing to do – except use a machine to give themselves electric shocks that were so painful, participants said they'd pay money not to experience them again. Sixty-nine per cent of men and twenty-five per cent of women were sufficiently discomforted by this that they began shocking themselves. The researchers concluded that most people seem to prefer to be doing something rather than nothing, even if that something is negative.[17] The neurobiologist Robert Sapolsky has argued that the brain's dopamine reward system, which guides our behaviour by giving us shots of pleasure, is more active not when we seize the thing that we're after, but in the pursuit of it.[18] Although the roots of our egotistical behaviour may be inherent, core cultural ideas are slowly but surely becoming more focused on self-admiration and self-expression, and there is not a shadow of doubt about that.

The Rise of Individuality

Since the days of Ancient Greece, the Western world has glamorised freedom. The default truth of our people has always been that the locus of power and control is the individual, and that what an individual requires to succeed is maximum freedom, whether that be from the repressive forces of society, from the self, or from regulation by the state. It was a collision of such freedoms that did much to cause the 2008 global financial crisis. It was a neoliberal catastrophe. As a result of the crash, in the US alone, more than 9 million homes were lost and almost 9 million jobs disappeared. In the UK, 3.7 million people lost their jobs – that's one in seven of all employees.[19]

Researchers have concluded that, in the UK, between 2008 and 2010, there were around a thousand *extra* suicides, nearly ninety per cent of them male, because of the crash and the period of difficulty that followed. There were also a surprising 30 to 40,000 more suicide attempts.[20] Additionally, according to a study in the *British Journal of Psychiatry*, in the same period, the estimated global figure of additional suicides comes out at 10,000.[21] When we feel we lose control and power over our own circumstances, we fail to function properly.

Of course, the point I am trying to make isn't that freedom is bad. It's a system. But like most systems, it creates a trade-off in outcomes. It has both positive and negative impacts. Many in the West have become wealthier since the 1970s and their standards of living have risen. Global free trade has helped lift millions more out of poverty in developing countries such as China and India. Globalisation is also a blessing. It has led to cheap imports and higher levels of immigration. Industry is embracing harsh new working conditions, such as 'zero hour contracts', which offer minimal job security and benefits. A recent study found 4.5 million people, nearly one in six of all workers, in England and Wales, were in 'insecure work'.[22]

In 1965, forty-five per cent of freshmen said they believed it was important to be financially well off, a figure that had risen as high as seventy-four per cent by 2004. High-school children in the 1970s were half as likely as those in the 1990s to believe 'having lots of money' was very important. It seems that over the past few decades there has been a significant change from internal to external values. A 2006 poll of British children placed 'being a celebrity' at the top of their list of the 'very best things in the world'. In their book *The Narcissism Epidemic*,

Dr. Twenge and Dr. Campbell point out that individualism is rising, including greater use of self-focused language in books and song lyrics, as well as the increased popularity of unusual baby names. When we grow up in a particular economy and society, it's natural that its values and beliefs will leak out in the things we say and do. It's in our TV programmes, on our supermarket shelves, on our mobile phones – it's everywhere.

The need to protect our ego is also predominantly seen in the way we remain in our comfort zones. The thing is, the more emotional we become, the less rational we become, and the less able to properly reason we become. In this attempt to quieten the stress in our heads, we begin muting, blocking, unfollowing, and unfriending. Safe in the digital, and often mental cocoon that we've constructed, surrounded by voices that flatter and conform to us, we become more and more convinced of our essential rightness. We become weak and more self-focused. I know you might question me here, but in all honesty, just take account of yourself – this applies to us all.

Seeking approval from social media followers and friends may not inherently be a bad thing, but the constant cycle of needing it definitely is. Getting accustomed to constant social feedback is dangerous, as is constantly being told you're beautiful. Why? Because when it gets cut off, and people stop giving you it, you start to feel bad about yourself and you seek out that hit again. What's more, the new 'famous' is made up of reality TV and social media influencers that seem too much more like us than those who have passed. For a long time, stars were elevated at the level of untouchable, but now anyone can be a star, and that is what makes everyone thirsty. All of this adds up to an increasing sense, particularly in the younger generation, that we have to maintain a continual state of perfection.

Although we will be discussing the use of social media shortly, I just wanted to mention a few things beforehand. Researchers are not quite able to tell us for sure whether any of this is a cause of rising depression, although two longitudinal studies have found that more social media use leads to more unhappiness whilst the opposite isn't true (and funnily enough, the unhappiness effect only really kicks in after two hours of use per day). So before you point fingers at me for using social media, some use of social media is fine, but it is also associated with diminished well-being and lower life satisfaction. Why? Because people are always looking at other people with better lives. Playing the individual ego game is a really dangerous game.

A large US study that traced parental attitudes through 2004 found some fascinating results. It asked, "If you had to choose, which thing on this list would you pick as the most important for a child to learn to prepare him (or her) for life?" The five choices given were 'to obey', 'to be well-liked or popular', 'to think for themselves', 'to work hard', and 'to help others when they need help'. American parents have always ranked 'to think for himself or herself' as the most important. Virtually everyone agrees that parents are now considerably more lenient than ever before.

Some parents believe that praise builds self-esteem, which, in turn, builds success. I mean, that's what we're told to believe nowadays. Parents also think that praise encourages performance and they assume that higher levels of praise encourages higher levels of performance. When children have done good work or they behave well, yes, praising is fine – in fact, that approach works better than punishing children for behaving badly. But in the last few decades, modern parenting has moved to a different model heaping on praise for the littlest achievements and even, sometimes, for poor performance. In her recent book *The Self-Esteem Trap*, Polly Young Eisendrath describes how treating children as 'special' leads to young adults who are self-absorbed and fragile in the face of hard work and negative feedback. They feel entitled to high-status occupations but quickly become discouraged when they aren't highly successful right away.[23]

I Want Fame

There is no doubt that reality TV stars and other celebrities have an important role to play in the spread of narcissism. Of course, not all celebrities are egotistical. But unfortunately the ones we hear about the most often are. One journalist wrote in an online survey, "I interviewed hundreds of well-known actors and actresses over a 10-year period, and this, basically, is how the interview went: 'I think… I believe… I am… My passion is… I'd like to think what I do makes a difference to the world… Me… Me… More Me… Major Me… did I mention Me? I am a role model to so many… I am, in fact, God incarnate." [They], and not only the mega-stars, were so self-absorbed, so self-obsessed, that my attendance at the interview wasn't totally necessary. They blurted out their Me-ness unprompted."

But fame isn't all it's cracked up to be – the loss of privacy and the constant scrutiny from one and all can get old very fast. An increasing number of us not only admire fame from afar but may even subconsciously wish to enter the circle of celebrities themselves. In a 2006 US survey, fifty-one per cent of 18 to 25-year-olds said that 'becoming famous' was an important goal of their generation – nearly five times as many as named 'becoming more spiritual' as an important goal.[24] A 2006 British poll asked children to name 'the very best thing in the world'. The most popular answer was 'being a celebrity'. This was followed by 'good looks' and 'being rich'. 'God' came in last.[25]

Magazines, TV shows, and movies allow adults to even fantasise about what you could do and buy if you were only famous enough. Many consumer products have become instant sellers simply because the right celebrity uses them. I first noticed this in India, when I saw gigantic billboards of Bollywood superstars holding certain drink products. Marketing manipulation aside, it's also about the belief that 'If they have it, then to become just a bit more like them, so should I'. Marketing and advertising in general discovered the trend towards self-admiration and fame a decade or so ago, and helped it grow even bigger. From 2001 to 2006, the US Army – of all things – recruited soldiers with the slogan 'An Army of One'. Today, everything is about 'you'. You can customise your shoes at the Nike store. You can choose your own ringtone. You can broadcast yourself on YouTube. You can blog to thousands of people online. Every major marketing campaign in the modern world is about empowering 'you', and this is the state of modern society.

It is clear that the Internet and the ego work hand-in-hand like a feedback loop, with egotistical people seeking ways to promote themselves online. The slogan of YouTube is 'Broadcast Yourself'. The name 'Facebook' explains it perfectly, with its subtlety of making you see and be seen by others. It's understandable that in previous generations they weren't given the same tools as us. We can't be blamed for growing up in a time when the likes of Facebook and Instagram are created specifically for us to talk about ourselves. As YouTube co-founder Chad Hurley said, "Everyone, in the back of his mind, wants to be a star." Bingo. We've given them exactly what they want from us.

Storymakers

In the 1960s, a surgeon by the name of Joe Bogen began cutting people's brains in half. Not as a hobby, but as a way to try and help those whose lives had been negatively impacted by frequent and serious epileptic seizures. As you probably know, the human brain has two separate hemispheres, these are joined by a large bundle of nerves called the corpus callosum. Seizures are known to begin at any one spot within the brain and then eventually spread to the surrounding brain tissue. If a seizure crosses over the corpus callosum, it can quickly spread to the entire brain, causing a person to lose consciousness, fall down, and suffer uncontrollably. Just as the army would blow up the bridge leading to the gate of their kingdom, to stop the enemies entering, Bogen had a similar incentive to sever the corpus callosum from the rest of the brain – to prevent seizures from spreading. At first, it seemed it insane. People believed and warned Bogen that there had to be a reason that the corpus callosum was the largest bundle of nerves in the entire body – it had to serve an important function. They were right. It allows the two halves of the brain to communicate and coordinate activity with one another. Yet, research on animals found that within a few weeks of surgery, the animals were pretty much restored back to normality. So, Bogen quickly took up the chance with human patients, and it worked. The intensity of seizures was tremendously reduced in the patients. So, nothing went wrong? To confirm the after-effects of the surgery, Bogen's team pulled in a young psychologist called Michael Gazzaniga, whose job was to study the effects on these subjects, who we will know call: *split-brainers*.

With his neuroscientist friend, Roger Sperry, Gazzaniga conducted some of the most profound research in the history of psychology – a series of experiments that would catapult Gazzaniga into an illustrious career as the 'grandfather' of cognitive neuroscience, and for which Sperry would eventually win the Nobel Prize in 1981.

The method of the experiments were fairly straightforward: an image was flashed, some questions were asked, and so on. What distinguished these experiments were split-brainers. Until Sperry and Gazzaniga's experiments, no one had noticed anything particularly strange about split-brainers. They were able to walk around leading seemingly normal lives. Neither their doctors, their loves ones, nor the patients themselves, had noticed that much was different. But things had actually turned out *very* different.

In order to understand their research, it'll help to familiarise yourself with two basic facts about the human brain. I know you probably think this is longed out, so if you want to pause here, take a deep breath and come back, that's fine. But this is important. The first fact is that each hemisphere processes signals from the *opposite* side of the body. So the left hemisphere controls the right side of the body (the right arm, leg, hand, and everything else), while the right hemisphere controls the left side of the body. This is also true for signals from the ears – the left hemisphere processes sound from the right ear, and vice versa. With the eyes it gets just a bit more complicated, but basically when a patient is looking straight ahead, everything to the right – in the right half of the visual field – is processed by the left hemisphere, and everything to the left is processed by the right hemisphere.[26]

The second important fact is that, after a brain is split by the procedure mentioned earlier, the two hemispheres can no longer share information with each other. In a normal (whole) brain, information flows smoothly back and forth between the two hemispheres, but in a split-brainer, each hemisphere becomes an island unto itself – almost like two separate people in one skull. Now, what both researchers did, through a number of experimental setups, was ask the *right hemisphere* to do something, but then ask the *left hemisphere* to explain it.

In one experiment, they flashed a split-brainer two different pictures at once, one to each hemisphere. The left hemisphere, for example, saw a picture of a chicken while the right hemisphere saw a picture of a snowy field. The researchers then asked the patient to reach out with *his left hand* and point to a word that best matched the picture he had seen. Since the right hemisphere had seen the picture of the snowy field, the left hand pointed to a shovel (because a shovel goes nicely with snow).

This probably seems normal, but wait. When the researchers asked the patient to *explain* why he had chosen a shovel, things started to surface. Explanations, and language generally, are functions of the left hemisphere, and thus the researchers were putting the left hemisphere to the real test. The *right hemisphere* alone had seen the snowy field, and it was the right hemisphere's unilateral decision to point to the shovel. The *left hemisphere*, meanwhile, had been left completely out of the loop, but was being asked to justify a decision it took no part in.

For the left hemisphere, the only valid answer would have been, "I don't know." But it didn't give that answer. Instead, it said it had chosen the shovel because shovels are used for 'cleaning out the chicken coop'. In other words, the left hemisphere, lacking a real reason to give, *made up a reason on the spot.* It pretended that it had acted on its own – that it had chosen the shovel because of the chicken photo, and it gave this answer casually, thinking it was factual. It had no idea it was making up a story. The left hemisphere, says Gazzaniga, "did not offer its suggestion in a guessing vein but rather as a statement of fact".

In another version, the researchers asked a patient – in his left ear (leading to the right hemisphere) – to stand up and walk towards the door. Once the patient was out of his chair, they asked him again, out loud this time, what he was doing. Now, his left hemisphere would need to respond. Again, this put the left hemisphere to test. Now, *we* know that the patient got out of his chair because the researchers simply asked him to do that. But, the patient's left hemisphere had no way of knowing this. But instead of saying, "I don't know why I stood up," which would have been right, it made up a reason and its own truth: "I want a Coke."[27]

What I am trying to get at is the fact that our minds will readily fabricate reasons to explain their own behaviour. This notion is known as 'confabulation'. The reason these studies were so important is because they showed, in quite a stark way, that the mind is a group of modules capable of working independently, and even, sometimes, at cross-purposes. This is the royal council of the mind. This is the antahkarana at work.

What Gazzaniga concludes from his years of research, including his later work on healthy patients, is that all human brains contain a system he calls the 'interpreter module'. The job of this module is to interpret, or make sense of, our experiences by constructing explanations: stories that integrate information about the past and present, and about the inside world and the outside world. It is the press secretary, or the royal announcer, from the group of ministers. It is what is responsible for strategically spinning the truth for the external audience. Isn't it funny how easily we claim to know our own minds, but we're actually strangers to ourselves?

Much of what seems real and true in the space around us, is not. The Mithila Matrix exists within our minds. We want to question the existence of an omnipotent being. We want to understand what is hereafter. We want to know why we are even here now. But how? The actual world that you see around you is monochrome and silent.

Sounds, colours, tastes, and smells exists only through our senses and in the production of our minds. What is actually out there are vibrating particles, floating chemical compounds, molecules, and colourless light waves of varying lengths. Our perceptions of these phenomena are generated within the mind. And our senses can only detect the tiniest fraction of what is out there. For instance, our eyes are able to pick up less than one ten-trillionth of the available light spectrum. That's it.

So it is the mind that creates our experience of the world. It then conjures up the ego (the blinded self) at its centre. The mind makes you a hero, manufacturing both the illusion of our being and its gripping narrative that we tell ourselves. It is so powerful that it inclines us to adopt self-serving beliefs about ourselves, and comforting beliefs about the world too. The most powerful of this is the moral bias. No matter what we do, and how many mistakes we make, the mind nudges us to conclude that we are ultimately a better person than most. In one study, participants guessed what percentage o time they exhibited a range of virtuous behaviours. Six weeks later, when asked again, they were also shown the average ratings of others. Most participants rated themselves as much higher than the average ratings. What they failed to realise was that the 'average ratings' for others were, in fact, *their own ratings from six weeks earlier*.[28]

How to Fool Yourself

The Sanskrit word for ego is ahankar. Note that this differs from aha<u>m</u>kar. It is what leads us to lie to ourselves. We are masters of self-deception. We repress painful memories, create completely false ones, rationalise immoral behaviour, act repeatedly to boost positive self-opinion, and show a suite of ego-defence mechanisms. At least one, if not more, of these will apply to you. Study after study shows that we often distort or ignore critical information about our own health in order to seem healthier than we really are. One study, for example, gave patients a cholesterol test, then followed up to see what they remembered months later. Patients with the worst test results – who were judged the most at-risk of cholesterol-related health problems – were most likely to misremember their test results, and they remembered their results as being better (i.e., healthier) than they actually were.[29] Smokers, but not nonsmokers choose not to hear about the dangerous effects of smoking.[30] People systematically underestimate their risk of contracting HIV (human immunodeficiency virus)[31], and avoid taking HIV tests.[32] We also deceive ourselves about our driving skills, social skills, leadership skills, and athletic ability.[33] The results are clear. The human mind cannot be trusted in the way it internally processes information from the external world.

It seems as though our ego and self-esteem are fragile and need to be shielded from distressing information, like the fact that we probably *won't* win the upcoming competition, or the high chance that we won't land that job interview after applying to a hundred different places. Or the fact that we may be sick with some lurking cancer that we haven't yet been diagnosed with. Self-deception is the mind's form of defence. But in reality, when we deceive ourselves about our health, achievements, or whatever for that matter, whether by avoiding information entirely or by distorting information we've already received, we *feel* like we're trying to protect ourselves from distressing information. But the real reason our ego needs to be shielded is to help us maintain a positive social impression. In reality, we don't personally benefit as such from misunderstanding our current state of health (I'd be surprised if you think so), but we benefit when *others* mistakenly believe that we're healthy. And the first step to convincing others is often to convince ourselves. As a colleague of Steve Jobs, Bill Atkinson, once said about the self-deception of Jobs, "It allowed him to con people into believing his vision because he had personally embraced and internalised it."[34] Our minds are so impressionable that whatever we think we believe, *can* quickly become our reality. You are probably beginning to see how this is coming to a full circle and almost a paradox. Our egos lead us to deceive ourselves, we then go onto deceive others (whether directly or indirectly), which only fuels our ego even further. This is the way that the monkey plays with the commander and the ministers. The monkey is the one that leads the senses (in the form of ministers) astray, to fulfil its needs. Why? Because *it* needs it. The ego needs it. The uncontrolled mind is the personified form of all the enemies we are discussing. Every enemy is the monkey itself. Many modern thinkers and philosophers are quick to assume and assert that the mind is one, but as social psychologist Jonathan Haidt puts it, "To understand most important ideas in psychology you need to understand how the mind is divided into parts that sometimes conflict." He goes on to explain how we assume that there is one person in each body, but in some ways we are each more like a committee whose members have been thrown together working at cross purposes. There are many ways and theories on how the mind is divided. It's the monkey, the commander and the ministers for us.

In his book *The Self Illusion*, Bruce Hood talks about 'The Looking-Glass Self', and its creator, the sociologist Charles Horton Clooney, who wrote, "I am not what I think I am and I am not what you think I am; I am what I think that you think I am."[35] This illusion of the ego, according to modern science, is thought to take form around the age of two. But according to Vedic teachings, it is believed to be intrinsic to the very nature of existence, and primarily the cause of rebirth. But we don't notice this in babies, who cry for attention from their parents and become the centre of their own world. We notice it, in most cases, at around two to three years of age, when children start interacting with other children, competing with them and joining tribes. And as we grow, we become more and more preoccupied with what others think about us. Our sense of self worth is a reflection of what we think other people think about us.

We then go on to form hierarchies of 'us' against 'them'. With these hierarchies comes our obsessional concern with status. We constantly seek validation. Why do we buy fast cars? Why do we want to own big homes? Why do we need all these things that we don't really need? It's because we like to signal our self-status to others. If others believe we're 'something', our looking-glass self interprets that as evidence that we *are* 'something'. We're self-conscious creatures. We use clues from 'out there' to try and tell us who we are 'in here'. And that is, how it pretty much goes until the end of our lives. We run away from insult and run towards good reputation and praise. The rest of our life is, I believe, motivated by feeling good about ourselves and trying to alleviate as much negative emotions as possible.

Look at it this way, we earn a salary and bring home an income, but for most of us the needs of basic food, housing and environment are satisfied, and so the majority of us are motivated to pursue validation from other people. A man struggling on the railway tracks of Mumbai doesn't care about validation and what others think of him, he is trying to make it through to the end of the day, but not us. Our lack of true authenticity means that who we are and how we behave tends to shift, somewhat dependent on where we are and who we're with. Different versions of us emerge depending on where we are, what we're doing, who we're with and how we feel. Our sense of who we *actually* are turns out to be critically dependent on what we believe others think of us. It's got nothing to do with what people actually think of you. It's what you think other people expect of you. Research has shown that if a person, especially someone who is psychologically vulnerable, is surrounded by others who are abusing them, then they'll be susceptible to believing that *that's who they truly are*.

Vanity and Uniqueness

Vanity is the number one symptom of the ego; it's actually a synonym for it. In the US, botox injections were given 3.2 million times in 2006, 49 times more than in 1997.[36] Last year, the figure was 4.4 million.[37] There was more demand during the pandemic of 2020 – when people were at *home*. We know it's not just an American obsession though, it's a global obsession. People are increasingly obsessed with their appearance, and if this isn't a clear symptom of an egotistical culture in love with their own reflection, what else is it? Agreed, beauty *is* and always *has been* a virtue, but this recent pursuit has reached new levels. A 2008 poll found that seventy-nine per cent of Americans would not be embarrassed if others knew they'd had plastic surgery. One out of three women said they would consider having cosmetic surgery, as would one out of five men. There's no doubt that so many people feel more pressure to look beautiful and perfect.[38]

It is easy to see how much of today's desire for physical beauty sprouts from the seed of self-admiration. Perhaps even the desire to look tan is the reason behind the jump in the link of skin cancer rate over the last two decades.[39] The emphasis on vanity appears in almost every aspect of society: the media, TV, the Internet, business, and even parenting. It seems that only education has remained relatively immune to focussing on physical appearance, maybe because of the typical stereotype that smart people are not necessarily good-looking.

The emphasis on appearance has not made humankind any healthier. Obesity is at epidemic levels, as it has been for the last decade. At the same time, anorexic actresses dominate TV shows. Neither extreme is good. Accepting that you don't look like a reality TV star is a good type of self-acceptance; taken too far, however, loving yourself *can* make you egotistical and narcissistic, and is also a risk factor for both eating disorders and delusional thinking that leads some people to become obese.[40]

Too much media, and too much gazing at carefully chosen and even Photoshopped photos on Instagram, gives young people a warped view of what normal appearances are. The media portrays a world of shining superheroes with nothing but emptiness under the cloak. Unfortunately, this is how people are becoming, maybe without being consciously aware of it: beautifully painted but clothed with an empty mind.

Just a few words on uniqueness. It's a recent phenomenon actually, so it's hard to fully grasp, but the desire to give a child a unique name has both been facilitated and dictated by technology. Some expecting parents now even Google names for their child before choosing one. Unique names aren't necessarily bad, and I don't mean to pass judgement on them. But, advantages and disadvantages aside, the trend towards unique names possibly says a lot about our culture.

Today, everything is supposed to be unique, including our weddings. The media and superstars also love to dispense individualistic advise – we've just spoken about this too. This gives rise to the feeling of being 'special'. This is narcissism; not self-esteem, not self-confidence, and definitely not something we should be wanting to put into the next generation. There is a major difference between being egotistical and self-confident. For example, you can tell your child they are good at English, or that they *will* be good at English if they work hard, without telling them they're special. Even though everyone cannot be special, everyone *is* unique. But even an overemphasis on uniqueness has negative consequences for individuals. Studies have found that teenagers who have a 'personal fable' of uniqueness believe that no one understands them. Young people with these beliefs are significantly more likely to become depressed and to contemplate suicide.[41]

Debunking Ego Myths

Myth 1: I can be whatever I want to be. Today's culture is obsessively focused on unrealistic positive expectations. Be happy. Be healthy. Be smart. Be rich. Be fast. Be popular. Be productive. Be admired. Be seductive. Be perfect. Don't get me wrong, I'm not saying we shouldn't be positive. But what I *am* saying is that all this sugar-coated positivity and self-help stuff we hear all the time, and that is continuing to grow, seemingly only fixates on what you lack. You watch YouTube videos or read the popular books on financial freedom because you feel you *lack* money. You shower in the morning and stand in front of the mirror and repeat those affirmations, telling yourself you're beautiful and that the day is going to be great because you feel you *lack* beauty and drive for the day ahead. You attempt radical visualisation techniques about being successful and famous because you feel you *lack* success and recognition.

Funnily enough, the constant fixation on the positive only reaffirms the reminder again and again of what we are lacking, of what we are failing, of what we are not. You might have heard of the phrase, 'the smallest dog barks the loudest'. It does. I don't want to be that dog and I'm sure you don't either. Someone that is truly confident, doesn't need to prove that he is confident. Someone who is seriously 'well-off' doesn't go wrong flexing their cars or watches. Someone who is happy doesn't need to stand in front of the world and scream, "I'm happy!" Either you are or you are not. We must be extremely careful as the world around us constantly bombards us with the message of more. *Buy* more. *Own* more. *Get* more. *Make* more. *Be* more. It's all a manifestation of the ego – of seeking validation and conformity to the world around us.

Myth 2: I should be happy, perfect and never have to suffer. Human beings are one of the few species on this planet that have the ability to think about their thoughts. Most other animals simply think and do. We think *about* what we think we're going to do. Five-hundred years ago, maybe even a hundred years ago, this wasn't an issue. Even today, you can observe the phenomena I'm about to describe in various countries and societies across the globe. Don't judge me on what I'm about to say, just take it with a pinch of salt. Today's society, particularly those heavily invested in consumer culture, have fed a whole generation of humans to believe that negative experiences like stress, anxiety, fear, guilt, etc. are not normal, and that feeling these is wrong. What's worse is that if I'm feeling down and miserable for ten minutes, I am likely to pick up my phone and open one of my social media apps. As soon as I do this, I'm bombarded with an infinite feed of photos and videos of people 'happy', 'successful', or, 'having it all figured out'. That's why I don't blame you for feeling this way if you do. Despite reading numerous books, watching countless TED talks, mindfulness and wellness podcasts, we are unable to sustain our level of peace and tranquility. Believe me, you won't. Never feel bad about feeling bad. Never feel sad about feeling sad. To put it bluntly, don't pity yourself. Stress-related health issues, mental disorders, and cases of depression have skyrocketed in the recent years. Material possessions won't lead to existential solutions. We keep seeking material comfort and answers, but we fail to realise that our crisis is not material – it is spiritual.

The British philosopher and writer Alan Watts referred to the idea of 'the backwards law' which gives the idea that the more we pursue feeling better all the time, the less satisfied we become.[42] Primarily because pursuing something only reinforces the fact that we lack it in the first place. Around 200 years ago, Swaminarayan echoed this in his teachings, in which he mentions that one has never become satisfied by indulging in seemingly positive experiences, nor will one ever be satisfied. Whether you believe in evolution or not, human beings have always been dissatisfied with whatever they have and satisfied by that which they don't have. It is this very dissatisfaction that has kept the homo sapiens fighting, striving, surviving, building and conquering until today. If pursuing positive experiences leads to negative experiences, then surely we can assume that accepting negative experiences can lead to positive experiences, right?

Suffering *always* serves a purpose. I know it's cliché to hear, but it's the truth. The most successful individuals and businesses may have had other factors at play, but obstacles and failures have had a great impact on the knock-on success that they have had. Similarly, suffering through our anxieties and fears allows for us to build the courage and perseverance to face such situations in the future.

I agree that some suffering is certainly more painful than others. There are levels to suffering, but we all suffer nonetheless. Some of us just cope better with it than others. Suffering, dissatisfaction and unease are an inherent part of life on this planet. I used to question this too, but then I explored the life of Pramukh Swami. He suffered much more than I will ever experience, much of it has gone unheard and unaccounted for. History will never even hear everything he has been through. But I know that if he can still say that suffering should be accepted and one should maintain faith, then why shouldn't I?

Myth 3: I am special. It's simple. More and more people seem to have the problem of entitlement, especially in developed countries. We feel that we *need* to feel good about ourselves, even at the expense of others. Unfortunately, simply feeling good about yourself doesn't do anything unless you have a valid reason to feel good. The actual measurement of healthy self-worth is not how you feel about your positive experiences, but how you feel and then act upon your negative experiences. When it comes to problems, we feel more pain when we feel more hopeless against the problem in front of us. In reality, there is no such thing as 'my problem', or, 'your problem'. Problems are universal, and there is a high chance that countless other people have faced a similar problem to you in the past, right now, or they will do in the future. What I'm trying to say is that we are not unique in our suffering.

Myth 4: It's out of my hands. I'm not responsible. I can't help it. How you let the pain and suffering that you encounter affect you is a *choice*. You *are* responsible for how you feel, don't push it onto anyone else. And it's okay to feel the way that you do. Accept your feelings for what they are, but remember that they are fleeting. We don't always have control over what happens to us, but we *always* have control of how we interpret events and circumstances in our life, as well as how we respond to them. Even choosing *not* to respond to events is a response. You are always presented with a choice, and whether you approach it actively or passively, that is a choice you always make.

This is where responsibility comes into play in our lives. The more we choose to accept responsibility for our lives, the more power we will hold over our lives. A lot of individuals hesitate to take responsibility for their struggles because they believe that *responsibility* is *fault*, but that's not the case. Just because you're responsible for your problems, doesn't mean that you're at fault for your problems. Faults come from the choices we've made. Responsibility comes from the choices you make now.

Myth 5: I feel offended. I'm a victim. We seem to be pushing more and more responsibility to other individuals or groups over the past few years, particularly with the rise of social media and the Internet. Even for the tiniest discomfort, we push responsibility onto others. It's so easy to do this as well. If someone makes a comment, someone, somewhere, is offended. We make out as though we're being oppressed and therefore we have a right to be outraged. It's attention-seeking. According to Ryan Holiday, this is known as 'outrage porn'. It's the idea that rather than reporting on real stories and pressing issues, the media find it easier, and more profitable, to find something offensive that will catch attention and engagement, broadcast it to a huge audience, let the outrage poor in, and then push it out further. Why have we forgotten that part of living in a democratic and free society means having to learn to deal with differing and divergent viewpoints, as well as with others, who we may not necessarily like. I'm not fond of news channels and especially social media as a news source, but if you do view your news on these platforms, approach them with skepticism and open-mindedness.

To sum up the myths, anything or anyone that tells you that 'every person is destined for greatness and is extraordinary' should be steered away from. This will do nothing but inflate your ego. It tastes good to the tongue, but you won't be able to digest it. The monkey loves it, the commander is confused, but ultimately, the king suffers. It's the spiritual crisis. The craving is of the ātmā, not the mind or body.

Take the Humility Pill

We are all tempted to talk and hype instead of act. This temptation exists across all levels of society. Facebook's 'What's on your mind?' Twitter's 'Compose a new tweet'. Instagram. LinkedIn. Your inbox. Your phone. The comments section at the bottom of the blog post you just read. Wherever we look, we see blank spaces begging to be filled with our thoughts, feelings, photos and stories. With what we're *going* to do, with how things *should* or *could* be like, what we hope will happen. The Internet and social media prodding you, begging you, soliciting *talk*. Almost everywhere you look, the performance that everyone gives is *positive*. It's more: Look how great my life is. Look how happy I am. It's rarely the truth that "I'm scared. I'm struggling. I don't know what I'm doing." We seem to think that silence is a sign of weakness, and so we talk, talk, talk, as though our existence depends on it. In truth, silence is strength.

The Greek Stoic philosopher, Epictetus said, "It is impossible to learn that which one thinks one already knows." The power of being a student is not only to keep us humble, it also places our ego and ambition in the hands of another. Regardless of whether that is a mentor, guru, or the higher power. False ideas about yourself will destroy you. At the same time, you must become your own teacher and critic too. A student is self-critical and self-motivated, always willing, and trying to improve their understanding so that they can move on to the next challenge.

Today, it's all about passion. Find your passion. Do what you're passionate about. Live passionately. Inspire the world with your passion. But, what if I told you that it is your passion that may be the very thing holding you back from progress and growth? Often, failure comes from passion. For some reason, we only seem to hear about the passion of successful people, but we forget that failures also shared the same trait. What we require is purpose. Purpose, we could say, is similar to passion but with boundaries. Purpose is passion with detachment and perspective. Purpose deemphasises the 'I'. Purpose is about pursuing something outside yourself, and greater than yourself, as opposed to merely seeking pleasure. We must make it about what we feel we *must* do and say, not what we care about and wish it to be.

Two thousand years ago, Plato spoke of the type of people who are guilty of 'feasting on their own thoughts'. The British writer, Alan Watts, also said, "A person who thinks all the time has nothing to think about except thoughts, so he loses touch with reality and lives in a world of illusions."

The reason ego is so hard to fight is because we all want one thing: status, or, success. We want to matter. We want wealth. We want recognition. We want reputation. We want it all because it's nice. The problem is that we're not aware that humility can get us there, and much more peacefully and quicker. Austrian neurologist and Holocaust survivor, Viktor Frankl, said, "Man is pushed by drives, but he is pulled by values." Success is intoxicating, yet to sustain it, we must remain sober. You can't learn that which you think you already know.

A sign of early ego is telling yourself stories. We so desperately like to believe that those who have great empires or success *set out* to build one. Why? So that we can indulge and take pleasure from planning our own. So that we can take full credit for the good that comes and riches and respect that may flood our way. Unfortunately, this type of story-crafting out of past events is a very human impulse rooted deep within us. Even more unfortunate is that writing our own narratives leads to arrogance. If we aspire to succeed, we must resist the impulse to reverse-engineer success from other people's stories. And, when we achieve our own, we must resist the desire to pretend that everything unfolded exactly the way we planned. It's rubbish. There is no grand narrative, and even if there is, it's not dictated by us. Humans are never content with what they have. We want what others have too. In fact, we often want *more* than everyone else has. But, we must remember that it is not about having more than others; it's about being what we are, and being as good at it as much as possible. We must sit down and think about what's truly important to us and then take the necessary steps to let go of the rest. Without doing this, if success comes our way, we will not be able to enjoy it, or not as much as we possibly could. Ask yourself why you're after what you're seeking. Be independent in your thinking and actions.

You may have heard the phrase, 'Ego is the enemy', and this is true. Ego *is* its own worst enemy. It not only hurts us, but it also hurts the ones close to us too. We suffer from it, and so do our family and friends. So do our clients, customers and colleagues. A critic of Napoleon put it perfectly when they said, "He despises the nation whose applause he seeks."

To develop humility in every aspect of our life is the antidote to ego. The word 'humility' itself is such a broad term, encompassing many habits that can be practiced in our life. We can all start somewhere. Muhammad Ali once said, "It's hard to be humble when you're as great as I am." Well, okay. This shows us how much ego can get to us. It makes us think that humility is a mere imagined concept.

Saint Augustine of Hippo said, "Do you want to rise? Begin by descending." In today's social media-obsessed society, the true essence of humility is slowly evaporating. In a world that celebrates individualism, over-confidence, narcissism, and self-entitlement, how does one really remain humble? And what do we stand to gain from keeping this virtue steadfast in our lives? Humility is not the same as humiliation. Each individual being *is* important to this world, but not enough to actually feel a sense of self-importance. It is definitely a paradox of sorts. When we forget the essence of humility, we are limiting what provides us with true wholesome human potential. Humility is not a facade to be put on for the outside world either, in fact, it is an internally cultivated virtue to be sought after.

When we experience an enduring state of humility, we are not only aware of our own faults and shortcomings, but there is also a subtle peace to our heart. We are able to identify our mistakes immediately, not to justify or reject them, but to work on them. A humble person is someone who has a strong sense of self-mastery. They know what they're good at and what they're bad at, but they don't seek praise or confirmation from others because they neither want nor need it. Humility and modesty are two different things too. The act of humility itself is to subdue the ego so that things are no longer all about us. On the other hand, to be modest is to protect the ego of others so they do not feel threatened or uncomfortable.

The truth is, humility empowers us greatly. Those who are humble experience profound peace in their lives. Rabbi Jonathan Sacks says humility 'is one of the most expansive and life-enhancing of all virtues'. As humans, it is a natural tendency to resist owning up to our own limitations. We instead, prefer to stay safe behind our cloaked identity, even from ourselves. But the first step to true humility is to honestly come to terms with our own shortcomings. Humility, ultimately, has nothing to prove, but everything to offer.

I love bringing up my favourite character whenever I can, so meet Alexander the Great. He was the most famous pupil of the philosopher Aristotle. It is believed that it was partially due to the teachings of Aristotle that this young man was able to conquer almost the entire known world at the time. Putting his narcissistic and egotistical thinking to the side for a moment, Alexander was brave and brilliant, and often generous and wise too. But still, it's clear that he ignored or forgot Aristotle's most important lesson when he left, and that's part of the reason he died at the age of thirty-two – thousands of miles from home – probably killed by his own men who were fed up of him. Business strategist and author, Jim Collins terms the 'undisciplined pursuit of more', as one the reasons the great fall, in his book *How the Mighty Fall*. This is what hits us all the most.[43]

Napoleon, who, like Alexander, also died miserably, said, "Men of great ambition have sought happiness and have found fame." What he means is that behind every goal of humankind is the drive to be happy and fulfilled, but when egotism grabs hold of the reigns, we lose track of our goal and end up somewhere we never intended.

American businessman and investor Howard Hughes was a millionaire by the age of eighteen. During his own lifetime he was known as one of the most financially successful individuals in the world. This was literally in the last century. Yet, whilst one his aides sought to reassure him as death creeped over him saying, "What an incredible life you have led," Hughes shook his head. He replied with the sad, emphatic epiphany that hits everyone close to death, "If you had ever swapped places in life with me, I would be willing to bet that you would have demanded to swap back before the passage of the first week." Think, after achieving so much, how can someone regret their life? Do we want to be in a similar situation?

When it comes to success and failure in life, it's important to remember that there will always be times when we do everything right, perhaps even perfectly, yet the results will somehow be negative. Failure, disrespect, jealousy, or envy, are all a part-and-parcel of our short existence on this planet.

Alexander had an unusual encounter with the famous philosopher Diogenes in Athens once. It is believed that Alexander approached Diogenes, who at the time was lying down, enjoying the summer air, and stood over him asking him what he, the most powerful man in the world, might be able to do for this extremely poor man. At this point, Diogenes could have asked for anything, and we can probably assume that Alexander would've delivered. But instead, what he requested was amazing. Diogenes said, "Stop blocking my sun." Luckily, Alexander didn't kill him. We could say that Diogenes had a grip over his ego. In fact, he may not have had a choice, spending a large part of his life as a slave. Psychologists often say that a threatened ego is one of the most dangerous forces on earth. To quote Fight Club, "The bigger the ego, the harder the fall." I want you to repeat this to yourself a few times. Maybe even write it down on post-it notes and stick it around your home. The bigger the ego, the harder the fall.

No matter how hard we try, there are always going to be things that we're not good at. Let go of the myth of perfectionism. Regardless of all the promises we make to ourselves and others, there will always be things we'd love to have, but we just can't. An assertion defining modern culture is that we can be anything we want to be simply if we dream and put our minds to it; if we want it badly enough, we will get it. Today, this message is leaking out to us everywhere: on tv, in the cinema, on social media, in advertising, in self-help books, everywhere. We then go on to internalise it, making it a very part of our being. But it's false. It is actually the dark lie that is at the very core of the ego. Here is the hard-hitting truth that no bestselling self-help book, famous motivational speaker, or blockbuster Hollywood star wants you to know. We are limited and imperfect. There's simply nothing we can do about it. Western culture prefers us not to believe that we're limited or defined. It wants us to buy into the fiction that we are open, free, nothing but pure, bright possibly; that we're born spotless with the same abilities, like a 'blank slate'. This seduces us into accepting the cultural lie that says we can do anything we set our minds to, that we can be whatever we want to be.

We should always take a step back to realise what we are getting drawn into. If you know someone from a humble background, consider what they would think about any indulgences you are considering. Humility is the opposite of narcissism; the opponent of the ego. Some people misunderstand humility as bad, equating it with shame or self-hatred. Humility is not the same as humiliation, as many conclude. True humility is a strength. It is the ability to see or evaluate yourself accurately and without defensiveness (notice how I said 'accurately', not 'negatively').

Overall, humble people are more connected to others. When you don't concentrate on fuelling the ego, it is easier to relate to others and the wider world. Humility is not only a virtue of great leaders like Mother Teresa, Martin Luther King Jr., or even Pramukh Swami Maharaj. We can all practice humility by not praising ourselves, remembering those that have helped and supported us, contemplating on those less fortunate than us, and truly valuing the lives of others.

You need to be compassionate to yourself too. This isn't egotistical, it is necessary. It means being kind to yourself whilst also accurately facing reality and taking check of your flaws. People who practice compassion for themselves experience less anger, fewer uncontrollable thoughts about themselves, less self-consciousness, more positive emotions, more happiness, and more constructive responses to criticism.[44]

Mindfulness may also reduce narcissistic behaviour and quiet the ego. Mindfulness is the awareness of the present moment, nothing else. It is the thought, the feeling, and the physical experience, without negative judgement. I know how simple this sounds, but we know it isn't. When we eat dinner, we might be thinking about what we have to do for work the next day; when someone walks by without acknowledging us, we might become lost in concern about out appearance or fantasise about retaliation. Not only do our thoughts continuously jump around, but they are also accompanied by keeping those of self-concerned judgements. Practicing mindfulness keeps us separate from the experience. As Swaminarayan explains in his teachings, "The one who looks from within is the observer. Only a fool fails to not realise this."[45] By practicing this form of mindfulness, not only do we see the world as it is, but it also has clear benefits for our relationships, reducing conflict and keeping it from getting out of hand.

Almost every world religion teach love, compassion, and forgiveness as their central tenets. "Do unto others as you wish them to do unto you" is a classic Judeo-Christian principle. Islam's prophet Muhammad said, "Not one of you truly believes until you wish for others what you wish for yourself." The Buddhists say, "Treat not others in ways that you yourself would find hurtful." The Talmud of

Judaism says, "What is hateful to you, do not do to your neighbour. This is the whole Torah; all the rest is commentary." Almost all the Vedic scriptures of Hinduism declare that the noble virtues of love, compassion, and forgiveness too. In fact, even atheism and secular humanism encourage harmonious, ethical relations with others. It is at the very core of human flourishing.

Personal change takes time and effort. The key to practicing personal change is to set goals – ones that we can stick to – that we can keep a record of. This isn't a quick fix, but it can be effective. The most fundamental truth is that no one can exist without one another. It is individualism is what makes us point fingers at others. Individualism is one of the most dangerous ideas of the modern world. Ultimately, individualism and independence, both are a myth.

It is because mankind are disposed to sympathise more entirely with our joy than with our sorrow, that we make parade of our riches, and conceal our poverty. Nothing is more mortifying as to be obliged to expose our distress to the view of the public, and to feel, that though our situation is open to the eyes of all mankind, no mortal conceives for us the half of what we suffer.
Adam Smith

I made my way into the room and bowed in front of him. It had felt like so long since I had last been in his proximity. Divinity, peace, and bliss could be, and is always, experienced in his direct presence. He has a magnificent aura to him that is uniquely divine.

He knew why I was here. I knew why I was here. I didn't need to explain myself. Putting the paper and pen on the side table, he took some water. I sat directly in front of him. Even if he did not speak I knew all my questions would be answered. He is a man of few words, but, his life speaks for itself. Just by observing his life and actions, one can take constant inspiration from him.

"When I was at school," he began in his usual quiet tone, "there used to be a saying that was repeated often, 'He that is down needs fear no fall. He that is low, no pride. He that is humble ever shall have God to be his guide.'"

"So whatever I do, I must keep my ego in check?" I asked.

"Exactly. The ego is the root of all negativity." He replied instantly.

"But it's so hard! We live in a world where we constantly *need* to identify with others and conform to society. Without it, we can't progress."

He laughed gently and then placed both his hands in front of him, facing each other, with his fingers stretched out.

"You see," he said as he locked his fingers and clasped his hands, "This is what has happened. You've become glued to this idea. Try separate my hands."

I was hesitant, but he told me again. I tried to gently pull his hands apart. I couldn't. I shook my head.

"You see? That is your mind. It has become glued to this limited type of thinking. This is the power of māyā. Ego fuels all negativity. You must completely destroy your ego. Especially on the spiritual path."

What he said started to make sense, "But if I let go of my ego, who am I? I have no identity!"

He pointed to my chest, "Here. This is who you are. Your only true identity is your ātmā. All the great people have remained humble. If you think you are something, you are nothing. If you think you are nothing, you are everything. You are not special by your own accord, but you are special due to your attainment. Keep this constantly in mind and remain humble. Then you will feel at peace…"

Desire: The Source of Suffering

> We say "I want peace."
> But it's when we remove I (ego) and Want (desire)
> from our lives, that we are left with nothing but peace.
> *Pramukh Swami Maharaj*

The Sanskrit word for desire is vāsanā, or, kāmanā – to want, long, or hope for something. Desires are fundamentally of five types: the desire to see, the desire to hear, the desire to smell, the desire to taste, and the desire to touch. Throughout Vedic scriptures, desire is singled out as the worst mental affliction. The Rāmāyan states: "If you satisfy desire, it results in greed."[1]

If one person was to get all the wealth, fame, luxuries, and sensual objects in the world, that person's desire would still not be satiated. Knowing that desires are the cause of misery, a wise person renounces desire. The Vedic scriptures compare worldly pleasures 'like a mirage seen by the deer', or, 'mruga-trishnā'. The sun's rays reflecting on the hot desert sand create an illusion of water. The deer, fooled by the illusion, thinks there is water ahead and runs to quench its thirst. Its dull intellect cannot realise it is the victim of deception. The more it runs towards the water, the further the mirage recedes.

Yogiji Maharaj, the guru of my guru, used to share a story of a man with a hundred camels. After a tiring journey through the desert, the man decided to rest with his camels. One by one, he got the camels to sit on the ground so that they don't wander off. As he got to the hundredth camel, he struggled to make it get to the ground. He got frustrated and with a loud scream and pull, the hundredth camel fell to the ground. At the same time, the other 99 camels that were on the ground got up. Yogiji Maharaj used this anecdote to compare it with the pleasures and problems of this world. He used to say that as one problem is resolved, another 99 crop up. He said that this is the very nature of the pleasures and problems of this world. It is the mind – the commander – that generates desires.

In the Shānti Parva book of the Mahābhārat, there is a popular story about 'the blind well'. It goes something like this. Once a prince went to the forest to hunt. Suddenly, a tiger attacked him. The prince fell down from his horse. As he had no bow or weapons to arm, he quickly ran to save himself. Whilst running, his foot got stuck in some weeds and he fell into a dry, dark (blind) well. As he was falling, he managed to grab hold of two tree branches that were luckily hanging over the edge of the well. He looked up and he saw the tiger growling over from the top of the well. He was accustomed to seeing in the dark, and so, when he looked towards the edge of the wall, he saw two rats – one black and one white – slowly nibbling at the branches his life was hanging on. He feared, and knew deep down, that very soon the branch would fall to the bottom of the well.

As the prince looked down into the well, he was frightened to see many snakes hissing and showing their fangs. Suddenly a drop of honey fell on his face. As it rolled down, he stuck his tongue out to relish the sweetness of the honey. He looked up to see that there was a honeycomb between the two branches that were practically his lifeline in the moment. As he gently shook the branch to try and get some more honey, bees started to sting him. Forgetting that the tiger was arching over the top of the well, the snakes were hissing at the bottom, the rats nibbling at the branch, and the bees stinging him, he simply adjusted his tongue to get as many drops of honey as he could. His sole focus remained on the honey. He was happy indeed. He didn't want to think about the precarious situation he was in. He was lost in the sweetness of the honey dripping into his mouth. So what was going to happen to him?

It's obvious. When the branch collapses after the rats have nibbled through, he would fall to the bottom and be finished off by the snakes. This analogy, shared in the Mahābhārat, perfectly explains the human predicament. The prince represents us. We are stuck in the dark, stingy well of this material world (māyā). Death (the tiger) is constantly chasing us, it will not leave until it devours us. The black and white rats nibbling away at the branch (time) represent night and day respectively. The hissing snakes represent the major problems we face in life. The bees represent the small day-to-day problems that we just deal with and don't give much attention. But what about the sweet honey we desire? These are the pleasures we love indulging in. Whether that be seeking fame, acquiring wealth, indulging in palatable food, or whatever, we are all slaves to our desires. Due to these small drops of honey in the form of pleasure, we forget to discern between the truth and untruth and face the reality of life. This story has a deep meaning to it, and I personally choose to contemplate on it on a regular basis. Maybe you could too.

We Are Possessed

John F. Kennedy was probably one of the most successful and inspirational presidents in American history. His mental stability and resilience during the thirteen fateful days of the Cuban missile crisis in October 1962 was truly remarkable. But we should not allow that shining moment hide the fact that, like all of us, he also had inner enemies haunting him and undermining his greatness. Kennedy told the British prime minister, in a moment of very uncomfortable honesty, that if he went without sex for a few days, he'd get headaches. This is a direct example of how most of us view lust. But before we condemn President Kennedy as a lustful addict, we should look towards ourselves. Do we not fall victim to our own forms of lust? Do we not know better and yet do the same?

In this direct form, Swaminarayan constantly emphasised on controlling lust, primarily to his sādhus. Nevertheless, he expected the control of *all* desires to be in *all* of his devotees. He said, "Lust, anger and greed are worse evils than devils." We will explore lust in the broader sense to encompass desire. In fact, the Sanskrit word for lust is kām, and it is the root word for desire – kāmanā. Lust is the destroyer of peace in all areas of our lives. Lust for a beautiful person. Lust for someone other than that who we're committed to. Lust for power. Lust for dominance. Lust for fame. Lust for what others have. A person who is enslaved to their urges is never free – whether you're a painter or the president. How many stories have you heard of great men and women who end up losing everything, and in some cases end up literally behind bars, because they freely chose to indulge in their endless desires – whatever they may be?

A common form of lust is envy. This is the lust for what other people have, for the sole reason that they possess something. We are envious of one person, and they envy somebody else. It's a never ending cycle. Surprisingly, we don't simply want what other people have – we want to hold onto everything we have now *and* add theirs to ours. Let me share a small story with you. A farmer finds a magic lamp. He rubs it, and out of thin air a genie appears, who promises to grant him one wish. The farmer thinks about this for a little while. Finally, he says: "My neighbour has a cow and I have none. I hope that his drops dead." As dumb as it sounds, you can probably identify with the farmer. I'm sure you can admit that similar thoughts have occurred to you at some point in your life.

Of all the emotions, envy is the most idiotic. Why? Because it is relatively easy to switch off. This is in contrast to anger, sadness, or fear. "Envy is the most stupid of vices, for there is no single advantage to be gained from it," writes French novelist Balzac. In short, envy is the most sincere type of flattery; other than that, it's a waste of time.

Many things can spark envy: ownership, status, health, youth, talent, popularity, or beauty. It is often confused with jealousy because the physical reactions are identical. The difference: The subject of envy is a thing (status, money, health, etc.). The subject of jealousy is the behavior of a third person. Envy needs two subjects. Jealousy, on the other hand, requires three: Prem is jealous of Shyam because he has just bought a new Audi. So, how do we curb envy? First, we must stop comparing ourselves to others. Second, we have to find our 'circle of competence' and fill it on our own. Create a niche where you perform best. It doesn't matter how small your area of mastery is. The main thing to remember is that you are the king of the palace.

If you think deeply, you will come to find that most desires are, at the core, irrational emotions. The wise have known for millennia that real pleasure is about freedom from pain and agitation, and that this could only come with controlling their desires.

In the Bhagavad-Gītā, Krishna calls desire the 'ever-present enemy of the wise… which like a fire cannot find satisfaction'. The Buddhists went on the personify the demon of desire in the figure of Mara. They said it was Mara who tried to tempt and distract Buddha from the path of enlightenment. Let's agree that none of us are perfect. We all have biologies and pathologies that will, and do, trip us up at times. What we need instead is a philosophy and strong moral conduct – virtue, or dharma – to help us resist what we can, and to give us the strength to pick ourselves back up when we fail and try to do and be better. This is a topic we delve into in the third part of the book. Materialism is the literal manifestation of desire, and is also one of the most obvious examples of the modern-day egotistical epidemic. We want more things, but not just any old thing. We buy products that confer status and importance – expensive cars, jewellery, clothing, a nice house, or anything else that displays status, power, and sophistication.

The book *Affluenza: The All-Consuming Epidemic* detailed the spending explosion of Americans over the last few decades, comparing the need for endless accumulation of stuff to a disease.[2] Today, advertisement slogans shamelessly promote materialistic entitlement as a virtue. A quick Google search shows that the entitled statement 'you deserve the best' has literally been used across the board, from air tours of the Grand Canyon, selling home loans and mortgages, mobile contracts, guitar lessons, health and gym club memberships, weight-loss supplements, and even life coaches who insist 'you deserve the best life'.

In 1976, sixteen per cent of American high school seniors said that 'having a lot of money' was 'extremely important'. This rose to twenty-six per cent in 2006. High school students name 'getting a good paying job' as more important than 'being ethical and honourable'. When the Pew Center for Research recently asked 18 to 25-year-olds about the most important goals of their generation, eighty-one per cent named becoming rich, more than twice as many as named helping people who need help, four times more than named becoming a leader in the community, and eight times as many as named becoming more spiritual ('becoming famous' came in second at fifty-one per cent).[3]

Anyone born after about 1967 belongs to a generation raised in a highly materialistic culture, especially in the Western world. Obviously, money is important in many ways. The attraction of money is understandable in a time when the necessities of life demand so much more from us. All but 43 countries in the world offer universal health care. Unfortunately, the USA and India are in that list. College tuition has also far outpaced inflation, fuel prices continue to rise, and even small houses are now out of reach for a lot of middle-class families in many areas of the Western world. But, what is less apparent is why we feel the need for money to buy material goods whose purpose is merely to tell the world – and even to prove to oneself – that we are important and successful.

Economists have found that the desire for conspicuous consumption is actually stronger in poor neighbourhoods than in more affluent ones. For example, people in South Carolina, USA, make around $10,000 less on average than those in California, but they spend thirteen per cent more on 'visible goods', for example, cars, jewellery, clothes, and personal care – all status symbols designed to make someone *look* well-off. People throughout history have aspired to be rich, but now wealth seems much more accessible. With modern media, wealth is much more visible than ever before. Reality TV shows also feature behind-the-scenes looks at the lives of rich and famous people. Being rich is paradise for the egotistical. In 2010, when Bhisham Singh Yadav, a New Delhi wheat farmer, spent over $8,000 to fly his son just two miles to his wedding by helicopter, it generated so much attention that the story made the pages of the New York Times, 7,300 miles away.[4] Bhisham, one of India's so-called nouveau riche farmers, who had been born into poverty, was now benefitting from the country's economic boom and appeared to be spending his money recklessly. He had just sold three acres of his farm for $109,000 and wanted to put on a lavish wedding for his son. Even without such windfalls, poor families around the world spend disproportionately large amounts of their income on luxuries when they could be buying necessities. The poorer the families are, the greatest the percentage of their meagre incomes they spend on things they don't need.[5] But again, why?

Yadav was being extravagant. He wasn't so rich that he could easily afford to spend a length of the money on a helicopter ride just to impress the wedding guests. He is not alone, however, as many use their wealth to signal their importance – even those who shouldn't have to succumb to vanity. When the daughter of Microsoft Founder Bill Gates, Jennifer, first met Donald Trump at a horse show gala that he had organised in Florida, she was surprised when he suddenly departed, only to return twenty minutes later by helicopter. Bill Gates concluded that Trump must have been driven away from the event so that he could make a grand return entrance.[6]

Whether you're an Indian farmer or an American business tycoon billionaire, it is just as important to be seen as being wealthy as it is to be wealthy. We like to show off, and one of the ways we do it is through our wealth. Designer clothes, expensive watches, or even a helicopter can increase approval by signalling our success. How lovely.

The psychologist Tim Kasser, author of *The High Price of Materialism*, has spent his career studying the consequences of valuing money and objects. He find that, on average, materialistic people are less happy and more depressed.[7] Even people who simply aspire to have more money suffer from poor mental health; they also report more physical health problems such as a sore throat, back aches, headaches, and are more likely to drink too much alcohol and use illegal drugs. Striving for financial success, apparently, makes people more miserable.[8]

Beyond maybe a brief feeling of excitement we get when we buy a new product and show it off to our friends, the pleasure of anything material is fleeting. Lots of things may be fun to buy, but no so many of them are fun to own. The boost to the ego that you get from beating the Joneses only fuels the ego, and lasts only until we get that new BMW or install a home cinema.

Almost every succeeding contemporary law textbook asks, but never answers, the question "What is property?" In truth, the issue is unanswerable since the definition of property changes all the time. We don't even know what property is! If you are holding this book, I'm hoping I'll be correct in assuming that you are financially stable. Yet, studies show that many of us who live in affluent societies pursue lifestyles that have the goal of accumulating as much stuff as possible, with the belief that this is our purpose in life. Humans are not happy to just live within the physical world; rather, we feel compelled to claim as much control over it as possible, believing that the more we have, the better off we will be. We spend our lives building sandcastles with turrets and moats to protect ourselves from invaders, only to have them swept away by the tides of time.

The prospect of death, in the same way that we began this journey together, should serve as a sobering reminder of the ultimate futility of our desire for possessions. Yet in 1859, when 450 passengers on the Royal Charter drowned off the north coast of Wales, whilst returning from the Australian gold mines to Liverpool, many were burdened by the riches that they could not discard so close to home. Our lives are often dictated by the accumulation of goods, and with each new generation, we abandon the majority of what was left to us in order to obtain our own new stuff.[9]

Many of us believe that getting what we desire will make us happy, but this isn't always the case. According to psychologist Dan Gilbert, this is known as 'miswanting', and it is a frequent human affliction.

Competition is also fuelled by ownership. We cannot all be winners in this one-upmanship game since there is always someone ahead of us and others behind us.

The global luxury market is estimated to be worth $1.2 trillion – personal goods account for £285 billion of the total. Branding is a product's visual identity and an important component of luxury products. Luxury ownership might signal affluence, yet strangely, it is typically the very rich who wish to appear cheap. When you go out of your way to indicate that you don't need to go out of you way, that is known as counter-signalling. It has almost become a badge of honour in Silicon Valley to wear jeans and trainers rather than costly clothing or suits, indicating that you are more interested in technology than prestige. With his standard hoodie and casual wear, Facebook's Mark Zuckerberg has certainly impacted this style.

It's obvious that conspicuous consumption and signalling are both just ways of competing with others. We purchase luxury products to signal our status, but this leads to an issue called luxury fever, in which we spend increasing sums of money in order to maintain our assumed status and stay ahead of others. As a result, there is always someone richer than us, resulting in again, a war of one-upmanship.

One of the motivating aspects that keeps buyers looking for new items is novelty. We desire the latest and greatest because we are tired with what we have and want something new. It's no surprise that advertisers make a point of emphasising that their items are 'new' or 'better', implying that you may anticipate something different. We assume we want more goods and money, but when you question workers on their daily commute, most indicate they would rather have more time. We believe that having more money would make us happier because we will be able to purchase more pleasures, but it is the luxury of time that we should value.

The ancient sages realised these truths, and so, they stressed on the need for us to limit our desires. The alternative is to, of course, suffer in the long run. But there's one more dangerous game we all play to try and fulfil our desires, and it's potentially more devastating than this. In fact, it could be the worst.

> **We have all the money we could ever dream of.**
> **We have all the fame you could ever wish for.**
> **But, it isn't love. It isn't health. It isn't peace inside. Is it?**
> *George Harrison, The Beatles*

The Game We All Play

We all seem to have an inbuilt need to achieve and maintain status. When we achieve some form of status, we fear its loss. This deforms our thinking and denies us the possibility of consistent peace in life. We raise ourselves so high above the animals that we probably appear to them as gods, yet we still behave like them – and often worse.

Our life is primarily driven by status. Of course, life isn't only driven by status. We're also motivated by other drives. We also seek power. We seek connections. We seek love. We seek wealth. We want to change society for the better. But, most human endeavours are to the ends of satisfying the desire of achieving status – a place in this world. If you were asked why you do the things that you do, I'm quite certain you wouldn't say, "Because of status. I love it." This would contradict the stories that we like to tell ourselves, and so, whenever we are in the presence of others, consciously or unconsciously, we know we are being judged and measured. And these judgements matter.

Put aside for a moment your beliefs about evolution, but today, we are as we have always been: tribal. We have instincts that compel us to seek connection and coalition with others and groups. Once we've been accepted, we strive to achieve approval and acclaim. When researchers analysed 186 premodern societies across the globe, they found that men of higher status "invariably had greater wealth and more wives and provided better nourishment for their children." This was, and remains, the secret of maximising our capacity for survival and reproduction: the higher we rise on the status ladder, the more likely we are to live, love and procreate. This is a fact. It's no surprise to discover that feeling deprived of status is a major source of anxiety and depression. When we're losing at the game of life, we feel hurt – it's natural – but there is always another road.

We humans value connection and status more than anything else in this world. We seek to bond with others, to secure *more* resources, and to ultimately seek status. But how do we do this? We do it, in part, by assigning value to objects. These 'status symbols' tell us, and others, how well we are performing. It ties in neatly to what we just spoke about in the previous section. For example, around three-quarters of arguments between children aged 18 and 30 months are over possessions, a figure that rises to ninety per cent when just two toddlers are present. We love status so much, that it is also evident in young children.

In one test, when participants were shown pictures of people wearing 'rich' or 'poor' clothes, they automatically assumed that those in wealthier looking outfits were significantly more competent and of higher status. This effect remained even when they were warned upfront of the potential bias, when they were informed that the clothing was totally irrelevant, and when they were told all the people worked in sales at a 'mid-size firm in the Midwest', earning around $80,000.[10]

The desire for wealth is not fundamental either. Studies show a majority of employees would accept a higher status job title over a pay rise: one survey of 1,500 UK office workers had around seventy per cent choosing status over salary, with creative assistants preferring 'chief imagination officer' and file clerks opting for 'data storage specialists'. Assuming you have enough money to live, it would seem relative status would make you happier than cash. Researchers have found that our reward system is highly active when we achieve *relative* rather than absolute rewards; we are designed to be at our best not when we get more, but when we get more than those around us.[11] Academics at the University of Oxford's Wellbeing Research Centre have found that, as we might expect, the less rich countries *do* see increases in happiness as the general standard of living improves. But for those already wealthy nations, over the long term, money makes little to no difference. Ultimately, money is a symbol of status, power is a symbol of status, and so is the size of the logo on your coat.

But what happens when status is stolen from us? What happens when we are reduced to absolute nothing? Not by our own wish, but against our own will. What happens when we are humiliated and reduced to nothing by others?

Ed grew up with an abusive mother, who was alcoholic, paranoid and extremely controlling. She'd criticise him in public and refuse him affection in fear that it would emasculate him. Ed was large for his age, and when he was ten, his mother became obsessed with the idea that he might just molest his sister. So what did she do? She locked him in the basement to sleep. He spent months down there, the only exit being a trapdoor under the space where the kitchen table usually stood. She'd regularly make fun of him, telling him that none of the clever, attractive young women at the university where she worked would ever come near him. His childhood was marked by constant rejection and humiliation. "I hade this love-hate complex with my mother that was very hard for me to handle," he said. This complexity with his mother made him feel "very inadequate around women, because they posed a threat to me. Inside I blew them up very large. You know, the little games women play, I couldn't play or meet their demands. So I backslid."

And backslid he well and truly did. He killed his grandmother, "because I wanted to kill my mother." He then murdered his mother. He severed her head and molested it before burying it in the garden, with eyes pointing upwards since she insisted others to 'look up to her'. He also killed and ate the remains of eight additional women, molesting some of the corpses and eating others.

There is an African proverb that says, "the child who is not embraced by the village will burn it down to feel its warmth." Of course, claiming Ed was provoked only as a result of humiliation would be naïve. Ed Kemper was diagnosed with paranoid schizophrenia by a court psychiatrist (though this was disputed). Ed Kemper's mother used to tease him about how she didn't think the high-status co-ed girls at her institution would ever date him. He murdered those girls, earning him the name the 'Co-Ed Killer', before finally killing his mother: "I cut off her head and I humiliated her corpse." After that, he pushed her voice box into the food disposal unit. "It seemed appropriate," he said, "she screamed and yelled at me over so many years." His psychological profiler at the FBI, John Douglas writes: "He was a man on a mission who'd had humiliating experiences with women and was now out to punish as many as he could," adding he was "someone not born a serial killer but manufactured as one."

Kemper had an IQ of 145. He was a near genius. Kemper revelled in his fame, displayed himself at service stations, flashing his handcuffs, and speculated eagerly about press coverage during a long journey with police officers following his arrest.

Ed Kemper is still alive at the time of publishing, with his next parole due in 2024. He remains one of the most prominent and notorious serial killers in the United States.[12]

This is just one crazy example of how status can play with our minds, but we've all probably heard countless stories of what people do when they feel humiliated. It is a principal cause of honour killings. These generally include a family plotting to murder someone they think has humiliated their family, usually with behaviours related to adultery, affairs, or being 'too Western'. In some scattered and small cases throughout Asia, it's been observed that communities believe the only way to reclaim a family's lost prestige is to kill those blamed. Victims may have declined an arranged marriage, engaged in extramarital affairs, or sought divorce. They could have wished to completely abandon their beliefs too. Some people are killed as a result of being raped, or others, simply for wearing jewellery. Almost all of the victims are unfortunately women, but the offenders are shockingly gender-diverse. Emerita Professor of Psychology, Phyllis Chesler discovered women were 'hands-on killers' in thirty-nine per cent of instances and co-conspirators in sixty-one per cent of cases in a small study of thirty-one cases spanning Europe and Asia. The exception was India, where women were always the killers.[13]

Humiliation is the total diminishment of status. It is the hell to its heaven. And it's dangerous. We all need status, but it needs to be healthy. Humiliation has been phrased 'the nuclear bomb of emotions' and has been linked to significant depressions, suicidal thoughts, psychosis, intense range, and severe anxiety, including symptoms of post-traumatic stress disorder. Professor James Gilligan, a criminal violence expert, characterises humiliation as the 'annihilation of the self'.

Social media serves as the ultimate arena in which to play the game. Something has happened to the world's 3.6 billion social media users in recent years. It's a status game on social media. It's all there: the selfie-takers and humble braggers; the health gurus and political campaigners, even the cancellers are there too. We will be exploring the world of social media in a short while, but we know it's obsessively compelling. We all want status and seeing others receive it creates an urgency to grab some for ourselves. We signal with the number of followers we have, and if we're fortunate enough to become one of the top-tier players, we can receive the 'verified' badge too. But it's only a rare few who achieve massive success across these platforms and become wealthy. Eleonora 'Lele' Pons, a YouTuber, was supposedly demanding $142,800 for a sponsored Instagram post in 2020, whilst another YouTuber Zach King was listed at $81,100. On the photo-sharing site, they had 41 million and 23 million followers, respectively.[14] Top YouTube stars, according to The Washington Post, earn between two and five million dollars a year on the platform alone.[15] One of the greatest sociological developments of our lifetime is the global rise of social media, but more on this shortly.

The trouble with status is that we are never satiated – no matter how much we achieve – it is a desire after all. We're always looking for more. This is the flaw of the human mind that must be overcome. The reason for never being satisfied by status is slightly different though. One explanation for the need for status, according to researchers, is that it's never truly possessed by the individual once and for all, because it's never truly acquired by the individual once and for all. Because it is bestowed by others, it may be revoked at any time, at least hypothetically. As a result, we continue to crave more and more.

When it comes to status, there is one universal principle that unites humanity though. We despise people who strut around in higher ranks above us. Politics, class, gender, and culture all play a role in this hostility. People feel perfectly comfortable being perfectly cruel about celebrities, CEOs, politicians, and the monarchy, as if they are immune to pain. Our ill feelings towards high status individuals has been captured in the lab. When participants read about someone famous, wealthy, and intelligent, brain areas linked in pain perception became activated. When they read of this invented person suffering a demotion, their pleasure system flared up.[16] Psychologists have observed this impact throughout cultures, with one study in Japan and Australia showing that participants took pleasure in the falling of a 'tall poppy': the higher their status, the greater the enjoyment of their degrading.[17] Another flaw in the human condition.

Did They Vote For Hitler?

In the preface of the book, I asked a question. How could such a cultured and brilliant people, like that of Germany, have voted a violent tyrant to be their leader? And then cheered him on hysterically, in squares crammed with thousands, as if he were a living god? Let's try tie up the loose ends of that question before proceeding.

Whether you hate him or like him, Adolf Hitler was, for a time, one of the most successful leaders in modern history. "Few, if any, twentieth-century political leader have enjoyed greater popularity among their own people than Hitler in the decade or so following his assumption of power," says historian Professor Ian Kershaw. Yet, since the end of the Second World War, many have wondered how the forces of irrationality and evil could have risen with such vigour in a developed country like Germany. It conflicts with our fundamental assumptions about human nature again. How could such a sophisticated and intelligent population elect a violent anti-Semite as their leader? And then go on to cheer him madly, as if he were a living god? However, when examined through the lens of the fight for status, the rise of the Nazis becomes somewhat understandable.

Prior to the First World War, Germany was Europe's wealthiest and most developed society. According to historian Professor Richard Evans, 'capitalist enterprise had reached an unprecedented scale and degree of organisation'.[18] Germany generated two-thirds of all the steel in continental Europe, half of its coal, and twenty per cent more power than Italy, France, and Britain combined. Many of its major industries, such as chemicals, pharmaceuticals, and electricity, were global leaders, and its businesses, like Siemens, AEG, BASF, Hoechst, Krupps, and Thyssen, were reputed for their high quality. Their farmers were equally successful. Germany grew one-third of the world's potatoes. Since the turn of the century, living standards had risen dramatically. As the war began, there was widespread belief that the superior Germans would win quickly, bolstered by spectacular successes on the Eastern Front and the fast capture of Poland. Even when Germany unexpectedly and shockingly admitted defeat, there was an anticipation that the conditions of peace, as outlined in the Treaty of Versailles, would be fair.

They weren't. "No one was prepared for the peace terms to which Germany was forced to agree," writes Evans. This entailed handing over vast tracts of land in Europe, renouncing their colonies elsewhere, handing over massive amounts of military equipment, including all of their submarines, destroying six million rifles, over 15,000 aeroplanes, and more than 130,000 machine guns, as well as adhering to severe restrictions on future military activity. They also had no Air Force, and paid the equivalent of nearly £300 billion in cash reparations. These provisions were widely perceived as an unwarranted national disgrace in Germany.[19]

That wasn't the end though. The Germans had to pay for their own war in addition to financing the expenditures of everyone else's fight too. The administration had anticipated that reparations and money from newly acquired industrial zones would flow inwards, rather than outwards, and had therefore printed and spent currency. Its loss contributed to a situation of hyperinflation incredibly terrifying.

The shock and bewilderment that spread across Germany's upper and middle classes was nearly unanimous. Germany had been brutally expelled from the ranks of the Great Powers and covered in what they considered to be undeserved shame. Germany was superior, and the Germans knew it. They looked at the shattered hierarchy and spun a self-serving story about how the defeat was orchestrated by strong and dark powers. Military commanders, among others, began to allege that they had been the victims of a 'secret, planned, demagogic campaign' by the deviants.

Then came the Great Depression, and by 1932, it was estimated that around 13 million individuals were living in out-of-work households. This was a time when antisemitism was very widespread across Europe. Many Germans embraced a comfortable delusion that stated Jews were to blame for the downturn, the Communist threat, and the unjust defeat of the First World War, along with its associated humiliations. There were around 600,000 practicing Jews in the German Empire at the time. In general, they were of high-status, upwardly mobile, economically and culturally successful, with notable families in banking and retail, with prestigious Jewish names in the elite fields of the arts, medicine, law, science, and media.

I think it's important for me to make it clear that whilst many Germans blamed the Jews for the humiliation of their people, only a minority supported the brutal acts against them. They were far more preoccupied with their wonderful journey towards national order, togetherness, and reestablishment. The most fundamental component of Nazi ideology was its focus on social solidarity – the idea of an organic racial community of all Germans – which was followed by strong nationalism and the Hitler cult. Antisemitism, on the other hand, was significant only for a small percentage of the population, and for a large number of them, it was simply incidental. Hitler, aware of this, took a public step away from antisemitism. Prior to 1922, he had been screaming against Jews incessantly; after that, and throughout most of the 1930s, he raised the 'Jewish Question' very rarely in his speeches. Many saw incidents of antisemitic violence as unfortunate but understandable. Hitler feasted upon this situation.

For the people of Germany, the promise of future status was far more potent than racial hate. Hitler's side positioned itself as youthful and forward-thinking, with unrivalled power, organisation, and desire to restore Germany's rightful place. He spun a magnificent fantasy that millions of potential voters couldn't resist: they were part of the elite Aryan master race.[20]

The tale he conveyed was that race, not class, was what mattered: "There are no such things as classes; they cannot be. Class means caste and caste means race." The Germans, he claimed, had been victims of "the greatest villainy of the century," and when he learned of their loss in the war, "everything went black before my eyes," and he cried. But their humiliation would stop when they united as one people. They'd soar to ever greater heights under his guidance in the form of a magnificent thousand-year Aryan kingdom: the Third Reich. Hitler began his ascent to the pinnacle of the status game.

On 5 March, 1933, Hitler's party won the election. But they won with fewer than fifty per cent of the vote. The Nazis, realising this, rapidly imposed their laws and symbols onto the population at large. Nonconformists would be 'purged' from their stations just three weeks after the election, with the option of cleansing their staff themselves, or having it done for them. The elimination of ideological opponents and Jews from positions of power continued: incorrect-thinking university professors, artists, writers, journalists, and scientists were fired, including twenty Nobel laureates, of which Albert Einstein and Erwin Schrödinger were included.

But the truth was clear: millions of Germans – more than half of the country – did not vote for Hitler or his part at the outset. How they won the people was by gradually shifting their values to accommodate every aspect of society. Within months of Hitler's appointment as Chancellor, party membership had quadrupled to two and a half million, prompting the government to declare a ban on any new memberships. By 1939, at least one-half, and most likely two-thirds of all Germans had joined some form of Nazi organisation.[21] Membership was essential to advance in one's job and for social mobility. As the goldrush grows, the game continues to attract more players, luring them in with spectacular prizes; as it rises in power, more and greater status is made accessible; and it gets even larger and more powerful.

Tyrants frequently begin by telling you something you already believe. When they arrive, they spin their enticing self-serving dream, promising that you *deserve* higher status, just as you'd always thought, and accusingly pointing fingers at those you'd always assumed to be your enemies – child abusers, big business, Communists, Jews. They accuse and gossip, and you become enraged, excited, and morally offended. You join in the status game. They tighten up after they've got you. Their views become more radical, precise, and are more strictly policed; second-self methods of domination are used too.

It's difficult and incomprehensible to fully understand how the Nazi tragedy came to be without understanding why Germans came to revere their leader as a god, and how they fulfilled the goals of the Berlin leader, Goebbels, who announced upon their victory in 1933 that they would win over doubters by working on them "until they have become addicted to us."

Hitler himself became extremely symbolic of the resurgent Germany, partly through successful propaganda. He climbed to the top of the status game, promising it to others, and thus became sacred – the equivalent of a living god – a person that symbolised all that the humiliated people of Germany cherished, and who, in fact, was their status.

But it's not only Germany that has been seized in this manner. Nations across the globe become dangerous when they are humiliated. Take a look at history and modern-day global events themselves. According to one analysis of 94 conflicts since 1648, sixty-seven per cent were driven by concerns of national standing or vengeance, with the next most important cause – security – coming in at a distant eighteen per cent. Many terrorist attacks are motivated by feelings of humiliation and complete loss of status. Osama Bin Laden stated in his first public speech following 9/11, "What America is tasting now is only a copy of what we have tasted. Our Islamic nation has been tasting the same for more than eighty years of humiliation and disgrace." According to researchers, one of the major motivations for suicide bombers is the shame and humiliation induced by foreign troops in their country.

Such feelings are considered to be especially intense in Middle Eastern cultures, where honour is highly valued, a mindset reminiscent of the grandiose American mass-killers who similarly wanted to restore their outrageous degrading via murder. The imperialists of the British Empire also told a self-serving tale in which they claimed to be guiding lower forms of life on a journey to the promised land of civilisation.

The large-scale slaughter of Jews began once the war began to go wrong for Hitler, with his nation and its lofty ideal collapsing. The worst part of Auschwitz, according to survivor Marian Turski, was the humiliation, not the cold, starvation, or the beatings. But, "just because you were Jewish, you were treated not like a human being, you were treated like a louse, a bed bug, like a cockroach."

For reasons like this, the psychologist Dr. Evelin Lindner, has determined that 'the most effective weapon of mass destruction' is 'the humiliated mind'.[22] Of course, these nightmares also contain a deep message. They reveal something about who we could be, as well as how we approach life and others. I'm not too sure on what the message is, and I don't think we're in a position to draw conclusions either. Some things in life are not meant to be understood, they are simply meant to be overcome. If we try to understand everything, we will fall deeper down the rabbit hole. It's not about ignorance – it's about waking up – just like Janak did.

Insatiable Beings

The famous pop musician Michael Jackson had a net worth of around £392 million in 2020. During his lifetime, he became one of the most famously loved singer and dancer. Yet, he once publicly commented: "I am always feeling lonely." What was he lacking? He had his family around him. He lived in luxury. He had millions around who loved him. But he felt lonely. Why?

Around two-thousand years ago, Alexander left in his attempt to conquer the Indian subcontinent. Before he left, he went to his mentor, Aristotle, who told him: "Alexander! You're going to the land known for its rishis. Make sure you don't return without meeting them!" After defeating the Indian king Porus, who reigned over the modern-day Punjab region at the time – whilst Alexander was making his return journey – he remembered the words spoken by Aristotle. He immediately instructed his aide Onesicritus to go and find him a rishi, or as the Greeks called them: Gymnosophists. There's much debate whether Onesicritus met the rishi in a forest on the banks of the River Indus, or in Taxila (located in modern-Pakistan), but nevertheless, he met one. He was called Dandamis. Alexander was quickly informed that there were in fact such rishis in this land, and so, Alexander commanded Onesicritus to go and bring this man to him, "Tell him that the supreme commander will shower him with jewels!"

When Onesicritus passed this message to Dandamis, he responded: "I don't need any of those useless items." When Alexander was informed of the response, he was furious and said, "Tell him that if he doesn't come, I will slice his head off his body!" Dandamis laughed at this, and responded: "I would live even without my head. That sword will only destroy this body, but I am the ātmā. No weapon can pierce my true being. It makes no difference to me if my head remains or not. Pick up your own sword and cut off my head! Death is nothing but a game to us!" Alexander was stunned and impressed when he was informed of Dandamis' response that he himself went to meet him. The conversation that followed between them is recorded by the Greeks as the Alexander-Dandamis colloquy.[23]

On one side, we have Alexander who has conquered almost two-thirds of the known world before he was thirty. Here he was, full of ego and desire. On the other end, we have Dandamis, who was satisfied from within – with no more desires. Who would you say was really at peace? History slaps us again and again with the fact that humans are insatiable beings. No matter what we get, or how much we get, we will never remain satisfied. King Solomon, the king of Israel around 3,000 years ago, was said to have 700 queens, yet he never felt at peace.

In the Vachanāmrut, Swaminarayan says, "The pleasure and pleasantness which are apparent through our senses are experienced only due to the ātmā. However, when the ātmā leaves the body, that which was once pleasurable becomes miserable."[24] Like this, all of the happiness we experience may seem like it is coming through our indulgence in desires, but in reality, we are experiencing the bliss of the ātmā. But we, insatiable beings, falsely believe it to be the indulgence of the sense pleasures. Swaminarayan gives the metaphor of a dog chewing on a dry bone and relishing the taste of its own blood. That's the dilemma.

In the Shānti Parva book of the Mahābhārat, Bhishma is laying on a bed of arrows. Prince Yudhishthir approaches him to seek guidance on the path to peace and liberation after this bloodthirsty conflict. At the time, Bhishma says, "There is more misery than happiness in life – there is no doubt about it."[25] The Buddhists and Stoics followed course with this truth, flourishing their philosophies based on this truth echoed in the ancient Vedic texts.

You and me are unhappy in large part because we are confused about what is valuable. We seek to fulfil our lust of desire through various means, and then end up where we were. In the 1970s, psychologists Shane Frederick and George Loewenstein termed this as 'hedonic adaption'.[26] Regardless of what we achieve – money, fame, success – every human adapts and the joy is only temporary. To illustrate this adaption process, they point to studies of lottery winners. Winning a lottery typically allows one to live the life of their dreams. It turns out, though, that after an initial period of exhilaration, lottery winners end up about as happy as they were before. They start taking their new Ferrari, jacuzzi, and mansion for granted, the same way they previously took their previous car, bathtub, and cramped apartment. For us, a less dramatic form of hedonic adaption takes place when we make consumer purchases. Initially, we delight in the OLED television or fine leather handbag we buy. But, after some time, we come to despise them and find ourselves longing for the new, latest television, or an even more extravagant handbag. Hedonic adaption affects us in every area of our life. We experience hedonic adaption in our career. We also experience hedonic adaption in our relationships. About 150 years before Frederick and Loewenstein, Swaminarayan said that if a person was to get all the wealth, luxuries, and sensual objects available in the world, that person's desire would still not be satiated. Knowing desires to be the cause of our misery, an intelligent person should set out to limit and renounce desire.[27]

The majority of our unhappiness comes from unfulfilled desires. We work hard to fulfil our desires, in the belief that on fulfilling them, they will give us satisfaction. The problem, though, is that once we fulfil a desire for something, we adapt to its presence in our life and as a result, we stop desiring it – or at any rate, we don't find it as desirable as we once did. We end up just as dissatisfied as we were before fulfilling the desire. Neurologically, when we get something we really want, we simply start to want more. Research in the nature of dopamine – which was previously believed to be the driving force behind desire and lust – proves that it is more complex than previously thought. In *The Molecule of More*, Daniel Z. Liberman explains that experts who studied the chemical found that when someone was introduced to something they greatly desired, the dopamine surge would diminish after it was acquired. It turns out, dopamine is not the chemical that gives us pleasure, but it's the chemical that gives you the pleasure of *wanting more*. Today, most of us are so deeply enmeshed in the mental state of 'wanting' that we cannot shift to the state of 'having', or fulfilment.[28]

After working hard to get what we want, we routinely lose interest in the object of our desire. Rather than feeling satisfied, we feel a bit bored, and in response to this boredom, we go on to form new, even deeper desires. One of the desires we mistakenly pursue is fame.

American philosopher William James famously said, "The deepest principle in human nature is the craving to be appreciated." To a greater or lesser extent, we all want to be appreciated – by our family, our friends, our followers. Those who don't actively pursue 'localised' fame still seek popularity within their social circles, or recognition in their work life. Social media is the mirror of this. Head over to your Instagram and see the posts that people put up for yourself. We are so convinced that gaining fame (in some very broad sense of the word) will make us happy. We fail to realise that fame, whether it involves being recognised globally or merely the admiration of our friendship groups, comes at a price.

If we seek social status, we are practically handing other people power over us. We then have to do things calculating if the 'others' will admire us, and so, we then refrain from doing that which they may frown upon. If we truly want freedom and peace, we must always be aware that other people will always judge. Most of us, after all, are obsessed with the opinions and views of others. We work hard, first to win the admiration of other people, and then, to avoid losing it.

To overcome this obsession, you must realise that in order to win the admiration of other people, we will have to change our values. To be more precise, we will have to live a life that is successful or fulfilling according to their notions of success and fulfilment. It is better for us to find like-minded people, who we share common values and beliefs with, in order for us to grow and find peace too. It is extremely difficult to conquer the desire for fame, even so, we must remember: No one is ever going to like or agree a hundred per cent with what we do. That is not an excuse for us to do whatever we want, instead, it is a call to introspect and look towards the higher values in our life.

> "I have all these desires within me." I said, "Is that good or bad?"
> He chuckled lightly, and then spoke, "Tell me, has anyone ever been satisfied by fulfilling their desires? What makes you think that is the epitome of happiness?"
> "It's the small joy that we get when the desires are fulfilled, isn't it?" I replied.
> "The Katha Upanishad says, 'When one eliminates all selfish desires from the heart, then the materially-bound jivātmā attains freedom from birth and death, and then becomes like Brahman.'"[29]
> He was right. When are we ever satisfied in life?

Anger: A Brief Insanity

Anger is not only counterproductive, it is destructive. Anger itself arises from egotism and desire. In fact, it often stems from the roots of unfulfilled desires. For example, if reality doesn't meet our expectations, anger arises almost instantaneously. Swaminarayan says that anger is like a rabid dog, in which, if the saliva of a rabid dog touches a man or cow, then they, like the barking rabid dog, suffer and die. Similarly, one who suffers from anger suffers and falls from the path of a good life.

Psychologists and paediatricians observe the emergence of emotional reactions in newborns. In the first three weeks, children manifest reactions of fear, anger and satisfaction. This makes obvious sense with the Vedic three-bodies belief. We are born with anger, and for the remainder of our life, we wrestle with anger.

Anger stems from egotism and has many unpleasant consequences. We can be angry with others, and sometimes even with ourselves. We project our anger on anyone who is unfortunate to come into contact with us in the moment. Our words and gestures indicate how angry we are, and it is also evident in our body language. Once anger has passed, we normally forget the words we used to hurt others, but the recipient remembers and remains hurt. In the Rāmāyan, the character Vali is mortally wounded, and so he speaks to Rama harshly. Yet, Rama doesn't respond in a fit of anger or aggression. He calmly listens to Vali and then talks to him.

The leaders that we truly respect, who stand head and shoulders above the rest, have been motivated by more than anger and hate.

Whether that is Pericles or Martin Luther King Jr., we find that great leaders are fuelled by love. I saw directly in Pramukh Swami, and today in Mahant Swami this same quality. To tolerate and to understand one and all.

Even apologising or doing after projecting our anger doesn't necessarily repair the damage already done. Consequences always follow. Anyone that is driven by anger is never happy. They are never at peace. They are never stithpragna. We must actively choose to drive out anger and replace it with love and gratitude – and of course, purpose.

For ninety-six minutes on a hot summer's noon of 1966, ex-marine Charles Whitman, positioned high up in the tower building of the University of Texas in Austin, fired 150 rounds, killing 14 people and wounding another 32 before being shot dead by the authorities. The University of Texas massacre was one of the first examples of a modern-day phenomena of mass shootings. Dunblane, Columbine, and Virginia Tech are just a handful of the recent tragedies in a long series of inexplicable killing sprees. Every time one of these atrocities occurs, we are left wondering, why? Why did someone – an ex-marine in fact – lash his anger out in this manner? In the instance of Charles Whitman, we seem to have an answer. He wasn't his normal self.[1]

Whitman talked of his impulsive aggression and the emotional anguish he was suffering in his prospective suicide note. Whitman had a history of violent outbursts and a difficult family life, but in the months leading up to the Austin rampage, he believed things were worse. "After my death, I wish that an autopsy could be performed to see if there is any visible physical disorder," he wrote. He further requested that when his debts were paid off, any money left over be used to conduct study to determine whether there was any reason for his behaviour. He was aware that something was wrong. And he was, sadly, accurate. There was a large tumour in the amygdala area of his brain, deep within his skull.

The amygdala is the part of the brain circuitry responsible for emotional actions; injury to this region can result in extreme swings in range and anger. Overstimulation of the amygdala causes both animals and humans to lash out violently. Whitman's tumour could have been the source of his impulsive anger throughout his life. Together with the fact that his family life was difficult, he misused amphetamines, and he had been under a lot of stress in the summer of 1966. Having an amygdala tumour would have hindered his ability to remain calm.

But, given that we know he had a brain tumour, was Whitman to blame for his actions? Was it Whitman who murdered those innocent individuals, or was it his tumour? How can a lump of cancerous cells lead someone to murder random people? There is something seriously wrong with the way we conceive about the relationship between brain, behaviour, and mind. The danger is that as our understanding of how the brain works advances, we will increasingly hear claims that people who commit crimes are not responsible for their conduct because of some neurological defect. Our choices and actions are greatly influenced by our mind and others, but who is the ultimate controller?

The Stoic philosopher Seneca said about anger, "No plague has cost the human race more." It's because of anger that we see people being killed and poisoned, and cities and nations ruined. Anger doesn't destroy cities and nations, anger destroys us individually. We live in a world, after all, in which there is much to be angry about, meaning that unless we control our anger, we will perpetually be angry. Being angry is a waste of our precious time and energy.

So does this mean if we see our close-ones being killed or our friend being raped we shouldn't feel angry? That we should stand there and do nothing? Not at all. We should definitely seek justice for wrongdoings, but to the best extent possible, we should remain calm in the process. Justice should be an expression not of anger but of caution. To avoid becoming angry we should always keep in mind that the things that anger us generally don't do us any real harm; they are instead mere annoyances. The Roman emperor, Marcus Aurelius, also offers advice on managing anger. He says that we should contemplate the impermanence of the world around us. By doing this, we will realise that many of the things we think are important in fact aren't, at least not in the grand scheme of things. The antidote to anger lies in mastering the ego. After all, the ego is the root of all suffering within the kingdom, and for its people too.

> "When desires remain unfulfilled, they result in anger. The world doesn't seem as it should to the mind, and so, it reacts with anger." He revealed. "That is why it always comes back to the ego. By conquering your ego, your conquer your mind. When you conquer your mind, you conquer *your* world."

The Fault of Fault-Finding

We will never move forward by pointing out the flaws of others, but only through finding our own.
Yogiji Maharaj

One of the most universal pieces of advice from across cultures and millennia is that we humans are all hypocrites, and in our condemnation of others' hypocrisy we only compound our own. We are blind to the logs in our own eyes. When a celebrity or well-known figure slips up, we so quickly and easily point fingers to them, but when we step out of line in a similar fashion, we try to justify our actions. Isn't it funny how we judge ourselves by our internal motives and everyone else by their external actions?

Social psychologists have recently isolated the mechanisms that make us blind. The moral implications of these findings are disturbing indeed, because they challenge our greatest moral certainties. But the implications can, and will be, liberating.

There is a Japanese proverb that says, "Though you see the seven defects of others, we do not see our own ten defects." From the person who cuts us off on the motorway all the way to the Nazis who ran the concentration camps, most people think they are good people and that their actions are motivated by good reasons. As Robert Wright put it in his book *The Moral Animal*, "Human beings are a species splendid in their array of moral equipment, tragic in their propensity to misuse it, and pathetic in their constitutional ignorance of the misuse."[1]

When Americans and Europeans are asked to rate themselves on virtues, skills, or other desirable traits (including intelligence, driving ability, sexual skills, and ethics), a large majority say they are above average. (This effect is weaker in East Asian countries, and may not exist at all in Japan).[2]

We judge others by their behaviour, but we think we have special information about ourselves – we know what we are 'really like' inside, so we can easily find ways to explain away our selfish acts and cling to the illusion that we are better than others.

In a study of a million American high school students, seventy per cent thought they were above average on leadership ability, but only two per cent thought they were below average. Everyone can find *some* skill that might be construed as related to leadership, and then find *some* piece of evidence that one has that skill.[3]

You cannot change these biases in other people. Emily Pronin at Princeton and Lee Ross at Stanford have tried to help people overcome their self-serving biases by teaching them about biases and then asking, "Okay, now that you know about these biases, do you want to change what you just said about yourself?" Across many studies, the results were the same: People were quite happy to learn about the various forms of self-serving bias and then apply their newfound knowledge to predict others' responses.[4] But their self-ratings were unaffected. The results show that each of us thinks we see the world directly – as it really is. We further believe that the facts as we see them, are there for all to see, so others should agree with us. If they don't agree, it follows either that they have not been exposed to the right facts or else that they are blinded by their own interests and leaning ideologies. It is this sort of thinking that gives us a world full of good and evil, and this brings us the most disturbing implication of the Vedic advice about hypocrisy: Good and evil do not exists outside of our beliefs about them.

In his book *Evil: Inside Human Cruelty and Aggression*, social psychologist Roy Baumister examined evil from the perspective of both victim and perpetrator.[5] When taking the perpetrator's perspective, he found the people who do things we see as evil, all the way from spousal abuse to genocide, rarely think they are doing anything wrong. They almost always think their actions are justified, especially in the moment. They often think they themselves are the victims. Is this what happened to Hitler? Napoleon? Alexander? Maybe. Maybe not. Even more interestingly was Baumeister's research literature, in which he found that victims often shared some of the blame. Most murders result from an escalating cycle of provocation and retaliation; often, the body could just as easily have been the murderer. In fifty per cent of all domestic disputes, both sides used violence. He also points out that, even in instances of obvious police brutality, there is usually much more to the story than what is shown on the news. (Remember, news programs gain viewers by satisfying people's need to believe that evil lurks in every corner of known land.)

People usually have reasons for committing violence, and those reasons usually involve some form of retaliation for a perceived injustice, or for self-defence. When George W. Bush said that the 9/11 terrorists did what they did because they 'hate our freedom' he showed a stunning lack of psychological insight. Neither the hijackers nor Bin Laden were particularly upset because the Western world allowed women to drive, vote, or show their faces in public. Rather, many Islamic extremists want to kill Westerners because they see America as being almost Satanic, the current villain in a long pageant of Western humiliation of Arab nations and populations. They did what they did as a reaction to America's actions and impact in the Middle East. However horrifying it is for terrorists to categorise all of the population into the category of 'enemy' and then kill them indiscriminately, such actions at least make psychological sense, whereas killing because of pure hatred for freedom doesn't. The major atrocities of the twentieth century were carried out largely either by men who thought they were creating a utopia or else by men who believed they were defending their homeland or tribe from attack.[6]

To tackle our seemingly inherent fault-finding nature, we can write down our thoughts, learn to recognise the distortions in them, and then think of more appropriate ones. This is kind of the basis of cognitive behavioural therapy too. When we extract a splinter it hurts, for a moment, but then we feel relief, eve pleasure. When we find a fault in ourselves it will hurt, for a moment, but if we keep going and acknowledge the fault, we are more likely to feel relief. It is this taking responsibility for our own behaviour that allows us to live in peace. By seeing the log in our own eye we can become less biased, and therefore less inclined towards argument and conflict. We begin to follow the perfect, focused way of living.

These are, in very brief, the main enemies that live within our kingdom. Of course, we could expand on them and talk about lust, avarice, jealousy, greed etc., but we'd be here too long. Hence, we've introduced ourselves to some of the key enemies and their consequences. Before moving on to how we can train the commander to handle these inner enemies, I want to talk about some of the fallacies and biases associated with the mind, and so, that's out next stop.

> "Why is it that wherever we look, we see people being selfish. It almost seems like we can't trust anyone… Why?"
> He nodded and smiled, but he didn't speak. He then picked up a book that was on the table next to him, and he opened it up to a page with a post-it note on it. Then he spoke…
> "See… here it says that everything is divine. In fact, everything *is* divine. We look towards people's external qualities and judge them accordingly, but we fail to see everyone's true identity as the ātmā."
> "Yes…" I replied, eager to hear more.
> "Due to the influence of the three modes of nature and *maya*, any individual's mind may be affected, and because of that people act and behave differently. But you should always remember that at the root of their being, everyone is divine. Realising this is key to achieving peace in life. Why? Because it's the truth."
> As he finished talking, my fellow swami walked into the room…

The Mind Games

By now, you've probably figured that the commander has it's own thinking and nature. I myself cannot say for certain whether the way that the commander thinks and works is down to evolution, or if it was moulded in that way throughout its upbringing. But, one thing is certain – he doesn't like listening to the king. Either that, or the monkey is very good at distracting him.

The commander has inherited so much power thanks to the king, that his ahankar (ego) has got the better of him. He believes that it is him that has the true say in what happens throughout the kingdom. He believes he is in charge of the ministers and all the subjects (senses). The king is always too busy tending to his garden to notice what the commander is really up to.

This very brief section is dedicated to understanding the flaws of the commander. If you want to look into these biases and logical fallacies further, I recommend reading the works of Daniel Kahneman and Nassim Nicholas Taleb – two amazing thinkers of the modern world. The reason I bring these 'mind games' up is not merely for the sake of accepting, but so that we can mould the commander to work as per the wishes of the king. For sure, it will take time and effort, but doesn't everything in life require persistent effort?

The Survivorship Bias

In today's world, success is made more visible than failures, and because of this we severely and systematically overestimate our own chances of succeeding. Behind every popular author, we will find another hundred writers who can never manage to sell their books. Behind them are others who have manuscripts lying around waiting to be published. Behind them are yet another hundred unfinished pages gathering dust in the drawers. And behind each one of these are a hundred people who – one day – dream of writing a book. The same goes for any field of human endeavour. Photographers, business startups, artists, athletes, architects, actors and even influencers.

This is what we call the survivorship bias. If enough scientists examine a particular phenomenon, a few of these studies are guaranteed to deliver statistically significant results through pure coincidence. For example, the relationship between red wine consumption and high life expectancy. Such (and I am certain, false) studies immediately attain a high degree of popularity and attention. As a result, you won't read about the other side of the story. People systematically overestimate their chances of success. To tackle this bias it's necessary to keep the 'be prepared for failure and obstacles' mindset at the forefront of our mind. We must also look at the wider picture. Behind every success, there are hundreds others who have failed. Yes, it is a sad walk down the lane of history, but one that will surely clear our mind, and also keep our ego in check. Always consider both sides of any story.

The Clustering Illusion

In 1994, Diane Duyser from Florida had an out-of-the-world encounter. After biting into a slice of toast and placing it back down on her plate, she noticed the face of Virgin Mary in it. Immediately, she stopped eating and stored the divine encounter (except for her bite) in a container. Twenty years later, in November 2004, she auctioned the still fairly well-preserved snack on eBay. She made $28,000. I know what you're thinking – what the hell?

This is the clustering illusion – a bias that arises from seeing trends in random events that occur in clusters, but are actually just random events. It's like when you see faces in the clouds or the outlines of people in rocks and mountains. The human mind seeks patterns and rules. It often goes one step further by inventing some of its own. We are oversensitive. Be skeptical of chance occurrences. Don't believe everything that your eyes see.

Social Proofing

You are walking through the city and notice a group of people, huddled together, staring and pointing into the sky. Without even thinking about it, you look upwards too. Why? Social proof. It's also sometimes known as the 'herd instinct', and it dictates that individuals feel they are behaving correctly when they act the same as other people. It's what makes the magic behind stock market panics, and it also exists in fashion, management, and diets. It can paralyse entire cultures and even lead to entire groups of people committing collective suicide. This phenomenon is rooted deep within our being. Thousands of years ago, in hunter-gatherer tribes, it was a good survival strategy. Today it may not be the case. The advertising industry greatly benefits from our weakness for social proof. Be skeptical and think twice before you act. You don't need to be a sheep. Become a lion. Live truthfully. Live spiritually. Live blissfully.

The Sunk Cost Fallacy

The sunk cost fallacy plays its most dangerous move when we have invested a lot of time, money, energy, and love into something. This investment becomes a motive for us to carry on, even if we are dealing with a lost cause. The more we invest in something, the greater the sunk costs are, and the greater the urge to continue becomes. Investors often fall victim to this fallacy.

The Concorde is a prime example of a government deficit project. Both parties – Britain and France – had long realised that the supersonic aircraft business would eventually flop, yet they continued to invest huge sums of money in it. Abandoning the project would lead to admitting defeat, a blemish on status. That is why this fallacy is often referred to as the 'Concorde effect'. It was the reason behind why the Americans extended their involvement in the Vietnam war. They thought, "We've already sacrificed enough for this war, why would we make the mistake of giving up now?"

I'm not saying it is wrong to invest in something, there may be many good reasons to do so, but we must be aware of the wrong reasons too. Rational decision making requires us to forget about the costs incurred to date. No matter how much you may have already invested in something, only your assessment of the future costs and benefits count.

The Confirmation Bias

This is one of the most popular biases. Prem wants to lose weight. He selects a particular diet from an online health plan and checks his progress on the scales every morning. If he has lost some weight, he pats himself on the back and considers that the diet plan is a success. If he has gained weight, he will probably write it off as a normal fluctuation and will forget about it. For weeks on end, he lives under the illusion that the diet is working, even though his weight remains the same. Prem is a victim of the confirmation bias – a harmless form of it – or is it? The confirmation bias is the minister of all misconceptions. It is the tendency to interpret new information so that it becomes compatible with our preexisting beliefs, theories and convictions. We filter out any new information that contradicts our existing views. But, unfortunately, facts do not cease to exist just because we choose to ignore them. Warren Buffet says: "What the human being is best at doing is interpreting all new information so that their prior conclusions remain intact."

We are forced to establish beliefs about the world, our lives, the economy, investments, our careers, and more. We deal mostly in assumptions, and the more nebulous these are, the stronger the confirmation bias. Many self-help 'secrets' and 'get-rich-quick' books are further examples of the blinkering storytelling that stems from the confirmation bias. These shrewd individuals collect piles of proof to pump up the most unoriginal theories.

The Internet is the breeding ground for the confirmation bias. To stay informed, we browse news sites and blogs, forgetting that the pages we often view mirror our existing values to some extent. Even worse, a lot of sites and companies now tailor content to personal interests, browsing history and cookies, causing new and divergent viewpoints to vanish from your radar altogether. We are pushed into virtual cages of like-minded people, further reinforcing our existing beliefs. Don't jump to conclusions, be open to divergent viewpoints, and be accepting of others and differences.

The Contrast Effect

In his book *Influence,* Robert Cialdini tells the story of two brothers, Sid and Harry, who ran a clothing store in 1930s America. Sid was in charge of sales and Harry led the tailoring department. Whenever Sid noticed that the customers who stood before the mirror really liked their suits, he became a little hard of hearing. He called to his brother: "Harry, how much for this suit?" Harry looked up from his cutting table and shouted back: "For that beautiful cotton suit, forty-two dollars." (At that time, it was a completely inflated price.) Sid pretended as if he hadn't understood: "How much?" Harry yelled again: "Forty-two dollars!" Sid then turned to his customer and reported: "He says twenty-two dollars." At this point, the customer would have quickly put the money on the table and hastened from the store with the suit before poor Sid noticed his 'mistake'.

Maybe you know the following experiment from your school days: Take two buckets. Fill the first with lukewarm water and the second with ice water. Dip your right hand into the ice water for one minute. Then put both hands into the lukewarm water. What do you notice? The lukewarm water feels as it should to the left hand and piping hot to the right hand.

Both of these stories epitomise the contrast effect. We judge something to be beautiful, expensive, or large if we have something ugly, cheap, or small in front of us. We have difficulty with absolute judgments.

Experiments show that people are willing to walk an extra ten minutes to save £10 on food. But those same people wouldn't dream of walking ten minutes to save £10 on a £1000 suit. An irrational move because ten minutes is ten minutes, and £10 is £10. Logically, you should walk back in both cases or not at all, right?

Here I leave you with a thought. Today, when we are bombarded by advertisements featuring supermodels and 'perfect' individuals, we now perceive beautiful people as only moderately attractive. Will this have an adverse effect on the next generation seeking a partner?

The Availability Bias

Are there more words in the English language that start with a 'k' or more words with 'k' as its third letter? Instinctively, you will probably go for the first one. But, there are more than twice as many English words that have 'k' in the third position than those that start with it. Why do most people believe the opposite though? Because we can think of words beginning with a 'k' more quickly. They are quickly 'available' to our memory.

The availability bias says that we create a picture of the world using the examples that most easily come to our mind. This is dumb, of course, because in reality, things don't happen more frequently just because we can conceive of them more easily. The commander plays his games. We attach too much likelihood to flashy, amazing outcomes. Anything silent or invisible we push to the back of our minds. We think dramatically, instead of quantitatively. If something is repeated often enough, it gets stored at the forefront of our minds – even if it isn't true. Spend time with people with differing viewpoints and that think differently to you. To overcome the availability bias, we need the input of others.

The Story Bias

I'm not here to bash the media, but facts are facts. The media is the haven of story bias. Say a car is driving over a bridge when the structure suddenly collapses, what would you see the next day on the news? There is no doubt we would hear the tale of the unlucky driver, where he came from, and where he was going. We read his biography: born somewhere, grew up somewhere else, earned a living as something. If he survives and can give interviews, we hear exactly how it felt when the bridge came crashing down. The crazy thing is that, not one of these stories explains the underlying cause of the accident. Where was the weak point? Was it fatigue? If not, was the bridge damaged? If so, by what? Was a proper design even used? Where are there other bridges of the same design? The problem with all these questions is that, though valid, they just don't make for a good story.

Stories attract us; abstract details repel us. Consequently, entertaining side issues and backstories are fuelled over relevant facts. Advertisers have also learned to capitalise on this. Instead of focusing on an item's benefits, they create a story around it. Objectively speaking, narratives are irrelevant, but the human mind still finds them irresistible. Whenever you hear a story, look towards the sender and their intentions. Choose facts over fabrication.

The Hindsight Bias

This is one of the most prevailing biases of all. We can call it the 'I told you so' fallacy too. On reflection, everything seems clear and inevitable. If a CEO becomes successful due to fortunate circumstances, looking back, he will rate the probability of his success a lot higher than it actually was.

The hindsight bias makes us believe we are better predictors than we truly are, often causing the mind to remain arrogant about our knowledge, and consequently, to take too much risk. Overcoming this bias isn't easy. Studies have shown that people who are aware of it fall just as easily as everyone else. It's practically the elephant in the room.

The Illusion of Control

Every single day, shortly before nine o'clock, a man with a red hat stands in a square and begins to wave his cap around wildly. After five minutes, he disappears. One day, a police officer comes up to him and asks: "What are you doing?" "I'm keeping the giraffes away." "But there aren't any giraffes here." "Well, I must be doing a good job, then!"

The illusion of control is the tendency to believe that we can influence something over which we have absolutely no control. This was discovered in 1965 by two researchers, Jenkins and Ward. Their experiment was simple, consisting of just two switches and a light. The men were able to adjust when the switches connected to the light, and when they didn't too. Even when the light flashed on and off at random intervals, subjects were still convinced that they were in control by the flicking of the switch. We hardly have control over most events in our life. Accept it and work with it.

The Outcome Bias

Say one million monkeys speculate on the stock market. They buy and sell stocks like crazy and, of course, completely at random. What happens? After one week, about half of the monkeys will have made a profit and the other half a loss. The ones that made a profit can stay; the ones that made a loss you send home. In the second week, one half of the monkeys will still be riding high, while the other half will have made a loss and are sent home. And so on. After ten weeks, about one thousand monkeys will be left – those who have always invested their money well. After twenty weeks, just one monkey will remain – this one always, without fail, chose the right stocks and is now a billionaire. Let's call him the success monkey.

How does the media react? It will pounce on this animal to understand its 'success principles'. And they will find some: Perhaps the monkey eats more bananas than the others. Perhaps he sits in another corner of the cage. Or maybe he swings headlong through the branches, or he takes long, reflective pauses while grooming. He must have some recipe for success, right?

The monkey story illustrates the outcome bias. We tend to evaluate decisions based on the result rather than on the decision process. We should never judge a decision purely by its result, especially when randomness and 'external factors' play a role.

The Paradox of Choice

In his book *The Paradox of Choice*, psychologist Barry Schwartz describes this phenomenon. First, a large selection leads to inner paralysis. To test this, a supermarket set up a stand where customers could sample 24 varieties of jelly. They could try as many as they liked and then buy them at a discount. The next day, the owners carried out the same experiment with only six flavours. The result? They sold ten times more jelly on day two. Why? With such a wide range, customers could not come to a decision, so they bought nothing. The experiment was repeated several times with different products. The results were always the same.

A large selection leads to discontent. How can you be sure you are making the right choice when two hundred options surround and confound you? The answer is: You cannot. The more choices you have, the more unsure and therefore dissatisfied you are afterwards. Think carefully about what you want. Realise that you will never be able to make a perfect choice. We live in the age of unlimited variety and choices. When will we be satisfied? Never.

The Halo Effect

Cisco, the Silicon Valley firm, was once a darling of the new economy. Business journalists gushed about its success in every discipline: its wonderful customer service, perfect strategy, skilful acquisitions, unique corporate culture, and charismatic CEO. In March 2000, it was the most valuable company in the world.

When Cisco's stock plummeted eighty per cent the following year, the journalists changed their tune. Suddenly the company's competitive advantages were reframed as destructive shortcomings: poor customer service, a woolly strategy, clumsy acquisitions, a lame corporate culture, and an dull CEO. All this – and yet neither the strategy nor the CEO had changed.

The halo effect occurs when a single aspect dazzles us and affects how we see the full picture. In the case of Cisco, its halo shone particularly bright. Journalists were astounded by its stock prices and assumed the entire business was just as brilliant – without closer investigation.

The psychologist Edward Lee Thorndike discovered the halo effect nearly one hundred years ago. His conclusion was that a single quality (beauty, social status, age, etc.) produces a positive or negative impression that outshines everything else, and the overall effect is disproportionate. Beauty is the best-studied example. Dozens of studies have shown that we automatically regard good-looking people as more pleasant, honest, and intelligent. Attractive people also have it easier in their professional lives – and that has nothing to do with the myth of (women) 'sleeping their way to the top'. The halo effect obstructs our view of true characteristics. To counteract this, go beyond face value. Dig deeper. Invest the time to do serious research.

Framing

C'est le ton qui fait la musique: It's not what you say but how you say it. If a message is communicated in different ways, it will also be received in different ways. In psychologists' terms, this technique is called framing.

We react differently to identical situations, depending on how they are presented. Kahneman and Tversky conducted a survey in the 1980s in which they put forward two options for an epidemic-control strategy. The lives of six hundred people were at stake, they told participants. "Option A saves two hundred lives. Option B offers a thirty-three per cent chance that all six hundred people will survive, and a sixty-six per cent chance that no one will survive."

Although options A and B were comparable (with two hundred

survivors expected), the majority of respondents chose A – remembering the maxim: A bird in the hand is worth two in the bush. It became really interesting when the same options were reframed. "Option A kills four hundred people. Option B offers a thirty-three percent chance that no one will die, and with a sixty-six percent chance that all six hundred will die." This time, only a fraction of respondents chose A and the majority picked B. The researchers observed a complete U-turn from almost all involved. Depending on the phrasing – survive or die – the respondents made completely different decisions.

Realise that whatever you communicate contains some element of framing, and that every fact – even if you hear it from a trusted friend or read it in a reputable newspaper – is subject to this effect, too.

The Self-Serving Bias

Do you ever read annual reports, paying particular attention to the CEO's comments? No? That's a pity, because there you'll find countless examples of this next error, which we all fall for at one time or another. For example, if the company has enjoyed an excellent year, the CEO catalogs his indispensable contributions: his brilliant decisions, tireless efforts, and cultivation of a dynamic corporate culture. However, if the company has had a miserable year, we read about all sorts of other dynamics: the unfortunate exchange rate, governmental interference, the malicious trade practices of the Chinese, various hidden tariffs, subdued consumer confidence, and so on. In short: We attribute success to ourselves and failures to external factors. This is the self-serving bias. It's rooted within our ego.

The Hedonic Treadmill

How well can we predict our feelings? Are we experts on ourselves? Would winning the lottery make us the happiest people alive for years to come? Harvard psychologist Dan Gilbert says no. He has studied lottery winners and discovered that the happiness effect fizzles out after a few months. So, a little while after you receive the big cheque, you will be as content or as discontent as you were before. He calls this 'affective forecasting': our inability to correctly predict our own emotions.

The Association Bias

Our brain is a connection machine. This is quite practical: If we eat an unknown fruit and feel sick afterward, we avoid it in future, labeling the plant poisonous or at least unpalatable. This is how knowledge comes to be. However, this method also creates false knowledge.

Russian scientist Ivan Pavlov was the first to conduct research into this phenomenon. His original goal was to measure salivation in dogs. He used a bell to call the dogs to eat, but soon the ringing sound was enough to make the dogs salivate. The animals' brains linked two functionally unrelated things – the ringing of a bell and the production of saliva. Pavlov's method works equally well with humans. Advertising creates a link between products and emotions. For this reason, you will never see Coke alongside a frowning face or a wrinkly body. Coke people are young, beautiful, and oh so happy, and they appear in clusters not seen in the real world. These false connections are the work of the association bias, which also influences the quality of our decisions.

Cognitive Dissonance

Suppose you buy a new car. However, you regret your choice soon afterward: The engine sounds like a jet taking off and you just can't get comfortable in the driver's seat. What do you do? Giving the car back would be an admission of error (you don't want that!), and anyway, the dealer probably wouldn't refund all the money. So you tell yourself that a loud engine and awkward seats are great safety features that will prevent you from falling asleep at the wheel. Not so stupid after all, you think, and you are suddenly proud of your sound, practical purchase. Cognitive dissonance is the state of having inconsistent thoughts, beliefs, or attitudes. It's overcome by regularly having conversations with yourself.

Neomania

How will the world look in fifty years? What will your everyday life be like? With which items will you surround yourself? People who pondered this question fifty years ago had fanciful notions of how 'the future' would look: Highways in the skies. Cities that resemble glass worlds. Bullet trains winding between gleaming skyscrapers. We would live in plastic capsules, work in underwater cities, vacation on the moon, and consume everything in pill form. We wouldn't conceive offspring anymore; instead we would choose children from a catalog. Our best friends would be robots, death would be cured, and we would have exchanged our bikes for jet packs long ago.

But hang on a second. Take a look around. You're sitting in a chair, an invention from ancient Egypt. You wear pants, developed about five thousand years ago and adapted by Germanic tribes around 750 BC. The idea behind your leather shoes comes from the last ice age. Your bookshelves are made of wood, one of the oldest building materials in the world. At dinnertime, you use a fork, a well-known 'killer app' from Roman times, to shovel chunks of dead animals or plants into your mouths. Nothing has changed.

How will the world look in fifty years? In his book *Antifragile*, Nassim Taleb gives us a clue: Assume that most of the technology that has existed for the past fifty years will serve us for another half century. And assume that recent technology will be passé in a few years' time. Why? Think of these inventions as if they were species: Whatever has held its own throughout centuries of innovation will probably continue to do so in the future too. Old technology has proven itself; it possesses an inherent logic even if we do not always understand it. If something has endured for epochs, it must be worth its salt. You can take this to heart the next time you are in a strategy meeting. Fifty years into the future will look a lot like today. Of course, you will witness the birth of many flashy gadgets and magic contraptions. But most will be short-lived.

The Default Effect

I've owned an iPhone for several years now. The gadget allows me to customize everything – data usage, app synchronisation, phone encryption, even how loud I want the camera shutter to sound. How many of these have I set up so far? You guessed it: not one. I'm just another victim of the so-called default effect.

In their book *Nudge*, economist Richard Thaler and law professor Cass Sunstein illustrate how a government can direct its citizens without unconstitutionally restricting their freedom. The authorities simply need to provide a few options – always including a default choice for indecisive individuals. This is how New Jersey and

Pennsylvania presented two car-insurance policies to their inhabitants. The first policy was cheaper but waived certain rights to compensation should an accident take place. New Jersey advertised this as the standard option, and most people were happy to take it. In Pennsylvania, however, the second, more expensive option was touted as the standard and promptly became the bestseller. This outcome is quite remarkable, especially when you consider that both states' drivers cannot differ all that much in what they want covered or in what they want to pay.

The Illusion of Attention

In the 1990s, Harvard psychologists Daniel Simons and Christopher Chabris filmed two teams of students passing basketballs back and forth. One team wore black T-shirts, the other, white. The short clip, 'The Monkey Business Illusion', is available on YouTube. (Take a look before reading on.) In the video, viewers are asked to count how many times the players in white T-shirts pass the ball. Both teams move in circles, weaving in and out, passing back and forth. Suddenly, in the middle of the video, something bizarre happens: A student dressed as a gorilla walks into the center of the room, pounds his chest, and promptly disappears again. At the end, you are asked if you noticed anything unusual. Half the viewers shake their heads in astonishment. Gorilla? What gorilla?

The monkey business test is considered one of the most famous experiments in psychology and demonstrates the so-called illusion of attention: We are confident that we notice everything that takes place in front of us. But in reality, we often see only what we are focusing on – in this case, the passes made by the team in white. Unexpected, unnoticed interruptions can be as large and conspicuous as a gorilla.

The News Illusion

Earthquake in Sumatra. Plane crash in Russia. Man holds daughter captive in his cellar for thirty years. Heidi Klum separates from Seal. Record salaries at Bank of America. Attack in Pakistan. Resignation of Mali's president. Do you really need to know all these things?

We are incredibly well informed, yet we know incredibly little. Why? Because two centuries ago, we invented a toxic form of knowledge called 'news'. It's to the mind what sugar is to the body:

appetising, easy to digest – and highly destructive in the long run. At the start of 2021, I began an experiment. I stopped reading and listening to the news. I deleted the news apps from my iPhone. The first weeks were hard. Very hard. I was constantly afraid of missing something. But after a while, I had a new outlook. The result after nine months: clearer thoughts, more valuable insights, better decisions, and much more time. And the best thing? I haven't missed anything important. People work as a news filter and keep me in the loop. You're probably thinking, "Why is Vinay being so anti-news?" Well, I'll tell you.

First, our brains react disproportionately to different types of information. Scandalous, shocking, people-based, loud, fast-changing details all stimulate us, whereas abstract, complex, and unprocessed information sedates us. News producers capitalise on this. Second, news is irrelevant. In the past twelve months, you have probably consumed about ten thousand news snippets – perhaps as many as thirty per day. Be very honest: Name one of them, just one that helped you make a better decision – for your life, your career, or your business – compared with not having this piece of news. No one I have asked has been able to name more than two useful news stories – out of ten thousand. A miserable result. News organisations assert that their information gives you a competitive advantage. Too many fall for this. In reality, news consumption represents a competitive disadvantage. If news really helped people advance, journalists would be at the top of the income pyramid. They aren't, they are quite the opposite. Third, news is a waste of time. An average human being squanders half a day each week on reading about current affairs. In global terms, this is an immense loss of productivity.

Take the 2008 terror attacks in Mumbai. Out of sheer thirst for recognition, terrorists murdered two hundred people. Let's say a billion people devoted an hour of their time to following the aftermath: They viewed the minute-by-minute updates and listened to the inane chatter of a few 'experts' and 'commentators'. This is a very realistic 'guesstimate' since India has more than a billion inhabitants. Thus our conservative calculation: One billion people multiplied by an hour's distraction equals one billion hours of work stoppage. If we convert this, we learn that news consumption wasted around two thousand lives – ten times more than the attack. A sarcastic but accurate observation. You're better off reading background articles and books. What you need to know, will come to you. One way or another.

The Modern Battles

Physically, we don't let people touch us, push us around, control where we go, or what we do. But when it comes to the mind, we are less disciplined. Why? In the modern world, we hand over our mind – willingly – to the media, television, social media, and even to other people. We sit down to work and the next thing you know, we're scrolling through Instagram. We sit down with our families, but within minutes we are all on our WhatsApp chats. We sit down peacefully on a bench in a park, but instead of looking inwards, we're judging people as they pass by. The astonishing thing is that we don't even know we're doing this. We don't realise how much time and energy we waste on it. We don't realise how inefficient and distracted it makes us. And what's worse – no one is *making* this happen. Regardless of what you think or believe, it's totally self-inflicted. Today's kids are on the frontline of these great battles; they are the first people not to know life without super-fast internet, ever-present smartphones and relationships that are shaped by social media. Figures from the Office for National Statistics (UK) show that suicides amongst girls aged 16 to 24 increased by eighty-three per cent in the six years leading up to 2019, and NHS figures show a forty-eight per cent rise in anxiety and depression in British children over the past fifteen. This pattern is likely to be similar across the globe. A 2017 survey by the travel company *First Choice* found that thirty-four per cent of kids wanted to be YouTubers when they grow up. Is something going wrong, or is this just the way it is? This is an optional section to understand the role and impact of media and technology in the modern world.

Your Personal Slot Machine

Every morning, the first thing most of us do is check our email, WhatsApp, Instagram, or the news. This is probably true for most of us. Eighty per cent of smartphone users check their phones within fifteen minutes of opening their eyes. The majority of us sleep with our phone under the pillow, or within arm's reach, and we instantly begin scrolling come morning. Your phone screams at you, "Here is what you missed whilst you were wasting your time sleeping!" The fear of missing out (FOMO, for short) is prevalent not only in teenagers, but throughout the vast majority of individuals in the modern world. We have allowed ourselves to become a commodity.

The majority of social media applications are injected with psychological techniques to keep you coming back for more. This could be in the form of 'likes', where our dopamine systems are hijacked and preyed upon, on the desire of us to be accepted and validated by others. The three dots that let you know someone is typing also means you're probably going to wait around to find out what they have to say, even if that means you swipe off the chat to avoid the read receipt. Infinite scroll now means that you never have to click 'next' and also that you never have a reason to cease mindlessly absorbing any content. The inventor of inline scroll, Aza Raskin, has since said he feels guilty for this creation, though he explained it away by saying "in order to get the next round of funding, in order to get your stock price up, the amount of time that people spend on your app has to go up." How can we forget push notifications? They call out from our phones at inopportune moments to let us know we've received messages or notifications, without letting us know what those messages and notifications are. This way, we're going to log into the apps in question to find out what is waiting for us. According to a 2019 Common Sense Media poll, the average American teenager spends over seven hours per day staring at a screen. Children of today are the worst victims of this.

During a talk at Stanford University's Graduate School of Business, the former Vice President of user growth for Facebook literally said that his children 'aren't allowed to use that sh*t' and that he feels 'tremendous guilt' for having created something that is 'ripping apart the social fabric of how society works'. When we feel depressed, anxious, lonely, or alienated, we often cease to value our own time and we become more than happy to waste it on things that we know will prove unfulfilling. I am not here to tell you to get off social media, or to stop using technology. Unless you're going int complete solitude (which I doubt you want to), it's near to impossible. I know this because I use it too. Social media and technology is here to stay; it's a part of everyone's daily life. But what is important is how we utilise these tools available to us, so that they don't affect our mental health, and so that we can find inner peace. A 2018 study carried out by Persil, claimed that by the time a British child is seven, they'll have spent double the amount of time looking at a screen (on average, 456 days), than they will have spent playing outside. The key lies in making sure that we control technology, rather than letting it control us. Young people today are predominantly unhappier than ever than ever before, and I don't think it would be a wild speculation to lay some of the blame at the feet of the things designed to hijack our minds.

A 2019 survey of nearly 2,000 US smartphone users found they check their phones an average of 96 times per day, that is around once every 10 minutes. This was a twenty per cent rise from just two years earlier.[1] Another study of 1,200 users revealed that twenty-three per cent check their phones within a minute of waking up, whilst another thirty-four per cent manage to wait between five and ten minutes. Congratulations. Only six per cent of people were able to wait two hours or longer.[2] I know it's hard to get away from our smartphones, even mine has become my constant companion.

I want to introduce you to the Dumbledore of the technology world now. If the magic of technology is Hogwarts, Dr. B. J. Dogg is Dumbledore. He is the creator of the Persuasive Technology Lab at Stanford University, Silicon Valley's favourite educational institution. Fogg's fame rose in 2007 when he began offering classes on how to use his persuasive techniques to build apps for Facebook. His students had amassed 16 million users by the end of the 10-week course, and made $1 million in advertising income in the process.[3]

In 2003, he published *Persuasive Technology: Using Computers to Change What We Think and Do*. He did this before the invention of the smartphone, and in this book he outlined his vision of a connected tomorrow: "Someday in the future, a first year student named Pamela sits in a college library and removes an electronic device from her purse. It's just smaller than a deck of cards, easily carried around, and is used as Pamela's mobile phone, information portal, entertainment platform, and personal organiser. She takes this device almost everywhere and feels lost without it." His ideas were further defined in the 'Fogg Behaviour Model'[4], which he named himself. According to this model, when three factors collide in a moment: motivation (we must want the thing); trigger (something must happen to trigger a desire to get more of it), and ability (it must be easy), then a person is compelled to act. Take, for example, LinkedIn. In it's young years, it had a hub-and-spoke symbol that graphically represented the size of a user's professional network. The bigger the icon, the greater the status. People desire status (there's your motivation), the symbol makes them want more (your trigger), and LinkedIn conveniently offered a simply solution, in the use of the site to generate more connections (that's ability).

If a programmer wants to create a certain action in a user, they should reward them with a sign of reinforcement once they have completed the required 'target behaviour'. The catch, though, is that positive reinforcement is inconsistent. You never know what you'll receive all of the time. Dogg likened it to gambling on slot machines: "Winning a payoff of quarters streaming into the metal tray is a reinforcer, but it is random. This type of unpredictable reward schedule makes the target behaviour – in this case, gambling – very compelling, even addictive."

We are judged every time we upload a photo, video, or comment. We eagerly await replies, likes, or uploads, and just like a gambler never knows how the slot machine will pay out, we're never too sure what we'll get in return for our contribution. Will we go up? Will we go down? The grand reward is different every time. This variation creates compulsion. We just want to keep pulling the lever.

Connecting or Disconnecting?

A 2019 study conducted by John Hopkins Bloomberg School of Public Health tried to make the leap from correlation to cause by taking into account the pre-existing mental health problems of participants in the year before their research. They followed 6,000 kids aged between twelve and fifteen and found that those who used social media for over three hours a day were twice as likely to develop mental health problems compared to those who unplugged. The set-up of the study suggested that it was more than likely that internet usage triggers mental health issues, rather than the correlation being in reverse.[5]

This is not a revelation. We know the internet is damaging. It's easy to come up with a list of potential easy the internet might cause emotional harm: cyberbullying, heightened self-consciousness, exposure to damaging and disturbing content, time-wasting, missing out on real-world experiences, substituting real friends for virtual ones. Nobody seems to be particularly infatuated with the internet, it's just there. But, it doesn't just affect kids. Without meaning to, we all find ourselves drawn into our phones, tablets and computers for hours on end. These internet binges are almost always followed by a kind of hollow, disappointed confusion. Where has the time gone? What have I done?

A 2007 UNICEF study of happiness in twenty-one economically developed countries ranked UK's young people last. But why are the British so unhappy? They have computers and phones. They have access to free healthcare and education. They are probably never going to experience hunger or war. So then, where is this unhappiness coming from? During my research for this book, I came across a number of subjects repeatedly:

- Poverty
- Academic pressure
- Bullying
- Domestic issues
- Body image issues
- Health problems
- Social media

The internet, most notably social media stood out. Why? Because it is a fairly recent phenomenon that is now occupying a central role in the lives of not just young people, but everyone across the world, and it is also changing how we perceive ourselves and the world around us. Should we stop using social media altogether? Well, studies that randomly assign groups to delete social media apps for four weeks find that, after those four weeks are up, these groups feel notably less depressed and lonely. However, similar studies also showed that people who used social media very moderately were slightly happier than those who didn't use it at all. Makes sense I guess, we all need to stay connected, particularly now more than ever. The 'optimal' level seems to be around thirty minutes a day.

So, where does the 'unhappiness' bit come from. In their book *The Teenage Brain*, Amy Ellis Nutt and Frances Jensen highlight the role of the THP hormone. In adults, when they are stressed, THP is the hormone that the brain releases to allow them to become less stressed. In younger people, however, THP does the opposite. Rather than taming the monkey, it is like letting it loose. They get stressed, THP shoots out, and they get more stressed. Social media increases stress (obviously), and stress in young people increase stress further, so it follows that time spent on social media isn't exactly 'unwind time'.

The most famous study on happiness is the Harvard Grant study. I recommend that everyone look into it. In this study, 286 men from the university were tracked from 1938 onwards, as they grew up, grew old, fell in and out of love, had children, work promotions, health scares, and existential panic attacks. After almost eighty years, only nine were still alive. The project continued by following their children, and it is still going on today. The results of the original study came as a surprise. They found that more than genetics, wealth, IQ, or any other variable, it was the quality of relationships that seemed to predict how happy the Harvard alumni reported being. This is a topic we discuss a little later. But this is relevant to the use of social media when we realise that most young people that think of socialising have little face-to-face interaction. Social media will never offer the same feelings of euphoria and joy that the earlier participants experienced. We are built to socialise physically, to read body language, exchange expressions, and exist beside one another through grievances, joys, sorrows, anxieties and all.

This all ties in neatly with conclusions reached by Johann Hari in his influential book *Lost Connections*. He argues that most mental illnesses are not the result of our brains going wrong, but of our lives going wrong in one way or another. He looks at cases of people diagnosed with 'endogenous' depression, which is basically depression that arises without any apparent outside cause, and sees that most suffered some kind of emotional trauma in the year leading up to their diagnosis or were living lives that left them disconnected from the environment, themselves, or other people. Most mental illnesses rise from or are triggered by disconnection in our day-to-day lives. We do not live in close communities, we do not generally work meaningful jobs, most of us are not free to spend long periods of time in nature.

Social media isn't designed to facilitate deep relationships; it is designed to keep you coming back by offering the illusion of popularity and interconnectedness. In 2017, almost fifty per cent of young people in the UK reported feeling lonely some or most of the time, despite the fact that they are permanently wired into systems that are meant to keep us connected. Loneliness is not just a moment of missing out, but it is a persistent sense of disconnection that has been shown to be harmful not only to mental, but also our physical health. A 2015 study equated the death impact of loneliness with smoking fifteen cigarettes a day.[6]

You may have experienced this firsthand. You have ever-increasing circles of friends and an ever-smaller amount of time to spend talking to each of them. Responding becomes a chore, especially when the other party can see that you've read their messages and not replied. The consequences of keeping so many 'friends' so visibly in your life is that you inevitably end up comparing your life to the lives of those around you. Unfortunately, we don't only compare cars, we compare our abs, brunches, yoga poses, and even emotional states. Is the beach they're on whiter than the one we visited? Is she happier than I am? Is he richer than I am? Healthier? Closer to spiritual enlightenment? This kind of race is emotionally destabilising.

It has been said a million times over by every self-help content creator that we are more connected but lonelier than ever. This interconnectedness means, necessarily, more manipulation, more bullying, more arguments, more instability. We are still people. Our faults are only magnified by the distance screens put between us, our ability to treat each other badly is only made worse by the fact that we don't have to sit in front of each other and watch the emotional repercussions of our behaviour. That we are talking to each other more, but through a medium devoid of any of the physical cues that true communication hinges on, is not necessarily going to be a good thing.

Suicide

I didn't really want to talk about suicide in this book because it's huge, complicated, and delicate. I'm not a trained professional either. Nevertheless, data from the Office for National Statistics (UK) shows that suicides amongst British 15 to 17-year-olds hit an all-time high in 2015 and the second highest in 2017. According to a 2007 Houston study of 153 survivors of suicide, around seventy-five per cent of suicide attempts were deliberated over for less than an hour, with twenty-four per cent of those thought about for less than five minutes.

Suicide is mysterious. It seems to go against everything we know about human nature in some subtle way. We're a species of progress. We do, strive, and fight. Whether our aims are good or bad, we push and push, building great cities, forging great empires, destroying climate and habitats and the limits of yesterday's fantasies, bending the forces of nature to turn magic into the everyday. We want things and we seem to get them; we're greedy, ambitious, relentless. Self-destruction seems to have no logical place in the grand scheme. It just doesn't fit. Except it does.

In 2016, a nineteen-year-old French girl called Oceane sat in front of her webcam, streaming a video of herself smoking cigarettes. She was using the live-streaming app called Periscope. As she smoked, comments flashed on her screen. They were mostly light jokes, despite what the girl was saying.[7]

Oceane told her viewers that she was going to kill herself. She explained that she had been raped and went on to give the name of her attacker. She said she wasn't doing it for attention, but to open people's eyes to what this person has done. No one in the comments really thought she would kill herself. The internet is known for its unending repository of empty threats. If someone cries, "I'll kill myself!" The replies come in, "Of course you will."

But as the viewers continued to watch, Oceane continued to stream, carrying her phone to the nearby train station of Égly, south of Paris. Those watching scrambled to alert emergency services. The next thing they saw was a policeman's face as he picked up Oceane's phone. She was dead.

Live-streamed suicides are the logical outcome of lives lived solely online. If you share everything else with the internet, why would you not share this? At the beginning of 2017, Netflix released a show called *Thirteen Reasons Why*, based on the book by Jay Asher. It revolves around the suicide of a girl called Hannah, who leaves behind a box of cassette tapes implicating those she has left behind. Each character listens to the tapes, learns Hannah's story and their role in it, and feels extremely terrible about themselves. How could I have been so thoughtless! They think. How could I have treated her like that!

In the wake of the TV show, online searches for 'how to kill yourself' jumped up, and some sources suggested that suicide rates amongst American males had increased by up to thirty per cent. In Britain, a twelve-year-old girl hanged herself three weeks after it was first shown, leaving behind a list of 'six reasons to kill myself'. We have to give some thanks to the media who have tried to alter its reporting of suicide over the past decade in an effort to deter copycat acts, but the internet has no such conscience. One way of understanding suicide is as a catastrophic breakdown in the human self. It's the most extreme form of self-harm there is. Even if you haven't actively plotted your own death, a lot of you may have surely experienced at least a fleeting thought: *I could end this. I could vanish.*

Sure, we mustn't put off the fact that overall rates of suicide in the UK and US have seen a general decline since the 1980s. But it's also true that the 1980s saw the introduction of new antidepressants that are known to be especially effective for severe depression, the type most likely to lead to suicide. Prescription numbers have continued to rocket since the early 2000s. Today, over a twelve-month period, between eight to ten per cent of the entire adult population of the UK and US use antidepressants. Today more people die by suicide than in all the wars, terrorist attacks, murders and government executions combined. According to the World Health Organisation, in 2012, 11.4 people out of every 100,000 died by self-harm compared to 8.8 people as a result of interpersonal violence, collective violence and legal intervention. It's projections indicate things are going to get worse. By 2030, it's estimated that the difference will have increased to 12 versus 7. In the UK, in 2000, 3.8 per cent of adults reported suicidal thoughts – a figure that had jumped to 5.4 per cent by 2014. In the US, suicide rates recently hit a thirty-year high. Between 2008 and 2015, the number of American adolescents and children receiving hospital after considering suicide or self harm doubled.

Men make up around eighty per cent of all suicides in English-speaking nations. But the really important point is, most people with depression don't kill themselves. Less than five per cent do. We live with our fears and negativity. If you're prone to social perfectionism too, your self-esteem will be dangerously dependent on keeping up roles and responsibilities you believe you have. One of the most critical functions of the human self is to make us feel in control of our lives. We love control. Although the worldwide data is relatively scant, it seems that in many countries women actually attempt suicide in greater numbers.

There is huge pressure in modern society to keep up with ideals of perfection. Spending on gym membership in 2015 alone rose by forty-four per cent. A government enquiry into the problem concluded, 'body image dissatisfaction is high and on the increase'. All males and females are apparently feeling increasing pressures to be perfect. And so the game goes on…

In 2018, psychologists analysed data from over 40,000 university students across the UK, US, and Canada and found levels of perfectionism, between 1989 and 2016, had risen substantially. Today we're living in the age of perfectionism, and this need to be perfect is the idea that kills us. It truly is the ego that kills us from within. It's the ego that wants to become perfect, and it's society and culture that tells the ego what 'perfect' actually is.

Regardless of all these modern battles going on in and around you, it is important to remember that you are the person who is in control of the person you'll become. I am no one to tell you how to use the internet, social media, or technology. This is a choice I leave up to you. But I do believe parents should be more cautious, because who knows what the future holds?

> I knew it was time to get up and leave. With a hectic schedule, my guru took out time for me and for that, I owed him immense gratitude.
> "Vinay," the fellow swami asked as I turned my head towards him. "Is there anything you'd like to say to Swamishri before we leave?"
> I turned my head back and saw my guru glimpsing continuously from me to him, probably waiting for me to say something.
> "Ummm… My mind…" I stuttered.
> "Ah yes! Your mind!" Laughed the swami, "Swamishri, Vinay tells me his mind seems to be all over the place."
> I looked towards my guru, who gave me a childlike smile. He wasn't finished. Humble wisdom was about to unfold.

Training the Monkey Mind

Running around the palace, the commander creates narratives. It goes to the king and fabricates stories of itself. The ministers and subjects also feed off the stories the commander creates. But what is the source of these stories that we tell ourselves? Is it the commander, or is it the monkey?

As an example, we want so desperately to believe that those who have great empires and businesses *set out* to build them. Why? So we can indulge in the pleasurable planning of our own. So that we can take full credit for the good that happens and the riches, respect, and success that come our way. Crafting stories out of past events is a very human impulse. But, writing our own narrative leads to arrogance.

Especially when we are aspiring, we must resist the impulse to reverse-engineer success from other people's stories. When we achieve our own, we must resist the desire to pretend that everything unfolded exactly as we'd planned. That's not how things work. There is no grand narrative (at least from our perspective). True success and peace doesn't come from grand narratives. Just look at how Google started. Larry Page and Sergey Brin weren't some evil genius masterminds, they were just two Stanford PhDs working on their dissertations. The founders of YouTube weren't trying to reinvent the television; they were trying to share funny video clips. Success comes from the cultivation of persistent effort, not from thin air. It's time we stop the commander and monkey from fabricating stories and begin the real training of the mind.

The Human Condition: The Vedic View

To begin with, I want you to recall the two parts of the mind: the Thinker (the commander) and the Feeler (the monkey). The monkey mind is the source of our emotions, and it is what gives suggestions to the commander on how to act. I also want you to recall the three bodies. The reason for this is to understand the root of our emotions from a Vedic perspective. Of course, we could've chose to take a modern approach to emotion and desire, and we've already briefly discussed desire in an earlier section. But, I feel that long before any modern philosophers or thinkers even began developing theories of the mind and emotions, the Vedic scriptures like the Upanishads, Bhāgavata-Purāna, and the Bhagavad-Gita already described satisfying theories. From all of my research, I strongly believe that the theories of desire and emotion, given in Vedic teachings are by far the most fulfilling descriptions. Based on Vedic scripture, Swaminarayan also provides extensive analogies and descriptions of this topic in the Vachanāmrut. In this section, we'll take a glimpse into these theories.

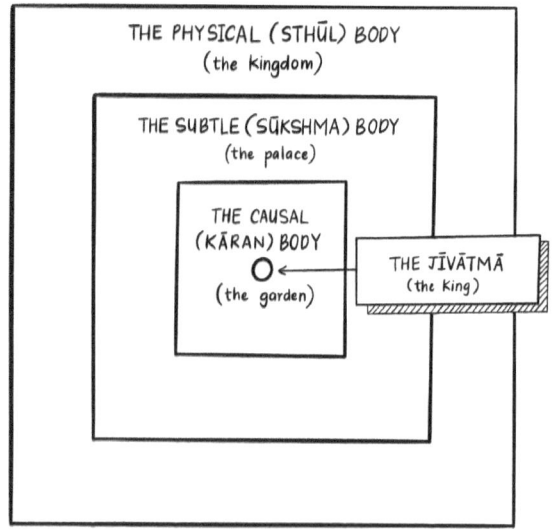

THE THREE BODIES

To recall, we are made up of the gross, subtle, and causal bodies. The gross bodies makes up our physical bodies and our organs. The subtle body is home to our antahkarana (made up of the four inner faculties). Emotions are the function of the manas (mind), and reasoning (cognition) is the function of the buddhi (intellect). The causal body is the seat of our desires (kāma), as well as our karma. It is also described as the root of ignorance, and it is believed to be the cause of rebirth in Hindu theology. The emotions we experience stem from desire (kāma). These emotions are experienced frequently on a daily basis, and they give us a lot of information about ourselves and others. The culmination of our desires from this lifetime, as well as our past lives, is known as vāsanā. For ease of understanding, and to differentiate between kāma and vāsanā, whenever the word 'desire' is used, we are referring to 'kāma', and 'vāsanā' is used for the culmination of desires.

Desires are connected with attachment, clinging, and yearning. They are usually directed towards an object of pleasure that is perceivable and can be remembered. This could be an object that has already been attained, or, something that is anticipated to give one happiness and pleasure. If it is attained and enjoyed, there is a clinging and yearning for more of that object. The ancient Vedic seers emphasised continuously that it is attachment which leads us to cling and yearn for more and more.

When we want to fulfil a desire, it is known as kāma, or, kāmanā. If the desire is expressed or fulfilled, the emotion experienced is known as santosha (satisfaction). If the object is not attained, there is krodha (anger). If it is obtained, there is lobha (greed), mada (pride), and moha (infatuation). If we find that someone else has fulfilled that desire, there is irshā, or, matsar (jealousy). As you might have probably figured out by now, all of these are obstacles in both our spiritual life and our personal life too. They are the inner enemies of the king. Hence, back to the earlier point, desire is the root of our suffering. Or, to be more clear, our inability to understand and work with our emotions is the cause of our mental suffering. According to Vedic thought, it is avidhyā (ignorance) that keeps one bound in this material world, as long as the mind is full of thoughts and feelings.

The Bhagavad-Gitā is the discussion between Krishna and Arjun. They are in the middle of the battlefield and despite of being one of the greatest warriors, Arjun has an emotional crisis, moments before the battle. He begins to question the purpose behind this war between him and his cousins.

> I feel the limbs of my body quivering and my mouth drying up.
> My body is trembling, my hair is standing on end,
> my bow is slipping from my hand, and my skin is burning.
> I am now unable to stand here any longer.
> I am forgetting myself, and my mind is reeling.
> *Bhagavad-Gitā 1.28-1.30*
> *[Paraphrased]*

This entire emotional state, that Arjun describes of himself, resembles that of anxiety and grief; one that we often experience throughout our life too. The Bhagavad-Gitā deals with the human condition. Arjun can be seen as a reflection of who we are – lost and bewildered by our own thoughts and emotions, guided by the divine Krishna. The crisis faced by Arjun is the crisis felt by the jivātmā – you and me. The emotions that Arjun is facing in the battlefield are the very form of human existence and condition, as well as the identity and experience of human suffering.

- *shoka:* grief about things that have come to pass
- *moha:* delusion about the present moment
- *bhaya:* anxiety about the future

How do we overcome this suffering? How do we rule over our emotions? The Vedic scriptures say time and time again that it is because of our mistaken belief (misidentification) and wrongful attachments to the vishays, beings, happenings, as well as our self-centred desires that are the root of our suffering. To simplify, we bring back the ego. Pramukh Swami often used to say that it is the identification with 'I' and 'mine' that is the cause of our suffering.

In the Bhagavad-Gitā, Krishna gives the Vedic view of the world as being a place primarily of suffering, from which one should seek moksha (liberation).[1] He describes the world as being dukhālayam (full of misery and suffering) and ashāshvatam (temporary). The human condition itself, according to the Vedic standpoint, is that every living being must undergo the process of rebirth until they become like Brahman, after which the process of rebirth is stopped.

The Vedic teachings give us methods by which the human condition can be reframed into a vision of meaning, purpose, and values, all of which serve the final part of the book. This is just a brief introduction to the Vedic viewpoint of the human condition.

Working with Emotions

Emotions, emotions, emotions. They define everything that we feel, think, say, and do. Today, most of our obstacles are internal, not external. Instead of opposing armies and enemies, we have internal tension. We have professional frustration. We have unmet expectations. We have learned helplessness. And of course, we still have the same overwhelming emotions humans have always had: grief, pain, loss, anxiety, etc. To prevent ourselves from becoming overwhelmed by the world around us, we must, as the ancients practiced, learn how to limit our passions and the control they hold over our lives. This is the master key to working with our emotions.

We will all face hurdles in life – fair and unfair. And we will discover, time and time again, that what matters most is not what these hurdles are but how we see them, how we react to them, and whether we maintain our composure. Where one person loses hope, another sees hope. Where one loses control of emotions, another remains still. From now, I want you to remember, no one or nothing *makes* you feel a certain way, you alone are the *chooser* or your feelings. Too often we react emotionally and lose our perspective. We ourselves can learn to perceive things differently, to rise above the illusions that others believe or fear.

> Would you have a great empire?
> **Rule over yourself.**
> *Publius Syrus*

America, in its race against the Soviet Union to send the first men into space, trained the astronauts in one skill more than any other: the art of *not* panicking. When we panic, we make mistakes. Our systems go into override. The monkey takes control. We become unresponsive and stop thinking clearly. We just react – not to what we need to react to, but to the survival hormones that course through our veins. It's obvious, 150 miles above Earth in a spacecraft smaller than a Renault Clio, this is death. Panic becomes suicide. So it needs to be trained out. But, that isn't easy. The challenges we face make us emotional, but the only way we can truly be at peace and lived a focused life is by keeping those emotions in check – if we can keep still no matter what happens, no matter how much external events may fluctuate – that is true peace. I saw this in the life of Pramukh Swami, and today, I see it in the life of

Mahant Swami. The skill of working with our emotions is one that needs to be cultivated so that we can focus our energy on trying to solve the problems in life, rather than reacting to them.

I just want to be clear that it isn't about not feeling anything. No one said you can't feel. If you need to take a moment, by all means, do it. Real strength lies in the *control* or, as Nassim Taleb put it, the 'domestication' of one's emotions, not in pretending they don't exist. So, feel, for sure, just don't fabricate stories for yourself. The key is to have conversations with yourself. It's about having conversations with Keshav. Then see how long the extreme emotions hold up. They won't last long. After all, our emotions and feelings are fleeting.

Man does not simply exist but always decides what his existence will be, what he will become the next moment. By the same token, every human being has the freedom to change at any instant.
Viktor Frankl

Perspective truly is everything. When we can dismantle something, or look at it from a new angle, it loses its power over us. In essence, how we approach, view, and contextualise a situation or challenge, and what we tell ourselves it means, determines how intimidating and trying it will be to overcome. Remember that wherever the head goes, the body follows. Positive action follows positive perspective.

Epictetus said, "In life our first job is this, to divide and distinguish things into two categories: externals I cannot control, but the choices I make with regard to them I do control. Where will I find good and bad? In me, in my choices." How powerful is this? Where will you find good and bad? In yourself. In your choices.

When we live in a society which so quickly takes the blame off us, and puts it on others, it's more important now than ever to understand and reaffirm what is truly up to us. Our emotions. Our judgements. Our creativity. Our attitude. Our desires. Our decisions. Our determination. And of course, our perspective. This is all up to us. Focusing exclusively on what is within our power only magnifies and enhances that power.

You must have conversations with yourself. Observe your thoughts, emotions, and reactions regularly. Until you don't understand what's going on in your head, you won't be able to work with it. Don't react. Just observe. Keep a journal if you must. This is the first step to working with your emotions.

Living In the Moment

Go down this list of some of the companies and businesses that were started during some form of depression, economic crises, or global challenge.

- *Fortune* magazine (90 days after the 1929 market crash)
- FedEx (oil crisis of 1973)
- UPS (Panic of 1907)
- Walt Disney Company (In the twelfth month after smooth operation, the market crash of 1929 happened)
- Hewlett-Packard (Great Depression, 1935)
- Standard Oil (Rockfeller bought out his partners and took over in February 1985, the final year of the Civil War)
- Costco (recession in the late 1970s)
- Revlon (Great Depression, 1932)
- General Motors (Panic of 1907)
- Proctor & Gamble (Panic of 1837)
- United Airlines (1929)
- Microsoft (recession in 1973-1975)
- LinkedIn (2002, post-dot-com bubble)

For the most part, these businesses will have had little awareness that they were in some historically challenging event. Why? Because the founders were too engrossed existing in the present moment – they dealt with the situation at hand. But what do we do? We live our own lives in discontent with the way things are.

Half of the companies in the Fortune 500 were started during a bear market or recession. Fifty percent. The point I am trying to make is that *most people* start from disadvantage. We grow through struggle. And guess what? We do just fine. This is universal. Those who survive and succeed do so because they take things day by day. They didn't look to yesterday or tomorrow. They lived in the moment.

Fortunately or unfortunately, this is something exclusive to humans. For all other species other than us, things are just the way are. Our problem is that we're always trying to figure out the *meaning* behind things – *why* things are the way they are. Ralph Waldo Emerson says, "We cannot spend the day in explanation."

Being present in the moment demands all of you. It *is* probably the hardest thing to do in the world. Most of us do not live in *this* moment.

In fact, we try, so desperately, to get out of it. How? By thinking, doing, talking, worrying, remembering, hoping, and even scrolling these days. We pay thousands of pounds to have a device in our pockets to guarantee we will never get bored. We sign up for endless activities and obligations, we chase money in accomplishments, always naïvely believing that at the end of it, we will get happiness.

Let me tell you the truth. There is no greatness in the future. Nor is there clarity, insight, happiness, or peace. There is only now. Greatness is now. Clarity is now. Insight is now. Happiness is now. Peace is now. Do the very best you can right now, in whatever you're doing. Don't think about what others might say. Don't dwell on the endless negativity and don't needlessly complain.

I've heard many people question whether today is the best time or the worst time to be alive, whether they are on a good career path or a bad one, or whether the challenge in front of them is intimidating or a smooth-sail. But what matters most is that right now is right now. In fact, now is the only time we have. It's not as easy as saying: *I will live in the present moment.* You have to embody it. Watch out for when the monkey mind wanders, and don't let it get away. Get rid of all distracting thoughts and ideas. And also remember, this moment doesn't *define* your life, it's just a moment *in* you life. Focus on the task in front of you. Focus on the now. Be here. Be *all* of you. Be present in the moment.

Think Like Steve Jobs

Steve Jobs was known to think differently. He was famous for what is called his 'reality distortion field'. Steve's early life had moulded him to think this way. He believed change was always possible. Let's take the design stages of a new mouse for an early Apple product as an example. Jobs had high expectations (obviously). He wanted the mouse to move fluidly in any direction – a new development for any mouse at that time – but a lead engineer was told by one of his designers that this would be commercially inviable. He said that Jobs wasn't being realistic, and that this wouldn't work. The next day, the lead engineer arrived at work to find that Jobs had fired the employee who'd said that. When the replacement came in, his first words were: "I can build the mouse."[2]

This was Job's view of reality at work. He thought different. He knew that to aim low meant to accept average accomplishment. He didn't want that. Accepted, for most of us, such confidence does not come as easy. So many people in our lives have fed us with stories that we need to be realistic or conservative. This is why you shouldn't listen too closely to what other people say (or to what the voice in our head says, either). That is, unless you are given critical feedback to improve yourself. Nevertheless, we should be cautious. Be open. Question. Think. Take feedback selectively.

Control Your Inputs

Napoleon made it a habit to delay responding to his mail till later in the day. He even told his secretary to wait three weeks before opening any correspondence. When he finally did open the letters and read what was in them, Napoleon loved to note how many supposedly 'important' issued had simply resolved themselves and he didn't even have to reply. He wasn't being lazy or negligent in his duties, but in order to be active and aware of what actually mattered, he was selective about who and what kind of information got access to his mind.

In a similar manner, he told his messengers to wake him up with *good news*. He used to say, "But when you bring bad news, rouse me instantly, for then there is not a moment to be lost."

We've already touched upon the fact that there is way too much coming at us. In order for us to think clearly, it is necessary that each of us figures out how to filter out the unessential from the essential. In the 1990s, political scientists began to study what they called the 'CNN Effect'.[3] Non-stop, 24-hour media coverage makes it considerably harder for politicians and CEOs to be anything but reactive. There's just too much information, every trivial detail is magnified under a microscope, speculation is rampant, and the human mind is overwhelmed. Today, the CNN Effect is a problem for everyone, not just for presidents and professionals. Each of us has access to more information than we would have done in a lifetime two generations ago. We like to tell ourselves that it's part of our job, that we have to 'stay informed', and so we freely give up our precious time to news, reports, meetings, and other forms of feedback. We must stop this. The monkey loves this. Epictetus once said, "If you wish to improve, be content to appear clueless or stupid in extraneous matters."

Learn to give things a little space. Don't consume news in real time. Be a season or two behind on the latest trends and cultural phenomenons. Don't let your inbox control your life. Here's another fact: If it is truly important, it will still be important by the time you get to it. Regardless of what you may think, there is a subtle play of ego in trying to stay up with everything. Likewise, there is ego in trying to appear like the most informed person in the room, the one will all the gossip, who knows every single detail about every single person's life. It's extremely difficult to train the monkey mind when you are drowning in information. It's the very mechanism lawyers use in attempt to bury the opposing side in paper. It's what intelligent operatives use to flood the enemy with propaganda. Is it any coincidence that the goal of these tactics is to create a *paralysis of analysis*? We do this to ourselves.

Roman emperor, Marcus Aurelius wrote, "Ask yourself at every moment, 'Is this necessary?'"[4] Thich Nhat Hanh says, "Before we can make deep changes in our lives, we have to look into our diet, our way of consuming. We have to live in such a way that we stop consuming the things that poison us and intoxicate us. Then we will have the strength to allow the best in us to arise, and we will no longer be victims of anger, of frustration."[5]

You must have heard of the saying: *Garbage in, garbage out*. Although this is usually applied to food, this is true for information too. It's a work of discipline. It means fewer alerts and notifications. It means using the 'Do Not Disturb' function to block incoming texts, calls, and emails. It means pushing away selfish people who bring needless drama in our lives.

The truth is that we are often afraid of silence. We are afraid of 'missing out'. We are afraid of being the bad person that says, "Sorry, I'm not interested." We'd rather make our lives miserable and hectic than make ourselves a priority. That is unless, of course, you want to change. Your mind is meant to be an important and sacred place. Keep it clean. Keep it clear.

The Paradox of Philosophies

Slow down and think deeply. No, don't think at all, just empty your mind. Do you notice the contradiction here? An eastern analogy says that the world is like muddy water. To see through it, we have to let things settle. We can't be disturbed by initial appearances, and if we're patient and still, the truth will be revealed to us. Appearances are misleading. We humans are quick to jump to conclusions. First impressions are misleading too. We are both disturbed and deceived by what's on the surface, by what others see. We make bad decisions, miss opportunities, or feel scared or upset. On the surface, there seems to be a clear contradiction, right? On one hand, we are told we must empty our minds to be fully present. We are told that we'll never get anything done if we are paralysed by overthinking. On the other hand, we are told to look within and think deeply if we are ever to truly *know* ourselves. So what is going on? The truth is, this is not a contradiction at all. It is life. We *must* get better at thinking, deliberately and intentionally, but only about that which matters. On the big questions. On the complicated things. On understanding what's really going on within our head, out there in the situation, and of life itself. Much of our distress comes from reacting instinctually instead of acting wit deliberation. We react too quickly. We make snap judgements. We're not stopping to take a step back and really *look*.

Just try this: Sit alone in a room and let your thoughts wander wherever they do. Do this for a minute. Work up to ten minutes a day of this mindless form of mental wandering. Then start paying attention to your thoughts to see if a word or goal materialises. If it doesn't extend the exercise to eleven minutes, then twelve, then thirteen… until you find the length of time you need to ensure that something interesting comes to mind. This state of mind is known as 'quietness without loneliness'. Some answers can only be found in the depth of solitude.

Why You Should Cultivate Silence

"We were all given two ears and only one mouth for a reason," said the Greek philosopher Zeno. What you notice when you stop to listen can make all the difference in the world. Too much of our lives today is defined by noise. Headphones go in. Screens on. Phones ringing. The quiet metal womb of the Boeing 737 I'm currently on, travelling at 600 miles per hour, is filled with nothing but noise. Everyone is trying to avoid silence. We'd rather watch the same bad series again and again, or listen to a tedious interview with an annoying celebrant, than to stop and absorb what is happening around us. We'd rather close our mind than sit there and have to use it.

If we want to think better and do better, we need to seize moments of silence. We have to learn to step away from the comfort of noisy distractions and stimulations. We have to listen more. Randall Stutman, who for decades has been the behind-the-scenes advisor for a number of the biggest leaders on Wall Street, once studied how several hundred senior executives at major corporations made use of their free time. The answers were things like sailing, long-distance cycling, listening quietly to classical music, scuba diving, riding motorcycles, and fly-fishing. All of these, he noticed, had one thing in common: *there was hardly any noise.*[6]

We limit our inputs and turn down the volume so that we can access a deeper awareness of what's going on around us. Mahant Swami often spends most of his day in silence. He speaks only when he needs to speak. In his silence, his actions speak for themselves. That is what we want to do. We want to cultivate silence. We can't be afraid of silence, as it has much to teach us. We must actively seek it.

Why You Should Write

On her thirteenth birthday, the German refugee Anne Frank, was gifted a small red-and-white 'autograph book' by her parents. It was designed to collect signatures and memories, but she chose to use it as a journal instead. In her very first entry on 12 June, 1942, she wrote, "I hope I will be able to confide everything to you, as I have never been able to confide in anyone, and I hope you'll be a great source of comfort and support."[7]

Twenty-four days later, Anne and her Jewish family were forced into hiding, in a cramped attic at her father's warehouse in Amsterdam. It's where they spent the next two years, hoping that the Nazis wouldn't find them. You might think Anne was a scared, frightened, lonely, and bored teenager, but her life was overwhelming. To her it was all unfair and unfamiliar. She needed somewhere to let out her feelings. Although Anne didn't write every day, she did write when she was upset or dealing with a problem. She also wrote when she felt confused or curious. She wrote in her journal as a form of therapy. She didn't want to unload her troubling thoughts on her family who also shared her conditions. She said, "Paper has more patience than people."[8] It's true, isn't it?

Anne used her journal to reflect. "How noble and good everyone could be," she wrote, "if at the end of the day they were to review their own behaviour and weigh up the rights and wrongs. They would automatically try to do better at the start of each new day, and after a while, would certainly accomplish a great deal." When I read this in her book, it made me think back to a similar exercise of reflection, spoken about by Swaminarayan in Vachanāmrut Gadhadā I-38.[9]

Anne Frank wasn't the only one to keep a journal. The list is endless, from the ancient to the modern.[10] Oscar Wilde. Marcus Aurelius. Queen Victoria. Ralph Waldo Emerson. Mary Chesnut. Brian Koppelman. Martina Navratilova. Benjamin Frankin. Pramukh Swami (in his earlier years). All journalers.

People like Leonardo da Vinci, kept their notebooks on them at all times. John F. Kennedy kept diary during his travels before World War II, and then as president he was more of a notetaker and a doodler (which has been shown in studies to improve memory).

Journal to silence the monkey in your head. Journal to teach the commander in your head. Journal to prepare for the day ahead. Journal to reflect on the day that has passed. Journals aren't for the reader, they are for the writer. They are to slow your mind down. They are to find peace with yourself. It is a way for you to ask tough questions to yourself. It's not just history, there's science to it as well.[11] According to one study, journaling helps improve well-being after traumatic and stressful events. Similarly, a University of Arizona study showed that people were better able to recover from divorce and move forward if they journaled on the experience. Keeping a journal is also a common recommendation from psychologists too, because it helps patients to stop obsessing and allows them to make sense of the many inputs – emotional, external, psychological – that would otherwise overwhelm them. In essence, this is the idea. We don't want to carry around baggage in our heads and hearts, so we pour it out onto paper. Instead of letting thoughts race around unchecked in your head, you force yourself to write then down and examine them. Putting your own thoughts down onto paper lets you see them from a distance. It gives you objectivity that is so often missed when anxiety, fear, and frustration fill our mind. There is no right or wrong way to journal either. It's all up to you. Once, twice, three times a day. Whatever. Find what works for you. The goal is to eventually shift from journaling to direct introspection. But that will take commitment, practice, and dedication. Work towards it.

Why You Should Learn to Let Go

Krishna says to Arjun, "You have the right to work, but never to the fruit of work. You should never engage in action for the sake of reward, nor should you long for inaction. Perform work in this world, as a man established within himself – without selfish attachments, and alike in success and defeat. For yoga is perfect evenness of mind." [12]But we love to be in control, don't we? The desire to be in control and to dictate the schedule and the process of everything we're a part of is a very human instinct.

Have you ever noticed that the more you want something, the more insistent you are on a certain outcome, the more difficult it becomes to achieve it? What we need in life is to loosen up, to become flexible, to get to a place where there is nothing in our way – that includes our own obsession with certain outcomes. In the religions born in India, the lotus flower is a powerful symbol. Although it rises out of the mud of a pond or river, it doesn't reach up towering into the sky – it simply floats, serenely on top of the water. The lotus also embodies the principle of letting go. It is beautiful and pure, but also attainable and low. It is simultaneously attached and detached. Only through reducing our aims are the most difficult targets within our reach.

Brain Work

Apparently, the ancient Greeks considered the brain a 'secondary' organ, whose only function was to cool the heart. Around first century AD, the Europeans believed that the brain was nothing but a cold, moist organ made up of sperms. No seriously, they actually thought that. By the time of the Renaissance, the brain was elevated to being the 'seat of the soul'. Leonardo da Vinci dissected many brains in attempt to find the elusive seat. Of course, he never found it, although he made a number of detailed diagrams of the brain from different angles.[13]

The ancient Vedic people were well aware of the supreme importance of the brain and thanks to the likes of Sushruta, they were performing complicated brain surgeries thousands of years ago. Contrast this with the Egyptians and the Greeks, who were pouring milk in both ears if the head (brain) was bleeding. Believe me, history is amazing if you look into it and then compare different civilisations.

How We Learn

Our brain is home to a hundred billion neurons. Each can grow 2,000 to 10,000 fibrous structures called dendrites. The neurons and dendrites interact with each another and pass information through chemical and electrical signals called synapses. The volume of these interactions surpass the number of elementary particles in the universe. The Vedic sages probably referred to this millennia ago, when they said, 'yatha pinde tatha brahmande'[14] (whatever is in the microcosm, i.e. the body, is also in the macrocosm, i.e. the universe).

In your lifetime, your brain will process around one quadrillion bytes of information. That's one, followed by fifteen zeros. We have an almost infinite capacity to learn. The brain is malleable throughout your lifetime.

A groundbreaking study on the brain sometime in the 1990s established that the human brain has the ability to regenerate itself. Many interesting studies that followed showed that the brain can not only regenerate itself, but it can make parts of itself bigger or smaller depending on what activities one is engaged in. London's Black Cab drivers are supposed to pass an incredibly hard exam about the city's roads, so that they can take their passengers along the fastest route possible. Scans of the brains of London cab drivers revealed that they have a larger hippocampus, an area of the brain associated with learning routes and spatial representations. The size correlated with the time that they had been driving cabs. This meant that being a cab driver in London changed the size of the hippocampus. Your brain is plastic.[15]

Newly formed synapses are fragile and can dissolve quickly. This is the process of forgetting. The stuff you do repeatedly is what makes the neurons that are wired together fire together, fortifying their connections – hence the importance of habits. If I asked you what five times five is, you'll be able to answer it quickly without having to think. The moment you read that line, twenty-five popped into your head. Your brain has already made and registered a strong neural connection for it. If I asked you what did you eat for dinner thirty days ago, chances are you will have completely forgotten. You may not even have had dinner that day. This is a case of dissolved connections. It's unnecessary information that you brain has decided to delete.

The brain is truly a marvellous gift we've been given by the divine.

Be careful though. Neural connections form for exactly what you do. Watching a series for the whole day will make you really good at binge watching series'. That is why the right habits are so important in our life. Practice may make one perfect, but wrong practice will make you perfectly wrong.

How To Be Productive

According to Dr. Barbara Oakley, professor at Oakland University, the brain uses two modes of learning – focused and diffused. The former is when you actively learn things from the external stimuli around you, which results in the creation of neural circuits in the brain. Typically, the brain cannot sustain this mode for more than thirty minutes. Focused activity for longer than this is physically tiring for the brain.[16]

The diffused mode is when you are more or less on autopilot – showering, driving, walking, and so on. You don't need to actively think about these activities as you do them, and thoughts in the brain are drifting from one to the next. This is the time when the brain processes the information it has acquired during the focused mode and gets those coveted flashes of insight.

Simply staring out of your window is diffused mode. Looking for somethings you stare out of the window is focused mode. Meditation is a brilliant way to encourage diffused brain activity. Try to never study or work on something for more than forty-five minutes in one go. Decide how long you want to engage your focused mode. To enter the diffused mode, get up from your desk, stretch and relax for about ten to fifteen minutes. This will give you brain some time to relax. Then return to your work and try tackling something else.

Another thing, don't multitask. The bottom line is that there is a very real chemical, electrical, and physical change that occurs in the brain when we do a particular task. If we hop to another task, it triggers a full-moon change. The brain cannot and does not know how to jump between changes effectively. Studies upon studies have shown that people who *think* they can multitask actually *can't* and *don't*. They have poor recall memory, hazy understanding, slumped productivity, and so on. Their cognitive abilities are also compromised. Do one thing. Focus and work on that.

While in focused mode, ensure you are also shielded from all distractions. One of the best things you can do is to switch of all notifications on your gadgets. You can always check your messages, emails, whatever after you're done with what is at hand. Those little pop-up notifications are the bane of creativity and productivity. I recommend everyone to read *Deep Work* by Cal Newport, *The 7 Habits of Highly Effective People* by Stephen Covey, and *Eat That Frog* by Brian Tracy. These are some of the best books I've read on productivity.

How to Develop Willpower

The truth remains constant: everybody who has accomplished anything worthwhile in their lives could not have done so without a strong sense of self-discipline. It is the dedication to practice that is important. The rest will fall into place. When you commit to a habit of practice that is beneficial to you in the long run, the effects begin to spread throughout your life. Aside from boosting our longevity, health, and energy levels, engaging in healthy practices for our bodies results in a number of other benefits. Being rigorous with ourselves is, in some ways, a terrific way to feel better about ourselves. Many self-disciplines are acts of self-care and beneficial behaviours that move us toward our goals.

Oscar Wilde was really onto something when he said, "I can resist everything except temptation." According to Roy Baumeister of Florida State University (an expert on mental strength), exercising self-control takes a lot of effort. He compares willpower to a battery in a metaphorical way. The purpose of a battery is to give electrical currents or energy to an object. But the disadvantage of batteries is that they have a limited lifespan and will ultimately run out. Baumeister illustrates that self-control is similar to a battery through a series of experiments. And if we over-exert our self-control battery, it eventually leads to 'ego depletion' (not to be confused with the normal ego).[17]

Self-control is strongest in the morning but gradually wears down over the day. Anything that saps our mental energy, such as a stressful day at work, the pressure to avoid carbohydrates for breakfast and lunch, or even regulating our emotions with a challenging boss, might actually work against us by the end of the night. As a result, how we structure our days has a huge impact on our self-control muscle, especially if you want to stick to discipline or form new habits.

As Jim Rohr, a well-known American motivation expert put it, "When the why is clear, the how is easy." We naturally and inevitably lose momentum if we are not constantly reminded of a long-term reward, gain, or clear purpose (the 'why'). Our minds require frequent reminders of why we do what we do. That is why visualising and believing official outcomes can help us re-calibrate our 'why.' More than a thousand years ago, Aristotle correctly stated that we are a product of what we repeatedly do. There is a psychological phenomenon known as synaptic pruning that demonstrates that as adults, we build our strengths through the things we do frequently – basically our habits.

One of the major sources of stress in our lives comes from the overwhelm of having a incredibly long list of things to complete. In my perspective, the key to success is to have the idea of 'progress, not perfection' at the forefront of our minds. In fact, in his book *Deep Work*, Cal Newport outlines a concept known as the chain approach. He says that the easiest way to consistently start deep work sessions is to transform them into a simple regular habit. The goal is to generate a rhythm for this work that removes the need for you to invest energy in deciding if and when you are going to go deep.[18]

According to new research, as discussed, the brain can only maintain intense focus for about forty-five minutes before losing momentum. The goal is to take as many brief breaks as possible during the day, interspersed with revitalising intervals that help enhance your brainpower and concentration levels.

Meditate Daily

Meditation not only has positive impacts on the body, but also on your mind. Meditation is not simply about postures, as it is often understood in the Western world. It is also about the way you control your breath, relax your body, and focus your mind. We've already touched upon how prāṇāyama is a form of meditation in itself. I wanted to take this section in the first part of the book, but I felt that it goes a layer deeper, and has benefits on both the mind and body, hence, I have included it here. Meditation enhances every aspect of life:

- You feel good about yourself and don't need a reason to be happy.
- Fewer things bother you.
- You experience less stress.

- You get the ability to effectively deal with pressure.
- You greatly improve your immune system functionality. You feel sick less often. And, even if you do, you recover much more quickly.
- You focus better and get things done to a better standard.
- Your memory improves.
- Your relationships improve. You feel more empathy.
- Meditation is known to reduce both physical and emotional pain. A study concluded that meditation is considerably better than morphine in decreasing the feeling of pain.

A series of studies have been carried out by Sara Lazar of the Neuroimaging Research Program at Massachusetts General Hospital. She is also an Assistant Professor of Psychology at Harvard Medical School. In a set of studies, the brains of long-term meditators were compared with those who didn't meditate. It was found that there was increased grey matter in the insula (which controls the autonomic functions like the sympathetic and parasympathetic we talked about earlier) and the sensory and auditory cortices. This implies that meditation can enhance our senses. Meditation helps us get so much more from the present moment too. Things look more beautiful. Nature looks prettier. People are nicer. Our experiences are enriched. [19]

The frontal cortex is the area of the brain associated with working memory and executive decision-making. It is well documented that it shrinks as we age, making it increasingly harder for us to remember things and solve problems. But, studies have shown that the brains of 50-year-old meditators have the same amount of grey matter in their pre-frontal cortex as normal 20-year-olds do.

There is also a considerable amount of scientific evidence to support the fact that having a long-term meditation practice helps decrease our cravings. Meditation aids self-control. Scientists at Duke University and Caltech studied the brains of 37 dieters while they looked at images of 50 different food items in a 2009 study. The findings revealed that the 'dorsolateral prefrontal cortex' (the part of the brain activated by those with strong willpower) is also the section of the brain that is highly active during meditation. As a result, the more you engage in meditative techniques, the stronger this part of your pre-frontal cortex, which is mostly responsible for willpower, becomes. This naturally occurs and results in a good feeling of self-discipline. By connecting your practice to an internal mood rather than an external reward, you can develop true self-control. Another study took a group of people who had never meditated in their lives and put them through an eight-week program where they learned and practiced meditation. It was remarkable what their 'before' and 'after' brain scans revealed. I know this next part may seem like jargon to you, but I'm going to try my best to keep it simple. Their brains showed significant 'thickening' in four regions:

- The posterior cingulate gyrus, which is associated with mind wandering and self-relevance. Basically, meditation can make you more attentive and also make you feel a greater level of confidence and self-esteem.
- The left hippocampus, which assists in learning, cognition, memory, and emotional regulation.
- The temporal-parietal junction, which is associated with empathy, compassion, and perspective. Meditation can make you more compassionate and you can see life from a broader perspective. Small things stop bothering you as much too.
- The pons (no, seriously that's what it's called), an area of the brain stem which is involved in the production of regulatory neurotransmitters.

The amygdala, which is associated with the fight-or-flight response of the brain – and the relevant behaviours we manifest for the likes of anxiety, fear, and stress – in general, actually got smaller. This change in the amygdala was correlated to experiencing a reduction in stress levels.

One of the tendencies of the mind is to vacillate between the past and the future. Have you noticed that whenever you feel angry, regretful, or guilty, it's always about something from the past? You never feel anger, regret or guilt about the future. It's impossible. Similarly, all the fear and anxiety we feel is only about the future. There is not fear about the past. You cannot be afraid of something that's already happened. The monkey mind loves this pendulum act, whirling us into the past and flinging us into the future, generating a scope of unhealthy emotions within.

The past is gone. You cannot do much about it. The future is yet to come, so why worry? All you really have is the present moment. Happiness is in the present. Peace is in the present. Life is in the present. Right here. Right now.

To end this part of the book, I want to bring in Patanjali, the father of Yoga and author of the Yogasutra. Patanjali says that for your meditation to really work, and for you to be established in a wonderful space, you need to do these things once you have learnt to meditate.

- Practice it daily, without breaks.
- Practice it for an appreciably long time (at least a few thousand hours). Though the benefits of meditation may become apparent in just a few days, for this to become our nature and form into a habit or lifestyle, takes a long time. Be patient and drop expectations. Trust the technique and yourself, then keep going.
- Honour, respect, and revere the practice. This last step is as important as the first two. Meditation isn't simply something we do. Feel it to be sacred and special – it is. Know that you are lucky to have the ability to meditate. Feel immense gratitude. This brings about an undeniable transformation.

"You know Vinay," he spoke. "You are not your mind. Nor are you your body."

"I guess. But I see my body in the mirror. I feel my thoughts and feelings. I feel all that. What else is there if not that?" I replied.

"You forgot already?" He laughed. "You are the ātmā!"

"But I don't feel the ātmā. I don't see it. I don't sense it."

He shook his head, "You say, 'This is *my* body,' right?"

I nodded in agreement. It is my body.

"You only say 'my' for that which you possess. You are the possessor of the body. You are not the body. Likewise, some people say, 'Please, *my* mind is disturbed!' So then if you possess the body and mind, how can you be them?"

This instant logic had be dumbstruck.

"You are the observer within," he continued. "You are the eternal ātmā. Whether you recognise that now, or years down the line, it doesn't cease to be the truth. Only when you realise this will you be able to truly diminish your ego. Only then will you realise that desires will never satisfy the quenching of the ātmā. Only then when you realise than anger and all these negative emotions serve no purpose. Only, and only then, will you be able to begin controlling your mind."

I was lost for words. I folded my hands in front of him. He folded his back. I smiled. He smiled back. That was my cue to leave.

SOUL

Hail The King

> The soul is neither born nor does it die.
> It is not slain when the body is slain.
> It is unborn, eternal, ever-existing and primeval.
> *Bhagavad-Gitā 2.20*

It's time to meet the true ruler of the kingdom – the king – our jivātmā. For time unknown, this king has ruled from kingdom to kingdom, with the supposed aide of various commanders and ministers. In reality, the king is strong and mighty, but due to the influential power of the commander and the ministers, it often seems as though they control the kingdom.

The ātmā is the same as the jivātmā, except for the fact that when the ātmā identifies with the body, mind, or senses, it is known as the jivātmā. We need to reignite that spark within our hearts. We want the king to successfully rule once again. But, there is an art in doing so. We need to understand the nature of the king. We need to understand what the ātmā is at its true essence.

How many of us feel that our values differ from our actions? How many of us feel that our purpose is misaligned? How many of us feel to maintain compassionate and close relationships with those close to us? How many of us feel that we lack real meaning in our lives? How many of us feel that we want a spiritual foundation in our life, but we do not know where to start? The final part of this book is my humble attempt at introducing and addressing the majority of these topics.

The Art of Dharma

Dharma gneyaha sadāchāraha
Know dharma to be righteous conduct.
Bhagwan Shri Swaminarayan

To properly understand the word 'dharma', we must begin with the Rig Veda, the oldest text of India, where we are told that the word 'dharman', the precursor to dharma, occurs sixty times and refers mostly to religious rites. By performing these rituals and traditional duties, Vedic people achieved a sense of order in their world. Dharma comes from the Sanskrit root 'dhri', meaning 'to hold, maintain, or keep', and by extension, in its noun form, 'that which cannot be taken away [because it is firmly part of something]'. Think of dharma as an inherent quality of something – that part of something that cannot be separated from it. Nevertheless, for thousands of years, the great have battled with the meaning of this elusive word and its true meaning. Scholars link dharma to 'dhārana', which means 'supporting', or, 'maintaining', and in this sense refers to 'the eternal laws maintaining all of creation'.

Later, in the Atharva Veda, 'dharman' becomes the more abstract noun 'dharma'. Here it does not simply refer to 'upholding' as an action or event, but to its result – a norm, a law or an established order. Scriptures like the Mahābhārat follow this idea, reminding us that 'the creatures are kept apart or upheld in their respective identities by dharma'. By the time we get to Manu, dharma's 'upholding' is incumbent on all qualified men; it is also the condition which preserves, is preserved, and destroys when it is violated. It protects it protectors. What I am trying to get at is that the notion of dharma is eternal, yet ever-changing, hence it is often difficult to limit it to one definition.[1]

Dharma is not about any one religion, denomination or belief system. Although it is often understood as religion, it is much more than that. Dharma is universal. Swaminarayan defines dharma as being righteous conduct as prescribed by the smrutis and shrutis.[2] Dharma is about living ones life with ethical principles and righteous conduct. Dharma is one's righteous duty in this world that upholds, sustains, and supports universal principles. Dharma is that which holds a person or object and maintains it in existence; it is the eternal law that governs its being. To live life according to dharma is to be in consonance with the true nature of things. Although dharma is universal, it'll differ slightly for every person. In the Bhagavad-Gitā, Krishna makes it clear that one should live their according to their own dharma, and not to that of others.[3] For the time being, you can understand dharma to be your purpose, calling, or duty in this life, and towards this world.

I'm not here to preach to you what your purpose or calling should be (I've already given you an introduction above). But I believe that dharma is essential to the focused life, primarily because it keeps us rooted and true to our values. Although we will talk about this shortly, at the end of the day, it is for you to contemplate on and work out. What I am definitely going to tell you though, is that most of the things modern society tells us about purpose, values, and meaning, are probably wrong.

The Search for Purpose

In order for us to stand any chance of finding meaning and purpose in our life, we need to first understand what's important to us. We need to start with our values. We all have values and we each have different values. Maybe you've not given too much thought to what your values are, but that doesn't mean you don't have any. Quite simply, your values are the things that are important to you and give weight to the way that you live, work, serve, and relate to other people.

Bronnie Ware spent several years working in palliative care in Australia, caring for patients in the last days and weeks of their lives.

She talked with her patients and listened to them as they looked back on their past. As a result of these conversations, Bronnie published a book called *The Top Five Regrets of the Dying*, in 2012.[4] In this book, she mentions the top regret that people expressed: I wish I'd had the courage to live a life true to myself, and not the life others expected of me. Doesn't this fit so perfectly with what Krishna said?

The first thing that stops most people from living a life that's true to them is the fact that they haven't actually identified what is true to them; they haven't clarified what their values are; what's meaningful and important to them. And so, identifying your own values is the first step towards living your own life – to living a life that's true to you.

We've been taught that if we work hard, we will be successful, and then if we are successful, we'll be happy. If we can just find that great job, get a promotion, lose 10kg, then happiness will follow. But recent discoveries, particularly in the field of positive psychology, have shown that this formula is actually backwards: happiness fuels success, not the other way around. When we are positive, our brains become more engaged, creative, motivated, energetic, resilient, and productive. This discovery has been repeatedly supported by research in psychology and neuroscience, management studies, and the bottom lines of organisations around the world. Having a set of values, and a sense of purpose is what gives real meaning in life.

Here's the hard truth. Many people hate their job, career, or what they do, but they don't hate it enough to change their path. Instead, they'd rather look for purpose and meaning outside of the nine-to-five grind. Ask yourself a series of important questions like: What difference can I make to give others a better life? Finding yourself is good, but losing yourself to something larger and more encompassing is great. What am I willing to go the extra mile for? This sense of fulfilment calls for you to make an effort, experience failure, yet have another go and learn from experience. What makes me forget about the passage of time? Think of the activities that you do through which you forget everything else, even sleeping and eating, because you become so immersed in what psychologists call the state of 'flow' and those on the spiritual path call tapping into the Higher Power.

For a minute, if we put aside the atrocities committed by Hitler on humanity, he was one of the most successful self-made people in the history of humankind. He went from being a cheap, failing painter, to the commander of an entire country with the most powerful military in the world in a matter of two decades. He also mobilised and inspired millions. He was sharp, witty and smart. He was intensely focused on his goals. But where he failed was in his dharma. Understand dharma here as values, or better, the accumulation of values in one's life. Because of his misguided values, tens of millions died. This is why it is of utmost importance that we define our dharma. Most of us fail to contemplate this. We obsessively focus on being happy, looking like a success in front of other people or online, and feeling good all the time. We fail to realise that if our values are not aligned with our sense of purpose, none of this is going to do us any good. I am not here to tell you which values are good or bad. I don't even want to push my own values onto you. The whole point of values is that they are adopted through one's own wish, not because someone tells you to.

The Dharma-Karma Life
Every moment of every day, whether we realise it or not, we are making conscious and unconscious choices of how we spend our time, on what we spend our time, and on where we direct our energy. Simply put, we make decisions to act. In Sanskrit, actions are known as 'karma'. Yes, that's right, the word is much more than just 'what goes around, comes around'. The true meaning of karma is action. Right now, you are *choosing* to read this book. That is a karma in itself. There are countless other things you could be doing, but right now, you are *choosing* to be here. In a few minutes, you might *choose* to put the book down and go grab something to eat, or to look at your phone and stop reading. Whenever such things happen, we make simple, value-based decisions. Our behaviour (or actions) follow the valuation accordingly. Basically, our karma is moulded based upon our values. Our values are constantly reflected in the way we choose to behave. Our dharma is reflected in our karma. This is critical, because we all say we believe and value certain things, but we never back them up with action. But we know that actions never lie.

In reality, our values are an extension of ourselves. They define us. When something good happens to something or someone we value, we feel good. When your child gets top marks in their class, you feel good – almost as though it is *your* achievement. To oppose this, if we don't value something, we feel good when something bad happens. In May 2011, when Osama Bin Laden was killed, people in the US cheered throughout the streets.[5] When Ted Bundy's body was driven by after his execution, people stood outside the prison and basically threw a party. When someone who is perceived as evil is destroyed, there is a great sense of moral victory in the hearts of countless. It's a slight paradox that when we are disconnected from our own values, we value scrolling through Instagram or posting our success stories online. We believe that we value ambition and hard work, and then our beliefs and ideas get disconnected from our actions and emotions.

The Higher Value
Just as we either value or devalue things and others in our life, we can value or devalue ourselves too. This is where a lot of the work of the self-esteem movement in the 1970s and 1980s came from. They wanted people to love themselves (self-love). People who love themselves get satisfaction from taking care of themselves and improving themselves. This form of love is important, but it is not sufficient in and of itself. If you only love yourself, you become self-absorbed and indifferent to the suffering of others, or the issues around you.

In the end, we all need to value ourselves but also something *above* ourselves. Whether that is God, your guru, some moral code and conduct, or cause, we *must* value something above ourselves to make our lives feel as though they have meaning. In fact, this is a prerequisite for meaning in one's life. Life definitely has a higher meaning, whether we choose to accept it or not.

If you make yourself the highest value in your life, then you will never feel the need to sacrifice for anything, and life becomes meaningless, simply chasing one high after another. You don't want that. I don't want that. No one wants that.

You Are What You Value
Our identity – that is, the thing that we perceive and understand as 'self' – is the aggregation of everything we value. In short, this is due to ahamkar, one of the four faculties of the antahkarana mentioned in the beginning sections of this book.

Values are the fundamental component of our psychological make-up and identity. We are defined by what we choose is important in our lives. Our life is defined by what we choose to prioritise. If money matters to you more than anything, then that is what will come to define who you are. If you feel self-pity towards yourself and believe you don't deserve love or success, then that will also come to define who you are – through your actions, your words, and your choices.

Any change in our 'self' is a change in the organisation of our values. When something painful happens, it devastates us because not only do we feel loss and sadness, but because we also lose something we value. And it is when we lose enough of what we value that we begin to question the value of life itself. We value our career and then it's gone. We value a partner and now they're gone. Things like this crush us. It questions who we are, our value and worth as an individual, as well as what we know about the world. It throws us into a kind of identity crisis, because we struggle to come to terms with what to believe, feel, or do anymore. The same is true for the positive in our life as well. When something amazing happens, we not only experience the happiness of the achievement, but we also have a change in the valuation of our 'self'. We come to see ourselves as more valuable and deserving. We add meaning to the world.

Which Values Do I Choose?
I don't feel I need to go into great detail about which values are healthy and unhealthy, nor do I want to push my beliefs onto you either. Good values are constructive and controllable, bad values are destructive, uncontrollable and stem from emotion alone. Bad values are damaging because relying merely on our emotions is dangerous in itself. Unfortunately, the majority of us mostly rely on our emotions without consciously realising it. Research confirms that most of us, for the most part, make choices based on our feelings, rather than basing our choices on knowledge or information. Research also shows that our feelings are usually self-centred, warped, and delusional.

People who live their lives solely based on how they feel find themselves on a sort of hedonic treadmill, constantly seeking more and more. The only way to switch that treadmill off is to decide and affirm that there is something that we value more than our own feelings. This is 'purpose', and finding it is one of the most important and enduring tasks you will take in your life. Our purpose should not merely be determined by that which feels good. When we value things outside of our control, in essence, we give up our life to that thing. The most obvious example of this is money. Agreed, you will have some control over how much money you make or have saved in your account, but… economies collapse, companies go under, people are laid off, and entire professions become automated thanks to new technology. If everything you do is for the sake of money, then when tragedy strikes, you will lose your false-perceived purpose for living a focused life. You must find values that you can control, or your values will control you.

Work

Between 2011 and 2013, the polling company Gallup conducted the most detailed study ever on how individuals around the world felt about their jobs.[6] Millions of workers across 142 countries were studied. They discovered that thirteen per cent of employees are 'engaged' in their professions, which indicates they are enthusiastic about, and committed to their organisation in a positive manner.

Sixty-three per cent said they are 'not engaged', which is characterised as 'sleepwalking through their workday, putting time – but not energy or passion – into their work'.

Furthermore, twenty-three per cent are 'actively disengaged'.[7] They, according to Gallup, 'aren't just unhappy at work; they're busy acting out their unhappiness'. Every day, these employees undermine the efforts of their engaged coworkers... Employees that are actively disengaged are more or less out to harm their company.

That means nearly twice as many people hate their jobs as love their jobs. One in every three British workers checks their e-mails before 6.30 a.m., and eighty per cent of British companies think it is appropriate to call staff after hours. For most people, the concept of 'work hours' is disappearing, so this thing that eighty-seven per cent of us hate is infecting more and more of our lives.

The most stressful situation for people is not having a lot of responsibility. It is having to put up with work that is tedious, boring, and soul-destroying. To do something where they die a little every day when they arrive to work, because their work affects no part of them that is truly them.

We spend the majority of our waking lives at work, and eighty-seven per cent of us are either disengaged or irritated by it. You are twice as likely to dislike your job as you are to enjoy it, and if e-mails are factored in, those work hours are extending across more and more of our lives – fifty, sixty hours a week. I get it – we have no choice – work is necessary. On an individual level, a few of us may be able to flee. If you can shift to a position where you are less constrained and have more autonomy, or if you are doing something that you believe is important, do it. Your feelings of anxiety and depression will most likely decrease. But, in a world where only thirteen per cent of people have meaningful work, that counsel appears almost cruel. Nevertheless, there are other ways to find meaning.

Your Moral Compass

Do you remember the times when you were full of joy? Like when you got your first promotion? Your brand-new car? That iPhone? What about that expensive ring? How happy are you today? Not much I'd assume. People who have achieved intrinsic goals become much happier as opposed to those who seek out such extrinsic goals. They are also less depressed and anxious.

According to twenty-two independent studies, the more materialistic and extrinsically motivated you become, the more anxious you will be. Other studies suggest, the more materialistic and extrinsically motivated you get, the more nervous you will become. Similar studies have been conducted in the United Kingdom, Denmark, Germany, India, South Korea, Russia, Romania, Australia, and Canada, with the same results.[8]

All of these materialistic values that advise us to spend our way to happiness appear to be true values; they appeal to the part of us that has developed to need some basic rules to guide us through life; yet, they do not provide us with what we need from values – a path to a fulfilling existence. Extrinsic thinking ruins your interactions with other individuals.

When you have a strong desire for material things, you begin to wonder about yourself all the time – how are people assessing you? It forces you to concentrate on other people's opinions of you, and their admiration of you – and then you're kind of tied into having to worry about what other people think about you, and whether or not other people will give you the rewards that you desire. Materialism makes you vulnerable to the world around you.

Unfortunately, in our culture, the urge is largely one way: spend more and work more. We live in a system that constantly distracts us from the things that are truly wonderful about life. We are being persuaded to live in a way that does not suit our basic psychological requirements, leaving us with a persistent, perplexing sensation of dissatisfaction. Here's a truth bomb for you: The more you believe that life is about having stuff, superiority, and showing it off, the more dissatisfied, sad, and nervous you will be.

The desire to discover important intrinsic values exists; it is a powerful element of who we are, yet it is easy to divert our attention. And we have an economic system that is based on doing just that. People aren't simply missing out on anything, such as fulfilling employment or community. They are also affected by the presence of something – an inaccurate set of values that tells them to seek happiness in all the wrong places and to ignore the possible human relationships that are right in front of them.

Most individuals are aware of all of this deep down. I truly feel that most people understand the intrinsic values that will provide them with a pleasant existence. However, I believe that one of the reasons people feel depressed is because society is not set up to assist how people live lifestyles, have employment, participate in the economy, or participate in their communities in ways that promote their basic values.

The questions people should ask themselves are, "Am I putting up my life such that I have a chance of success as my inherent values? Am I associating with the right people, who will help me feel appreciated rather than making me feel like I made it?"

In today's culture, we end up on a sort of materialistic autopilot. We have advertising thrown in our face telling us that we will feel better (and less stinking, and less disgustingly shaped, and less all-around worthless) if we buy some specific product; and then buy something else; and buy again. And again. And again, until your family eventually buys your coffin. Intrinsic motivation is constantly present. It's been dormant for a long time. We simply need to bring it into the open. We don't make or allow space for these crucial dialogues to take place, which leads to increasing isolation and discontent in life.

Your Life Purpose

Chances are, if you are reading this book, then you will probably have been lucky enough to ask yourself: "What is my purpose in life?" So, let's take a step back into history. For the vast majority of it, meaning and purpose were found in creating tribes and small communities with the single aim of delaying death as much as possible (which was only a few extra years). The purpose back then was simple: Do whatever we need to do to stay alive.

But obviously, over time, the magnificent *homo sapien* adapted and learnt how to overcome and defy a large number of ways to die. And then, at some point in human history, we turned to figuring out ways to make ourselves more healthier, more comfortable, more entertained, and so on. Whilst progress is rewarding, and it has its inherent benefits, it's also left our species wondering what we should do with all the time that is left now. It's a struggle the majority of us have gone through, or will go through, at some point in our life. What do I want to do with my life? What am I passionate about? What am I bad at?

Putting aside all spiritual beliefs for a moment, read this. We exist on this planet for some undetermined period of time. During this time we do 'things'. Some of these things are important, others aren't. The important things are what give our life meaning and joy. The unimportant things are just there to waste away at time. And so, let's end this section with where we began this book – your death.

We all know that we're going to die. One day, eventually, the moment will come and take us away. The question is no longer when we will die, because we all have to accept our mortality. But instead, the question is, how will we die? Cancer? Heart attack? Pneumonia? Choking? An accident? We just don't know. But, what we do know is that when we think about our own death, this is how we typically picture our final moments. The hospital beds. The beeping machines. The crying family. The ambulances. We seldom think about all the time leading up to those final moments. Death is the work-in-progress over the course of your life – each breath, each bite, each swallow, each laugh, scream, cry and sigh – they each bring us one step closer to our demise. So, there is a better question to ask instead of when we're going to die. How are we travelling towards the end of our journey? If everything that you do each day brings us closer to death in its own unique and subtle way, then what are we choosing to let kill us? Ultimately, it is death alone that will give you perspective on the true value of your life.

Living Within Dharma

Dharma, the Hindus believe, is at the core of all morality. It is believed that it should be the principle driving force behind all of our actions. Dharma is not simply religion or holiness, but rather moral and civic excellence in the course of one's daily life. It is a sense of righteousness that emerges from within our ātmā and is made real through the actions we take. The rest of the Eastern and Western world alike, have also put emphasis on dharma, although through different terms. The Stoics called it virtue, and believed it to be the highest good.

If you're not particularly comfortable with the notion of dharma, understand it as the discretion between right and wrong. Consider a dharmic life as worthwhile for its own sake. No one is less serene than the person who does not know what is right or wrong. No one feels worse about themselves than a cheater or liar, even if they are showered with rewards for their cheating and lying. Life is meaningless to the one who decides their decisions hold no meaning.

The gift of free will is that in this life we can *choose* to be good or we can *choose* to be bad. The choices we make in that regard will determine whether we experience peace or not. You need to sit down and examine yourself. What do I stand for? What do I believe to be important? What am I really *living* for? When we sit down and examine ourselves in this manner, deep down within our hearts, we find the answer. The only thing holding us back is the hectic life we live today. The realities of pursuing a career, and surviving in the modern world, come between us and self-introspection.

The Mahābhārat is the battle of dharma. Throughout the text, we hear stories of the characters fighting their own inner enemies, in attempt to find their dharma. The epic famously proclaims eleven times, "Where there is dharma, there is victory." This verse is used in the emblem of the Supreme Court of India today. The Chinese philosopher Confucius wrote that the "gentleman is self-possessed and relaxed, while the petty man is perpetually full of worry."

It's possible to get ahead in life by lying and cheating and just being downright awful to other people. Many people may do just this. It might even be a quick way to rise to the top. But it comes at the expense of not only your self-respect, but your inner peace too. Each of must cultivate a moral code – our dharma – a higher standard that we love almost more than live itself; it becomes the foundation of our life. You must sit down and ask: *What's important to me? How am I going to live and why?*

Integrity – Living with Truth
If you open up any dictionary you will know that the word 'integrity' evolved from the Latin word 'integritas', meaning 'whole', or, 'complete'. Predictably, it is also related to the word 'integrate', which means 'bringing together'. In this sense, if one were to look at it from an abstract angle – being in integrity with oneself is akin to an integration of our outer life and our inner life. It is almost like two sides of a battle merging together creating a union. Being in integrity, therefore, is not just for other people – in fact, the virtue helps to make us feel better and more complete. A question to ask yourself: Do I live my private life with the same consistency as I live my public life? Charles Marshall's famous quote sums up living within dharma

beautifully. He defined integrity as 'doing the right thing when you don't have to – when on else is looking or will ever know – when there will be no congratulations or recognition for having done so'.[9] This will be the ultimate test of dharma for us.

The Highest Dharma

The Bhāgavata-Purāna states, "It is said that great personalities almost always accept voluntary inconvenience because of the suffering of people in general."[10] Similarly, during the Yaksha Prashna, when Yudhishthir is asked what the highest dharma is, he responds saying 'compassion is the highest form of dharma'.[11] Both can be understood in a similar way, as it is only when we have compassion, that we will act with non-violence.

Patanjali, in his Yogasutra mentions 'ahimsā', meaning 'non-violence', which actually means more than not harming other beings. It also means to act with positive intent: to be kind and loving, to wish for another's spiritual and material well-being, to be compassionate. The very credo of Pramukh Swami's life was, 'In the joy of others, lies our own'. By being compassionate to others, we only enrich our own lives. For over six decades of his life, every action he carried out was with the sole intent of compassion. Such compassion, according to almost all the Vedic scriptures, is the highest expression of dharma. This is especially true when compassion extends far beyond one's ability, not just to their own group, but to the whole of humanity and all living beings. This is echoed in the Vedas, which state that non-violence should extend beyond our relationships with other human beings to include all living creatures. A Sanskrit phrase says, 'para dukha dukhi', which basically means 'empathy': to feel one's pain when they suffer, and to feel one's joy when they're happy.

As the seemingly most advanced form of life, human beings should be the ones taking care of the environment and all living creatures. Understanding and practicing the principle of ahimsa – not just non-violence, but empathy and compassion too – is a basic tenet of the focused life. It is held sacred by Hindus and Buddhists, and it is also inherent within the Golden Rule of the Judeo-Christian faiths. To genuinely be compassionate, to feel one's suffering as your own; to make the serious, lifelong attempt, as much as possible, not to inflict pain on another living being, whether directly or indirectly – through our thoughts, words, or actions – is ahimsa. This principle underscores the importance of a pure diet too. Again, I don't want to push my own values onto you, but, the unnecessary suffering caused by slaughtering animals in the name of food is not only heart-wrenching, but it has negative effects on one's mental and spiritual life. Hence, Hinduism encourages a vegetarian diet. The higher our dharma, and the more we're willing to live by it, the more meaningful and fulfilling our lives will become.

Whilst we're talking about non-violence, you might ask, "Since plants also feel pain when we eat them, how is consuming vegetarian food any less violent than non-vegetarian food?" But, the essence of ahimsa is to consciously minimise pain to others. When we kill an animal, bird, or fish, we will see them fighting for their life in fear and pain because of their enhanced nervous systems. The psychological and physiological makeup of species on the lower levels of the food chain, like plants, is such that they have extremely undeveloped senses and nervous systems, and therefore minimal (note, I don't say complete absence) of pain. Ahimsa is based on the doctrine of double-effect, to avoid causing the least pain possible. The doctrine of double effect, in ethics, says that if doing something morally good has a morally bad side-effect, then it's ethically okay to do it providing the bad side-effect wasn't intended. By the law of nature, we have to eat to survive, but our diet should be as compassionate as possible. The world is made in such a way that it is impossible to be a hundred per cent non-violent, but shouldn't we try as much as possible?

Sometimes, I truly wonder what would happen if we showed children the horrors of the slaughterhouses. I also wonder whether after this, they would still continue to eat meat. Society has programmed children to eat meat as if it just magically grows on supermarket shelves. By the time they're old enough to make a connection between live animals and what's on their plates, they've been so culturally habituated to their diet, that they rarely question its acceptability. Again, this gives rise to another truth. Most people are good at heart, but from birth, they have been inundated by the media and society at large, and so they believe what they do is good. They never learn to consider the suffering of other animals and creatures.

Recently, I have researched extensively into modern-day dairy and slaughter industries, to see their connection. When calves are born, the industries keep the females and normally kill the bulls for meat. The cows are often kept in inhumane conditions until their milk productions drops off and it no longer becomes profitable to keep them alive. Then, most of them are crammed into trucks and sent off to a slaughterhouse. This form of recent awareness and apparent growing compassion in the world, has led many thoughtful people turning towards vegetarianism or veganism, in which animal products are avoided. In the majority of Indian spiritual traditions, however, even in Gujarat, people are encouraged to take milk products from places where cattle are loved and protected throughout their natural lives. Unfortunately, these places are rare. In Sarangpur, cattle are cared for, and the milk they naturally produce is then used throughout the complex. In a similar manner, crops are harvested through advanced systems like drip-irrigation systems, to make the entire campus almost a self-sufficient village of its own.

Karuṇā is a Sanskrit word meaning 'compassion', which itself literally means 'to feel for others'. The Oxford dictionary defines compassion as ;the feeling or emotion, when a person is moved by the suffering or distress of another, and by the desire to relive it'. Karuṇā goes beyond mere sentiment. Karuṇā is not something you just feel, but also something you act upon. Similar to ahimsa, karuṇā is essential to the focused life.

When I think of compassion, I think of the likes of Pramukh Swami, Nelson Mandela, or Abraham Lincoln. There is a story about a town drunk, who was sleeping on the road in his own vomit. One winter night when Lincoln and his friends were passing by. Lincoln took the man home. And in his second inaugural speech, he made the remarkable and unforgettable statements that are still remembered today, "With malice towards none, with charity for all, with firmness in the right as God us to see the right, let us strive on to finish the work we are in, to bind up the nation's wounds." It is in binding up another's wounds that we offer true compassion.[12] It is in the joy of others that we find true joy for ourselves.

Acts of compassion are innumerable: hug a friend, donate to victims of a disaster, volunteer, give thoughtful advice, or in rare cases like that of Pramukh Swami and his swamis, dedicating your entire life tending to the problems and pains of others, to bring them onto the path of joy and peace. Compassion is not merely an act, it's a way of living that we cultivate, and it brightens up our world, as well as that of others.

Every spiritual leader, philosopher, and thinker have pointed to compassion as the most human, and humane, quality. The German philosopher Arthur Schopenhauer stated bluntly, "Compassion is the basis of all morality." Compassion is immediate. We are moved by the suffering that is right before our eyes, and we're less likely to be stirred by pain halfway across the world. Compassion probably has an evolutionary purpose for the survival of our species, especially newborns and young children. It is the hallmark of perhaps the most important kind of love in our species: that of a mother and child. The brains of mothers show a distinct and powerful response to their baby's distress – certain parts of their brains light up in response to a newly-born infant, and different parts of the brain continue to light up months after as the relationship evolved.

Research at Princeton showed that a brain area called the insula, located within the cerebral cortex, is associated with empathy and compassion. Pilot studies with Buddhist monks also show that regular compassionate meditation could permanently be changing brain patterns, leading to greater feelings of happiness.[13] I know that in today's world, compassion has become a sort of buzzword, but it actually stops us from imposing suffering, and in that sense it can also be seen as a part of our moral compass.

Is Compassion Natural?
What happens when a person in need is not right next door to us, or when the situation is woven with many complexities though? American neuroscientist, Joshua Greene's work points to a higher-order kind of compassion that can help broaden our care in such cases. In one of his experiments he asks people what they would do if a bunch of people are hiding in a basement during the war, and there are enemy soldiers outside, and a baby starts to cry. You know if the soldiers hear the cry of the baby, they will find you and kill you all. The only way to prevent this is to smother the baby to death. And the awful question is, is this okay to do, ethically speaking?[14]

Brain imaging studies show that it takes people quite a bit of time to come with an answer. Are you still thinking about it? A part of the brain called the anterior cingulate cortex lights up. One thing we know about this area of the brain is that it lights up when we feel conflicted about our response. And we also see a part of the prefrontal cortex light up – the part that is responsible for cognitive control. With two parts of the brain lighting up together, it's as if peoples first response is pure compassion for the baby. At the same time, they can reason out that one death may be better than many. Their brain is spending time choosing the less automatic response. And those people who finally agree that one death, even if it is that of an innocent baby, is better than a whole group dying have high activity in the cortex – the executive control area – than the people who just finally say, "No, don't smother the baby, no matter what." When those close to us suffer, we are stirred by a kind of visceral response. But in more complex situations, we reason out a higher-order compassion that benefits those who are far away or is geared towards the greater good.

> **Compassion is the highest form of dharma.**
> *Prince Yudhishthir, Mahābhārat*

We were walking out of the ashram towards the main mandir compound.
"How was it?" Asked the swami.
"Amazing, as always. I have so much to think about and to practice in my life. It's a wake-up call more than anything for me."
He smiled, "You know how long you were in there for?"
"No," I shook my head cluelessly.
"For at least half an hour. I don't know what you spoke about, but it must have been *something*."
Meeting my guru after a long time was unexpected and unreal. The individual who I looked up to, always there, guiding me and holding my hand. I felt so lucky. I felt humbled. I felt grateful. I felt truly fulfilled.
"We spoke about so many things." I said as we continued to walk…

The Art of Knowledge

To some, this section may seem sceptical, nevertheless, I suggest you read on with an open mind. Dale Carnegie said, "Knowledge is only knowledge if it is applied." So often, we think that the more we know, the better. We believe that knowledge is power, but it is only power if it is practiced in our daily life. We will discuss truths in this part of the book – my truths or ancient truths – regardless, they are experienced by us all to some greater or lesser extent.

Thich Nhat Hanh says, "On the surface of the ocean there is stillness, but underneath there are currents." What is happening on the surface of the water doesn't matter; it is what's going on below that can kill you. Today, when we are living in a society of material comfort and moderate external peace, we lack inner comfort and peace. History proves this time and time again. Imagine Tiger Woods, who like so many successful people, got less happy the more he achieved. He got less freedom. He got less sleep, until it came to him only with medication. Even with a beautiful and brilliant wife, whom he loved, even as the undisputed champion of golf, he was miserable, tortured by a crushing anxiety from which he felt no relief. It cost him almost everything. What was he lacking?[1]

We are incapable of seeing what is essential in the world if we are blind to what is going on within us. Since ancient times, people have strived to train and control the forces that reside deep within them, knowing them to be the source of true joy and serenity. You may conquer empires or rule cities, but if you fail to control yourself, it is all for nothing.

Discontent: The Longing for Happiness

Around one in five US adults is taking at least one drug for a psychiatric problem; nearly one in four middle-aged women in the US is taking antidepressants at any given time; around one in ten boys at American high schools is given a powerful stimulant to aid their focus; and addictions to both legal and illegal drugs are now so widespread that the life expectancy of white men is declining for the first time in the entire peacetime history of the United States. We live in a culture of discontent.

Discontentment is not merely a lack of hope in one's life. it is the direct absence, or lack of, meaning and purpose in one's life. Hopelessness is rooted deep within our minds; but it is amplified to all layers of our being. It is the root of most anxiety, stress, depression, and mental illness. Depression too, stems from a lack of hope. It is the belief that the future is meaningless.

We seem to think that as we make progress in the world, things will get better. But, in fact, the opposite is true. The better things are getting, the more desperate, hopeless, and anxious we are all feeling.[2] In recent times, authors like Hans Rosling and Steven Pinker have been presenting cases to show how it's wrong to feel pessimistic, and that things are, in fact, better than they've ever been, and that it'll continue this way too.[3] Both have written arguably good books with numerous charts and figures to present their cases. They both explain, in great detail, the biases and incorrect assumptions our minds carry that make us think that things are worse. They argue that progress has continued, uninterrupted, throughout modern history. People are more educated than ever.[4] Violence, has trended down for decades, maybe even centuries.[5] Racism, sexism, discrimination, and violence against women are at their lowest points in recorded history.[6] We have more rights today than ever before in history.[7] Half of the planet has access to the internet.[8] Extreme poverty is at an all-time low globally.[9] Wars are smaller and less frequent than at any other time in recorded history.[10] Children are dying less, people are living longer.[11] There's more wealth today than ever before.[12] We've cured most diseases.[13] Okay, yes, they're right. These are by far some of the best books I've read too. They give facts, and they're important ones too. But do they make you feel any better about yourself? About your values? About your purpose? Did we forget that every coin has two sides?

For all the good news published today, take a look at these statistics. In the United States, symptoms of depression and anxiety are on an eighty-year upswing amongst young people and a twenty-year upswing amongst the adult population.[14] Not only are people experiencing depression in greater numbers, but they're also experiencing it earlier on in life, with every generation.[15] Since 1985, men and women have reported lower levels of life satisfaction.[16] This is partly due to increased stress levels in the past thirty years.[17] Drug overdoses have recently hit an all-time high (opioids being the worst). Across the US population, and probably across the globe too, feelings of loneliness and social isolation are increasing. Nearly half of all Americans now report feeling isolated, left out, or alone in their lives.[18] Social trust is not only low across the developed world but plummeting, meaning fewer people are putting their trust on the government, the media, and even one another.[19] In the 1980s, when researchers asked survey participants how many people they had discussed important personal matters with over half a year, the most common answer was 'three'. By 2006, it was 'zero'.[20]

We mustn't forget that the environment is in crisis too. The craziest people have access to nuclear weapons, or are pretty close to getting them. Extremism – in all forms, on both the right and left, both religious and secular – continues to grow across the world. Simply put, yes, we are the safest and most prosperous human civilisation in the history of the world, yet we feel the more hopeless and disconnected than ever before. We lack purpose. We lack meaning. We lack true values. This is the social paradox. One fact, that you've probably heard but it's never been backed up, shockingly sums it up. The wealthier and safer the place you live, the more likely you are to commit suicide. Yes, we've made magnificent progress in health, safety, peace, and material wealth over the past few centuries, but these are statistics of the past, not the future. The better the world gets, the more we have to lose. The more we have to lose, the less we feel we have meaning and purpose in life.

At its most basic, the concept of positive thinking is simple: decide to think happy and successful thoughts – banish the spectres of grief and failure - and happiness and success will follow. For a civilisation so fixated on achieving happiness, we seem remarkably poor at the task. The numerous benefits of modern living have done so little to improve our collective happiness. Higher economic growth does not always lead to happy societies, just as increased personal income over a certain threshold does not always lead to happier citizens. Better education does not help either. Neither does a wider range of consumer products. Neither do larger and finer dwellings, which appear to serve primarily to afford the luxury of additional space in which to feel glum. No wonder we are dissatisfied.

If you're looking for long-term solutions, self-help books aren't going to help you either. We want neat, book-sized solutions to the difficulty of being human, but when the packaging is removed, the themes of such books are usually boring. For example, evidence shows that venting your anger does not eliminate it, and visualising your objectives does not appear to increase your chances of achieving them.

There are good reasons to argue that the notion of 'seeking happiness' is wrong in the first place. Religions have never placed much emphasis on it, at least in this world; philosophers have surely not been unanimous in embracing it either. John Stuart Mill said, "Ask yourself whether you are happy and you cease to be so."

As I read numerous books and research studies, I realised that there was something that all those psychologists, philosophers, and even the rare self-help guru had in common. The unexpected conclusion to which they had all arrived, in their own unique ways, was that the desire to be happy is frequently the very thing that makes us unhappy. Our persistent efforts to erase the negative – insecurity, uncertainty, failure, or grief – are exactly the things that drive us to feel uncomfortable, nervous, doubtful, or unhappy.

Isolation: Imprisoned Within

Usually, loneliness is a temporary state as one adjusts to new surroundings, but when it is used as a punishment and is reinforced over days, months, or even years in solitary confinement, it can be one of the cruelest ways to treat another human being. Physical torture and malnutrition are horrifying, but some who have suffered imprisonment say that the worst part was the isolation. Of his time in prison on Robben Island, Nelson Mandela wrote, "Nothing is more dehumanising than the absence of human companionship," and he knew men in prison who preferred getting half a dozen lashes with a whip as opposed to being in solitary confinement.[21] It is estimated that

25,000 US convicts are currently imprisoned in tiny cells, deprived of all meaningful human contact. Some of them spend years secluded in this way. These aren't necessarily the most violent offenders. Prisoners have been 'locked down' for no reason other than reading the incorrect book.

Suffering: A Mental Construct?

One by one, researchers shuttled a group of people down a hall and into a small room. Inside was a single box computer console, with a blank screen and two buttons. That was it. The instructions given were simple: stare at the screen, and if you see a blue dot flash on it, press the button that says, 'Blue'. If a purple dot flashes on the screen, press the 'Not Blue' button. Each participant had to look at a thousand dots. And when a participant finished, the researchers brought in another participant to repeat the same process. This went on with hundreds of participants at various university institutions. Were the psychologists trying to torture the subjects? No. In fact, the aim of this experiment was achieved. It explained much of what we see in the modern world.

The psychologists were researching what is called the 'prevalence-induced concept change'.[22] To keep it simple, we'll call it PICC. Here's what happened. Most of the dots shown were blue. Some were purple. Some of them were some shade between blue and purple. What the researchers discovered was that when they showed participants mostly blue dots, everyone was pretty much accurate in determining which dots were blue and which weren't. But as soon as they started decreasing the number of blue dots, and showing more shades of purple, participants began to mistake purple dots for blue. It seemed as though their eyes distorted the colour purple and continued to seek a certain number of blue dots, regardless of how many were actually shown. You're probably thinking, so what, right? We miss seeing stuff properly all the time. And also the fact that if they have to look at a thousand dots, they're bound to make some mistakes. But that wasn't the point. The aim was to see how humans distort their perceptions to fit their expectations. When the psychologists had enough data for this, they moved on to varied forms of the experiment. For example, they showed participants pictures of faces that were to some degree threatening, friendly, or neutral. To begin with, they showed them more threatening faces. But as the experiment proceeded, they showed less and less (like they did with the blue dots), and the same effect occurred. The fewer threatening faces participants were shown, the more they began to misread friendly and neutral faces as being threatening.

Then, the psychologists went one stop further. It's one thing to see things as threatening when they're not, we do it all the time, but what about our moral judgements? What about the belief that there's more evil in the world than there truly might be? They had the participants read some job proposals. Some were unethical and involved shady stuff. Some were perfectly normal. Others were somewhere in between. Again, the researchers began by showing a mix of ethical and unethical proposals. Then, slowly, they showed fewer and fewer unethical job proposals. Yet the same effect occurred. Rather than noticing that more proposals were ethical, people maintained the perception that the majority of the proposals were unethical.

This PICC effect suggests that, basically, the more we seek to find threats, the more we will actually see them, regardless of whether they are there or not. We see this happening in the modern-world. Violence used to be where someone caused another physical harm. Today, many people use the word to describe even a slight level of discomfort, or even the presence of a person they dislike. 'Trauma' used to specifically mean an experience through which a victim was affected to a severe extent, that they could no longer function properly within society. Today, a mere unpleasant social encounter to a few curse words or images are considered 'trauma'. Even worse, the better things get, the more we perceive threats when there may be no threats, and then, the more we get upset about them.

Emile Durkheim, the French founder of modern sociology, gave a thought experiment in one of his books: What if there were no crime? What if there emerged a society where everyone was simply respectful and non-violent and everyone was equal? What if no one lied or hurt each other? What if corruption didn't exist? What would happen? Would conflict cease? Would stress evaporate? Would everyone live in peace?[23]

He said no, and in fact he said that the opposite would happen. He suggested that the more comfortable and ethical a society becomes, the more minor violations would become magnified in our minds at least. If everyone stopped killing each other, we might not necessarily feel good about it. We'd just get equally upset about the smaller indiscretions in life. Developmental psychology also argues something similar when it says that protecting people in a bubble from problems or adversity doesn't make them any more secure, safer, or happier; it makes them more vulnerable and insecure. Basically, our emotional reactions to problems are not determined by the size of the problem, and instead by how much our minds amplify the problems to fit the degree of our expectation of the experience.

Pain: Inherent to Reality

On 11 June 1963, in Vietnam, three Buddhist monks stepped out of a car. One placed a cushion on the street, at the centre of an intersection. The second monk, an older man named Thich Quang Duc, went to the cushion, sat down in the lotus position, closed his eyes, and began to meditate. The third monk opened the boot of the car, took out a five-gallon canister of gasoline, went up to Quang Duc, poured it over his head, covering him in fuel. With his robes soaked in gasoline and an expressionless face, Quang Duc recited a short prayer, reached out to pick up a match, and in his seated position he struck it against the asphalt, and then set himself on fire. He was instantly engulfed in flames.

Screams erupted as his skin turned black, his robes disintegrated, and a repulsive scent started to fill the air. Many fell to their knees, others were simply stunned and shocked and what had just happened. Yet, as he burnt, Quang Duc remained perfectly still.

News of Quang Duc's act of self-immolation rapidly spread. It angered millions across the globe. The reason for this act was in direct protest against the narcissistic leader of Vietnam at the time (something you can look into yourself). Five months later, the tyrant leader of Vietnam, along with his family, was assassinated. The image of the burning monk had clicked something in everyone's mind. Even President John F. Kennedy said that 'no news picture in history has generated so much emotion around the world'.

This photo triggered something primal and universal in humans. It went beyond politics or religion. It tapped into something far more fundamental to human experience: the ability for the *homo sapien* to endure enormous amounts of pain. I can't sit still for two minutes, and here was a monk that was burning alive, yet he didn't move. He didn't scream. He didn't even open his eyes to take one last look at the world he was leaving behind. There was something pure to this act.

And despite the horror to the incident, he rose above his mind, and today it is still breathtaking and inspiring. You see, pain is inherent to our reality. No matter how good or bad your life gets (or is), pain will always be there. If we try to avoid pain, we avoid stress, chaos and tragedy, and thus, we become fragile. Everything that we do, we are, or that we care about is a direct reflection of this choice. Unfortunately, our tolerance for pain in modern society is diminishing rapidly. Not only that, it is also generating greater amounts of emotional fragility.

As human beings, most of us not only fear death, we fear pain too. Many scientists and thinkers also believe that one day we will become immortal – that we will surpass death. They believe that biotechnology will somehow enable us to replace and restore our bodies indefinitely, allowing us to live forever. I know it sounds like science fiction, but some even go to the extent of claiming that this technology will be achieved within our lifetime. I personally don't believe this. Pain and death are psychologically necessary because it gives stakes in life. We have something to lose.

At the core of all emotion is pain. Negative emotions are caused by experiencing varying levels of pain. Positive emotions are caused by alleviating pain. The ancient Vedic seers knew this, and they elaborated upon how humans continuously endeavour to alleviate pain and attain positive experiences. Ancient philosophers knew this and they constantly taught us that instead of seeking a life of happiness, we should seek one of character, with the ability to sustain pain, and learning to make sacrifices where necessary. In fact, it wasn't until fairly recently (the Enlightenment period), in the age of science and technology, and the promise of never-ending growth, that thinkers and modern philosophers came up with the idea summed up by Thomas Jefferson as 'the pursuit of happiness'.

Coming to terms with pain is essential for meaningful spiritual growth and personal transformation. Any behaviour pattern centred on the avoidance of pain becomes the gateway to suffering itself. We must learn not to be afraid of inner pain and disruption. We must learn to remain steadfast. Everything in life is a temporary experience. Wise beings do not wish to remain enslaved by the fear of pain; they rise above it. They allow it to be what it is.

Somehow, we have seem to forgotten what the ancients kept telling us. No matter how much wealth is generated within society, across the globe, the quality of our lives are not determined by external factors but instead by the quality of our character, and it is the quality of our character that determines our relationship to emotions like pain. Just to put it into perspective, at the time of writing, at least 820 million people are starving or undernourished, and by the time you finish reading this section, more than a hundred people, in the United States alone, will be beaten, abused, or killed by a family member – in their own home. What happened to the progress of society? The pursuit of happiness is itself the road to dissatisfaction. Our thirst will never be quenched in fulfilling our pursuit of desires to indulge in the world around us. This needless pursuit is at the root of all corruption, addiction, self-pity, and self-destruction. We must rise above pain, realising it serves a purpose. To numb pain is to numb ourselves.

When Bad Things Happen to Good People...
This is one of the most intrusive thoughts that come into our minds when we hear news not only of tragedy, war, and destruction, but also when things are personal too. We are inclined to categorise events into logical boxes, but unfortunately, that's not how the world works. Bhishma gives us a glimpse of this knowledge in the Mahābhārat. He says that it is difficult to know for sure why good people suffer, simply because the answer is beyond our perception. But, he also goes on to explain that when we understand the bigger picture of reality, we realise that the Higher Power's compassion on any soul is perfect.

The general Vedic view of evaluating destiny is to look at cause and effect (the law of karma). But the real knowledge is deeper than this. The truth is, the nature of everything in this world is temporary, fleeting, and constantly changing. Therefore, loss in this world is inevitable for everyone. He who comes, is destined to go. The Bible echoes this too: "Make your treasure not in this world where thieves plunder, rust corrodes, and moths destroy, but in the kingdom of God. That kingdom is within you."

It's easy to say, I know. When tragedy strikes the innocent, it confuses and bewilders us. But when we look back to the stories of Rama, Krishna, Swaminarayan, and even modern-day individuals like Nelson Mandela, or, Pramukh Swami Maharaj – if they have been able to remain stable amidst bad events and circumstances, why can't we? Maybe we'll never fully understand the 'why' behind tragic events occurring in people's lives, but do we have to? The world may seem cruel, horrible, and meaningless to us, and at that point, we may question our faith. But, as we dive deeper into our spiritual connection with the ātmā, however, our perception of life and the world around us transforms. In the focused life, faith plays an integral role. Faith isn't just about being religious, it's really a shift in understanding and consciousness. It's not as much about understanding what happens after we die as it is about transforming ourselves now. Faith is what allows us to see that both happiness and misery are not random occurrences, but those that aid us in our development into realising our true self, and freeing ourselves from the bondage of the mind.

God: The Higher Power

In undergoing a twelve-step program, many addicts struggle most with step two: acknowledging a higher power. Addicts often fight this one. At first they claim it's because they're atheists or because they don't like religion or because they don't understand why it matters. But they later realise that this is just the addiction talking – it's just another form of selfishness and self-absorption. Subsequent steps ask the addict to submit and let go. The second step really has less to do with 'god' than the other steps – it's the letting go. It's about attuning to the universe and discarding the toxic idea that we're at the center of it. As soon as you can attune your spirit to that idea, the easier, happier, and more focused your life will be. Why? Because you will have given up the most potent addiction of all – control.

The most common objections come in the form of: "I don't believe in

God," or, "There is no evidence," or, "Look at evolution and science." But why do we forget that logic and faith are two completely different things? Accepting a higher power is about surrendering; it is about faith. Look, you can accept this higher power as you understand him. Mother Earth. Destiny. Fate. The Higher Power. God. It's up to you.

When we consider life, that itself is beautiful. The odds are stacked so much against us. Whether you look at it from a spiritual perspective, or simply a scientific perspective, the chances of you sitting here, reading this book right now are basically zero per cent. And yet, here you are. Simply knowing and reflecting on the fact that we are a literal speck in the cosmos always fills me with amazement and wonder. As you're reading this, we're literally on a big rock orbiting a star, hurling through space at sixty thousand miles an hour. Consider that for a moment. We're on a giant boulder speeding across the universe right now.

There are around 100 billion other planets and more than 300 billion stars doing the same thing within our galaxy. There are an estimated 2 trillion galaxies within the universe, beyond the Milky Way, each with its own, millions of planets and billions of stars. Let's just do the maths for a moment. With an estimated 2 trillion galaxies and 100 billion planets for each galaxy, that means there could be 200 quintillion (that's 2 followed by 23 zeros) other conceivable worlds. A figure of that magnitude is virtually incomprehensible. I often still look at photos of the Earth taken from space to remind me of this vastness and my own nothingness.

We may never know for certain how things came to be, but the only thing we know for sure is that everything had to happen exactly as it did. Everything had to be perfectly designed, otherwise how would any of us be here? We've already won the lottery simply by being born. Remember this constantly. If you're from a spiritual background, you can add to this the thought that you have been placed on this planet at a perfect time – for a perfect reason – to perfect your self.

We've only managed to identify five per cent of the matter in the universe so far. The remaining ninety-five per cent is a complete mystery. This mystery is what we call dark matter and dark energy. We can measure it because it affects gravity, but we have no idea what it is. We have no idea what it is doing either. Consider the fact that even the brightest minds on the planet have no idea what's going on here. Because we can only see 0.0035 per cent of the electromagnetic spectrum, a vast universe of things remain unseen and hidden among all that dark matter. We, as humans, have limited receptors. Another example is that whilst babies get made inside us, we have no understanding how to actually 'create' kids. Do we have any idea where the intelligence to make the lungs, eyes, and spinal fluid all sync up to work together, properly originated? Or how does consciousness enter and leave our bodies? Not even a fraction of this knowledge is known to the modern man. The most we can say is that the same force that created the universe created us.

We're a self-proclaimed intelligence species, but it's much more likely that we're an exceedingly unintelligent species in comparison to whatever or whoever runs this universal show. Dolphins, arguably the smartest animals on the planet, perform the same things today that they did 10,000 years ago. They used to live in the ocean, and they still do. But we used to live in caves, and now we've almost worked out how to get to Mars, manufacture self-driving cars, and create technology that allows us to talk face-to-face with anybody, anywhere, at anytime by using our phones and laptops. So, not only are we extremely fortunate to be here, but we also have the opportunity to learn, grow, and evolve. And all that thanks goes to the higher power.

In his 1978 commencement speech to the students of Harvard, the Russian novelist Aleksandr Solzhenistyn spoke of a modern world where all countries – capitalist and communist alike – had been pervaded by a 'de-spiritualised and a religious humanistic consciousness'. Yes, realism is important. Pragmatism, scientism, and scepticism are too. They all have their places to varying degrees too. But still, you have to believe in *something*. You just have to. Otherwise life is empty, cold, and meaningless. Is it any coincidence that the vast majority of people who we look up to, or that did good in the world, believed in a higher power? Is it not interesting how leaders who end up truly tested by turbulent times end up sincerely relying on some measure of faith and belief to get them through difficult times? Whether that is during the Apollo mission or as the motto of the United States (In God We Trust), it is the best strategy to a focused life.

Francis Crick, the British biologist known to have deciphered the helical structure of the DNA molecule said: "An honest man, as now, could only state that in some sense, the origin of life appears at the moment to be almost a miracle, so many other conditions which would have had to have been satisfied to get going." American astronomer, Alan Sandage, was a firm believer that it was science that brought one to the truth of the universe. That was until he looked into the sky, and then refreshed his beliefs: "If there is a God, he must be true to both science and religion."

Apollo 11 astronaut Gene Cernan, was the eleventh person (and the last till date) to walk on the moon. After observing the Earth from the moon he became convinced of the existence of a higher power and creator. He said, "Science and technology got me there, but when I got there and I looked back home at the Earth, science and technology could not explain what I was seeing nor what I was feeling. The design and fine-tuning of the universe seemed to carry God's fingerprints. There was too much purpose. There was too much logic. Science and technology could not give me the answers I was looking for, and I came home with a conclusion that it's just too beautiful to have happened by accident. There must be something that you and I, all of us, don't fully understand about the creation of the universe, about the miracle of life itself. Looking at the Earth in all its wonder, in all its splendour – it's all dynamics; it's alive. It's not tumbling through space. It's not moving aimlessly. It's moving with logic and purpose. It's too beautiful to have happened by accident. What I'm saying is there is a creator of the universe. There is a God."

Similarly, the likes of Einstein, Newton, Edison, and other well-known pioneers of science also believed in a creator or divinity. And it's when almost all the wise people of history – scientists, philosophers and thinkers alike – agree, we too should pause and reflect. It is next to impossible to find an ancient philosophical school that does not talk about a higher power (or powers). At the most fundamental level, the only thing that matters to any true father or mother – or creator – is that their children find peace, meaning, and purpose in life. They for sure didn't put us here to judge, control, and kill each other. In reality, we have such little control of the world around us, so many inexplicable events created this world so perfectly, that it works out almost exactly the same way as if someone created it.

Pramukh Swami once said, "Man believes that he does everything. That he makes the world, family, and society happy. But this is arrogance, and where ego operates there is always downfall. God is the all-doer. It is he who does everything. God is the doer of this world, our life, and our country. When we have faith in God's doership, we can truly realise the ātmā, attain success in life, and be happy and peaceful in all ways."

There is a divine intelligence behind this universe. The Bhāgavata-Purāna says, "Learned transcendentalists who know the Absolute

Truth call this non-dual substance Parabrahman, Paramātmā, or Bhagwān."[24] Various spiritual traditions mention that an aspect of God is found in all beings. The Vedic texts call it 'the inner guide', or, 'the witness'. In Sanskrit, just as the individual soul is called the ātmā, whereas God as the inner guide is called paramātmā, which means 'supreme soul'.

From a spiritual perspective, we understand the mind that we wish to master, to be made of māyā. So, to conquer the commander, is to have subjugated māyā. Only one who conquers the mind can be said to have conquered māyā. The Shwetashvatara Upanishad states that maya is the energy (prakruti), and God is the energetic to whom it belongs.[25] The word 'māyā' is derived from the roots mā (not) and yā (what is). Thus, māyā is 'that which is not what it appears to be'. According to Vedic teachings, it is this māyā which is the very form of ignorance that envelopes all living beings and creation. Although it is enveloping us, it is only through transcending it that we can realise our true nature. All the inner enemies can be seen as products of maya, but by our own efforts, it is impossible to conquer it. The only way to overcome it is through surrenderence to God or Guru. Again, in the Shwetashvatara Upanishad, it says, "Your efforts and the grace of God, both are essential for success."[26] And so, our own self-effort can never suffice.

This leads us on to the very brief topic of faith. Having faith is inevitable. We all must rely on some degree of faith. We pay our mortgage because we have faith that money is real and that credit is real. We have faith that happiness exists and is possible to achieve. We have faith that living longer is worth it, so we strive to stay safe and healthy. Simply put, there's no such thing as an atheist. In the end, it's all faith.[27] Religious beliefs and their constituent group behaviours are a fundamental part of our nature. It's impossible *not* to adopt them. If we think we're above religion or God, and that we can use logic and reason alone, well then we're wrong. We all must have faith in something. We must find value somewhere. It's the only means to psychologically survive and thrive.

But I get it, we all have differing beliefs and values. Maybe you're not ready to accept this just yet, and that is fine. There's no rush. Just know that this step is open to you. Waiting. And if, and when, you're ready, it will help significantly in living the focused life.

Guru: The Personified Truth

It is a fact that in our corporate and professional life, the easiest way to move forward is to find a mentor who can guide and coach us. Such mentors have first-hand experience of the path, having 'been there and done that'. Dating back to ancient times, the word 'guru' has signified a *spiritual* teacher, mentor, or master – a person capable of guiding others to awaken to their true eternal self – the ātmā. In one of its meanings, 'gu' signifies 'darkness' and 'ru' means 'to destroy or eliminate'. Thus, the guru is the personality who destroys the darkness of ignorance from within us, bringing us into the light of the truth.

All the Vedic scriptures declare in unison that divine knowledge is to be received through the guru. The Mundaka Upanishad says, "To know the Absolute Truth, approach a guru who knows the scriptures, lives by them, and who is Brahman."[28] The Bhāgavata-Purāna says, "Seekers of the Truth should surrender themselves to the spiritual master who has understood the conclusion of the scriptures and is the very form of Brahman, leaving aside all material considerations."[29] Krishna says in the Bhagavad-Gitā, "Learn the truth by approaching the spiritual master. Inquire from him with reverence and render service unto him. Such an enlightened saint can impart knowledge unto you because he has seen the truth."[30]

The principle of guru-disciple succession can be found in many great religious traditions. In India, several successions are said to have started at the dawn of creation. Others began with the earthly appearance of a particular avatar or were given prominence by the teachings of a particular saint. Each guru in a succession is responsible for preserving and disseminating his or her tradition's teachings. By studying with a teacher from an unbroken line, we receive the original revelation, and by serving our teacher, we honour all the saints in that succession, and in all other true successions.

The paramparā system is intended to protect knowledge from misappropriation and adulteration. The analogy is given of receiving a ripe mango from the top of a mango tree. Several people climb the tree and form a line. The person on top hands the mango down to the person below, who passes it down to the next person, until the mango reaches the ground unbruised. The guru connects us to the current of truth that flows through scripture, while the community of aspirants confirms that truth by living its spirit. The guru is even more necessary since spiritual knowledge is not immediately perceptible to us. Furthermore, in the practical application of spiritual wisdom, we encounter many doubts and difficulties. To resolve this, the guru plays an essential role. But, there is a difference between a material and spiritual teacher. Whilst material teachers require only theoretical knowledge about a subject, the spiritual teacher has both theoretical knowledge and practical realisation too. In the Bhāgavata-Purāna, Krishna states his close bond with a true sadhu (synonymous to guru here), "The sadhu is my heart, and I am the heart of the sadhu."[31] Adi Shankaracharya, one of the foremost philosophers of India said, "If one has not attached one's mind at the feet of the guru, then of what use is life!" The famous English writer, Somerset Maugham, on meeting the renowned sage, Raman Maharshi in India, writes, "It is a mistake to think that those holy men of India lead useless lives. They are a shining light in the darkness. When a man becomes pure and perfect, the influence of his character spreads so that those who seek truth are naturally drawn to him."

To find such a guru is probably the greatest spiritual blessings that one can receive – I certainly feel this way – I feel fulfilled and content with my life, and that credit goes to my gurus: Pramukh Swami Maharaj and Mahant Swami Maharaj. In the BAPS tradition that I belong to, Swaminarayan's divinity continues, through the living, breathing spiritual guru, to guide, bless, and inspire spiritual aspirants seeking the truth, as well as humanity at large.

For several decades, Pramukh Swami Maharaj had perceived the pulse of individuals and society, identifying their areas of concern, and presenting practical solutions. This was possible due to his long-standing experience of having personally counselled thousands of individuals of all ages, from all strata of society, delivering over 22,000 discourses to audiences ranging from two to over 200,000; having read and replied personally to over 750,000 letters dealing with an incredibly wide range of personal, familial, business, social, spiritual and other issues.

Although he was not ranked as an outstanding orator, his sweet and soft voice, simple thoughts, and spiritual experiences conveyed profound spiritual wisdom. Sometimes serious, sometimes humorous, his discourses were heard with pin drop silence. As one who had spent his entire life in the service of others, Pramukh Swami Maharaj's teachings were accepted by all as being above any self-interest or bias, and also because his words resonated with profound philosophical insights that provided practical guidance. But the main reason why his words were received with so much trust and faith was due to the fact that he embodied what he preached. Every single piece of advice that he gave was lived as an integral part of his life. Former Solicitor General of Canada once said about Pramukh Swami, "You are so pious and pure that if the whole world took you as an example, it would be free of war, crime, and self-destruction. I think you have valid answers to life's toughest questions." Former president of India, Dr. A. P. J. Abdul Kalam called Pramukh Swami his "ultimate teacher," who taught him how "to remove 'I' and 'me'".

Throughout his life, Pramukh Swami Maharaj's mind remained light as a feather, despite fulfilling the difficult role of leading the activities of one of the fastest growing Hindu denominations in the world. His every action was an offering aimed only at pleasing God and his guru. He firmly believed this, and that is why he was able to accomplish every task with such perfection.

Today, Mahant Swami Maharaj – the current guru of BAPS – reaches out to the aspirants and others through vicharan (spiritual travels), public assemblies, personal meetings, correspondences, and phone calls. During these encounters, countless experience inner peace, joy, and self-confidence. Many find solutions to problems and find strength to abide by dharma. They are inspired with family unity, divine faith, and countless other virtues. Taking the refuge of a true guru is the easiest, shortest, and surest path to attain not only the highest truth, but also bliss – right here, right now. The guru guides, encourages, and blesses an aspirant to also attain moksha (ultimate liberation).

Ātmā: Waking Janak Up

The American biologist, E. O. Wilson says, the loss of any other species – ants, for instance – would result in 'major extinctions of other species and probably partial collapse of some ecosystems'. In terms of actual biomass too, our presence is negligible – mathematically, the total mass of the human race can be stacked like sardines into a space measuring just one cubic mile. That's all we are. Yet look at what we've done. We've stripped the forests. We've exhausted the soil. We've drained the rivers. We've almost emptied the earth of its natural resources. We've poisoned the land, water, and air with numerous toxic chemicals, and dozens more feast inside each of our bodies daily. At best, human beings are unnecessary and expendable. This is eye-opening and fundamental to knowing our true nature and purpose in this world, especially during our short stay here.

In a world where we are all engrossed in physical and mental identities that bind us, we somehow struggle to make time to even ponder upon our true self, let alone understand it. This form of self-inquiry is more important today, when so many of us struggle to find meaning in life. In Vedic literature, both the Upanishads and the Bhagavad-Gitā, begin with a thorough analysis of one's true identity.

The Bhāgavata-Purāna states, "After innumerable births and deaths, we achieve the rare human form of life, which, though temporary, grants us the opportunity to attain the highest perfection. Therefore, a sober human being should quickly endeavour for the ultimate perfection of life, as long as the body, always subject to death, has not expired. After all, sense gratification is available in the lowest and most gross species of life, whereas ultimate liberation is possible only for a human being."[32] The essence of the Bhagavad-Gitā too, is Krishna telling Arjun that his true self is the ātmā – the eternal soul. Everything that we experience is through the atma. The ātmā uses the body and mind as tools (or so it supposed to) to experience everything around us. The reason that we identify with the body and mind is because of the direct experiences they provide us, along with our attachment to these sensations.

Swaminarayan regularly emphasised upon the insatiability of the panchvishay[s], loosely translating to 'five senses'. It is better understood as 'the indulgence of desire *through* the five senses'. We spend so much of our time seeking out ways to satisfy our panchvishays through our physical (sthūl) and mental (sukshma) bodies, mostly thanks to the causal (kāran) body, that we often identify ourselves to at least the first two. But this is the illusion. No matter how amazing your car is, it simply cannot function without you as a driver. Fortunately, the driver can always function without the car. You are not your body, nor the mind. You are the eternal ātmā. This ātmā is not one with the body; it is the observer living inside it – it is the 'I' that is experiencing.

For so long, the commander, his monkey, and the ministers of the kingdom have been ruling freely. The king has been sleeping. It's time we wake Janak up. It's time we wake up the ātmā within us, because, that is where true strength, bliss, and power resides.

Certain schools of philosophy propose that the world and cosmos do not exist – they say that it is all an illusion, a dream that we'll all one day wake up from. If we briefly skim through Janak's story, we'll probably assume something similar. But, that is only the tip of the iceberg. In reality, the world, cosmos, soul, and everything around us is very much real, they are divine too – created by the divine energy of the Higher Power.

When the sage, Ashtavakra, told Janak that one dream ends when he opens his eyes, and another ends when he closes his eyes, it is best understood that he was referring to the temporary nature of the world. This experience of life we may call dreamlike. The dream is that we identify with the material body and material world around us. We also fail to realise that whilst we're in this temporary world, we have the intelligence and opportunity to free ourselves from this seemingly-inherent suffering, and instead, live a life filled with peace and happiness. It's important that we understand this dream philosophy correctly, otherwise, if recklessly applied, it can make us both irresponsible and negligible to those around us, and towards the world too.

We've also talked about suffering. It is a universal experience that affects all forms of life to some greater or less extent. We all suffer physically, mentally, or emotionally. But it is as we develop a deeper level of self-awareness – aligning our identity with the ātmā – that we learn to acknowledge suffering without identifying with it. Ultimately, the goal is to transcend it. I never believed that it was physically possible to transcend suffering, it all seemed mystical to me at one point, but don't they say, a great teacher brings his words to life through his own example? Whilst studying the life of Pramukh Swami, I came across numerous occasions throughout his life where he had detached from physical, and what we may call, mental suffering too. Sometimes that would be in the form of physical pain, like his bypass, gall bladder operation, cataracts, or even falls in his final years of life. At other times, it would be issues that would make us dejected like the incident of acquiring land for the London mandir. In all instances, Pramukh Swami reaffirmed to those around him, that the nature of existence is suffering and that we should accept what comes our way, understanding it to be the will of God. Suffering, he said, could be transcended, that is, if one continuously contemplates and believes themselves to be the ātmā. He wasn't simply preaching; he embodied this truth at every step of his own life – till his very last breath.

The Art of Detachment

Detachment is a difficult topic to talk about in such a limited time. Human life in itself is multi-faceted. We live in the world, so we must wear many hats. We have family, professional, social, and spiritual commitments, as well as much more. In the process of trying to balance all of these, we often experience a plethora of problems, such as stress, anxiety, fear, burnout, among many others. Stress, anxiety, and it's numerous counterparts are truly damaging. I'm not here to bombard you with facts, statistics, and it's knock-on effects. That's all stuff you can look into yourself. But it's true that whilst we march forward in the progress of humanity, when it comes to conquering the mind, humankind seems to be frozen in time. With social media taking over almost every aspect of our lives, an increasing number of people complain about feeling stressed out, anxious, and the likes.

Stress causes a range of negative emotions like tension, fear, distress, apprehension, and anxiety. On the physical level, it causes health problems such as headaches, acidity, ulcers, inflammation, increased blood pressure, obesity, and heart disease. Swami Vivekananda once said, "Life is the continuous unfoldment of a being under circumstances tending to press it downwards." Stress has its benefits, we cannot completely rid of it. We need it – it's built into our system, and so, the goal isn't to eliminate stressful situations. Instead, we want to eliminate the emotional stress that is generated within us, whilst appropriately responding to situations and events that occur in life. The stress that we experience is directly dependent on our own inner mental state, and not on any external situations.

The Essence of Karma Yoga

We can debate what the causes of our stress are, but we know that they will differ from person to person. If we wish to truly be free of stress, we need to look at its root cause – the flawed mentality that leads to it in the first place. And so, the first step in the art of detachment is to try and understand the origin of stress.

Stress develops when we are attached to the desire of a particular outcome, and we are worried that things may not turn out the way that we desire. It is obvious that stress is caused by our own attachments to a particular outcome and our unwillingness to accept the possibility of other results. The solution for stress is simple – we must try to give up attachment to preconceived or wishful outcomes of our own efforts. This doesn't mean that we should simply go with the flow of life as a passive participant, we must always put in our best efforts, but without attachment to the results. Krishna instructs Arjun in the famous Bhagavad-Gītā verse, "You have a right to perform your work, but you are not entitled to the fruits of those actions."[1] This is what Krishna refers to as karma yoga.

I know this may seem like a difficult concept to grasp, so let me try put it into an example. A banker in a bank received and disbursed thousands of pounds. Whilst doing so, he experiences neither anxiety nor stress, although he works with great care and diligence. But, if he withdraws his own salary and accidentally drops a bundle of notes on his way home, he may feel terribly stressed and anxious when he discovers his mistake. This is an example of an individual who is attached to his own money, whilst at the bank, he is simply performing his duty. This may be a very abstract example, but from my own experiences, I have seen karma yoga in action in the life of Pramukh Swami.

Despite leading and overseeing over 160 activities across the globe, Pramukh Swami never felt an ounce of stress in anything he did. When asked on numerous occasions how he was able to remain at peace and ease, he said, "Man believes that he does everything. We think, 'I will make the world, family, and society happy.' But in reality this is arrogance, and wherever the ego operates, there is bound to be downfall. The truth is that God is the doer. It is he who does everything. We do nothing. Having such faith, one can realise their atma, attain success in life, and be happy and peaceful in all ways."

For ninety-five years, Pramukh Swami's life depicted this at every moment. He truly worked without attachment to outcomes and results, and hence, he was always able to remain at peace. Today, Mahant Swami lives the same way. Their state of being is echoed in the Bhagavad-Gitā, where Krishna says, "The person who gives up all material desires and lives free from a sense of greed, proprietorship, and egoism, he alone attains perfect peace."[2]

Of course, this also gives rise to another question: If we give up attachments to the results, won't that decrease our drive, motivation, performance and effectiveness for the work at hand? But history shows us that when we become free from negative emotions like tension, anxiety, and nervousness (stemming from our addiction to having things turn the way we want them to), our effectiveness and performance will only increase. Joshua Baker, who's authored a bestselling book, *Simplify: 7 Guiding Principles to Help Anyone Declutter Their Home & Life*, writes, "Not just the outcome, but the process that experiencing happiness only upon achieving an outcome for our efforts robs us of countless moments along the way." If we simply focus on the present moment, on the joy of the work at hand, we can experience the joy of work. We can then give our best efforts and let the results flow as they do. Becker also concludes that 'results-only' focus is short-sighted and distracts us from applying ourselves to that which we can control, which is our time and energy. If we believe that happiness can only be experienced in the future, on reaching a certain goal or outcome, we miss out on enjoying the journey towards the goal – which is only in the present.

In simple terms, a karma yogi is one who keeps their mind equipoised, whilst engaging in the turmoil of worldly duties. Karma Yoga is the synthesis of both karma, 'action', and, yoga, 'union with God'. This is how Pramukh Swami lived. This is how Mahant Swami lives. This is how I want to live. The main focus of the Krishna's teachings in the Bhagavad-Gitā surrounds karma yoga. It teaches us not to artificially renounce our work, thinking of it to be cumbersome; but instead, to be in internal equilibrium even whilst performing complex tasks, and detaching from the outcomes.

We have a desire to be in control and to dictate every aspect of our life. But the reality is we are only in control of a small number of things in life. Once we accept that most things are outside of our control, the key is to let go of our desire to control the outcomes. Learning how to ride the waves rather than seeking to stop them happening is what this is all about. What we need in life is to loosen up, to become flexible, to get to a place where there is nothing in our way – and that includes our own obsession with certain outcomes. Only through reducing our attachments, can we truly live the focused life.

What Fire Can Teach Us

Action is natural to us – it is almost innate. If we trip and fall, our body's instant instinct will be to protect us. We extend our hands forward to stop us from smashing our face against the ground. We touch a flame, and instantly the body pulls away. We don't think, we don't complain, we don't argue. We simply act. But when it comes to our day-to-day lives, we fail. We fail to act when we need to. When something needs doing, we distract ourselves. Or sleep. Or wait. Or procrastinate. We don't act. To some, it feels better to ignore or to pretend. But deep down we know that this isn't going to help us in any way. We often forget the truth that in life, it doesn't matter what happens to us, or where we come from. What matters most is what we do with what happens and what we've been given. No one is going to save us. We must learn to save ourselves.

In the late nineteenth century, Thomas Edison wasn't the only individual playing with incandescent lights. But he was the only person willing to try six thousand different filaments – including one made from the beard hair of one of his own men – inching closer each time to the one that finally worked. In applying all of his physical and mental energy – in never giving up and striving to act – Thomas Edison outdid impatient competitors, investors, and the media to discover, in a piece of bamboo, surprisingly, the power to light up the world. [3]

What stands in our way isn't going to just simply disappear. Margaret Thatcher famously said, "You turn if you want to. The lady's not for turning."[4] Too often, we think that great success comes from flashes of insight or genius, but in fact, it is slow work, and repetitive action, that gives promising outcomes. Working at it works. It's that simple. But it isn't easy. We must persist in our efforts – always.

Sometimes we get discouraged, and that's fine. But it isn't okay to give up. To know that we may feel like giving up, yet maintaining ground and still moving forward – that's real persistence. Life is supposed to be hard. We shouldn't ask questions of to why it is, or, why on us. We just have to act. When setbacks come your way, respond twice as hard. Keep persisting. Keep acting. That is the art of action with detachment.

Thomas Edison was sixty-seven, when he was returning home one early evening from his day at the laboratory. Shortly after his dinner, a man came rushing into his home screaming that a fire had broken out at Edison's research and production campus just a few miles away. Fire engines rushed to the scene, but they too, failed to put out the flames.

Fuelled by the various chemicals in the various buildings, flames continued to shoot up into the sky, threatening to destroy Edison's lifelong empire. Edison didn't run and scream, nor did he become stressed or angry. He made his way calmly through the hundreds of shocked onlookers and devastated employees, trying to find his son. "Go call your mother and all of her friends," he told him with excitement. "They will probably never see a fire like this again!"

You're probably thinking he was crazy, but wait. Edison then calmed his sulking son and said, "It's fine! We've just got rid of a lot of rubbish." Now this reaction is shocking – in an amazing way. But then, when we think about, could there have been any other appropriate response? What else could Edison have done? Cry? Got mad? Screamed at his employees? Ran home? And then, where would that have got him? We already know the answer: nowhere and nothing. He accepted the result of what had happened, regardless of it not even being his fault.

A similar incident took place in 2009, at Delhi Akshardham. At the time, this was the crown creation of Pramukh Swami Maharaj. In the month of June, the inner sanctum of the Akshardham temple was damaged by a fire. The six murtis, including the 11-foot murti of Bhagwan Shri Swaminarayan had toppled and were damaged when the platform gave way. When swamis saw what had happened, how did they react? Some of them obviously became distraught. A small accident had caused so much damage, and how would Pramukh Swami residing 800 miles away in Mumbai react to this event? The swamis immediately called Pramukh Swami, who listened calmly and carefully to the details of the incidents being narrated. Once they had finished, he replied calmly, "Whatever has happened, it is God's own wish. Don't be upset. Instead, we should accept the wish of God, and what will be reconstructed will be even more magnificent."

This reaction seems almost fictional, but it was very real. Pramukh Swami persevered for decades to build this magnificent temple on the banks of the river Yamuna, as a tribute to the vision of his guru, Yogiji Maharaj. Yet his response and mental stability at the time were unmatched. It gave hope to the swamis and all those present to move forward with utmost faith and resilience. This is just one, but there are numerous such incidents throughout the life of Pramukh Swami, where he has maintained the pinnacle of mental stability and acceptance, understanding whatever happens to be the wish of God. Now, regardless of our beliefs, to do great things, we *need* to be able to endure tragedy and setbacks. I pray and hope that we don't have to face and endure as much as Edison or Pramukh Swami did, but nevertheless, we've got to love what we do and all that it entails – both the good and the bad.

Natural ups and downs will surely come in our life, but whether we choose to come out the other end with personal growth or personal fears, that is up to us. Which of these dominates our life is completely dependent on how well we view the situation at hand. Change can be viewed as exciting or frightening, but regardless of how you may view it, we must all face the fact that change is the natural way of life.

The focused life is one of constant transformation. In order to grow, we must give up the struggle to remain as we are, and learn to embrace change all the time – at any time. We usually try to solve our inner conflicts by defending ourselves. But it turns out that the life you live in order to protect yourself from the problem is a perfect representation of the problem itself.

We have to learn to find joy in every single thing that happens. We have to act, and then detach from the outcome. We don't get to choose what happens to us, but we can always choose how we feel about it. Initially, it may seem a little crazy to feel gratitude for things that we never wanted to happen in the first place. But now, I hope you know, that opportunities for growth and peace lie within adversities. In overcoming them, we only emerge stronger, sharper, empowered, and of course, happier.

The Art of Bhakti

The word 'bhakti' is popular throughout Indian tradition. In a very simplified sense, it means 'unconditional devotion and love for God'. To give some setting to this word, around the sixth century, a bhakti movement developed in the Indian subcontinent, particularly by the wise men who extracted the essence of the Vedas. They put less emphasis on the formalities of ritual and caste.

Most of these individuals, expressed their divine love and devotion for God through philosophy, songs, and poetry. These revelations were gradually expanded by their disciples and were thus organised into schools by the likes of Ramanuja (1017-1137), Madhva (1238-1317), Nimbarka (ca. eleventh century), Vallabha (1479-1531), and Chaitanya (1486-1533). Bhakti was given even greater emphasis, and flourished even further in the eighteenth century with Sahajanand Swami's (the initiation name of Swaminarayan) travels throughout India and settling within Gujarat.

Swaminarayan, on many occasions and through his teachings, emphasised that regardless of whatever endeavours one performs, ultimately, all of them form the basis for bhakti. He taught, and showed, how it is through bhakti, that one can unveil the inner peace and bliss that intrinsic to the ātmā, and thus connect with the Higher Power. In this very brief section, I describe some of the key aspects of the dharmic life through bhakti. Again, I ask you to keep an open mind as you read on.

Seva: Selfless Service

To love is to serve. In the joy of others, lies our own. The greatest fulfilment in life can be found through selfless service. In Sanskrit, the word 'seva' is somewhat synonymous to this. For simplicity, understand the word to encompass acts of selfless service and giving with pure intention. In the modern world we often live contrarily to this notion. We live in a world of give-and-take; we live in a world where everything has a price. We don't feel the need to serve others if it doesn't benefit us. And so, we have been brought up to believe that this is the only true way to live. But is it?

There are many reasons that seva can be beneficial. The first is obvious, it gives us a sense of meaning. But, it also increases our social activity, introduces us to novel and potentially exciting activities, and because we genuinely try to improve the world, we develop an increased self-esteem. One of the biggest benefits of selfless service is that it is mostly done as part of a collective group.

Whether we consciously know it or not, many of us will work long hours, or fill up our time with other activities, so that we remain distant from other pain. Some of us use the office as a space to hide, to avoid harder, more emotionally intense work, like being a good partner, friend, parent, or child. What we often do is we confuse the term 'leisure' with 'amusements'. These are the short breaks and welcomed distractions that come alongside work. These moments are necessary, but they don't require much of us. Aristotle said, "Amusements are more to be used when one is at work, for one who exerts himself needs relaxation, and relaxation is the end of amusement, and work is accompanied by toil and strain... we should be careful to use amusement at the right time, dispensing it as a remedy to the ills of work."

The American poet and visionary, Ralph Waldo Emerson said, "It is one of the most beautiful compensations in this life that no one can sincerely try to help another without helping himself." We live in a world where everything is based on reciprocity. We give and receive. We breathe and exhale. We live and we die. The entire cyclical cosmos is such. The more we give, the more we receive.

We must strive to make seva a core part our life. Socrates referred to true leisure as 'the most valuable of possessions'. When we get it right, we see improvements in every aspect of our lives. True love for humanity and creation is expressed through seva of those in need, and this love expands to inspire us to serve those outside our own societies, or even species. As we gain a deeper understanding of our true inherent nature as the ātmā, we appreciate that serving others becomes a very form of devotion to the higher power, and this is one of the most valuable gifts of life. With this awareness, we can recognise opportunities to perform seva within our families, friends, society, or wherever we are.

Seva is the most powerful force on the planet. I learnt this from the life of Pramukh Swami. Giving is a form of love that we can count on, because it is always within our choice; it's always within our power to give. The startling findings from many studies demonstrate that if you engage in helping activities from a younger age, you will *still* be reaping health benefits sixty or seventy years later. Service in high school predicts good physical and mental health all the way into late adulthood. It reduces mortality significantly in later life, even if you start late. Doug Oman of the University of California at Berkeley followed almost two thousand individuals over the age of fifty-five for over five years. Those who volunteer for two or more organisations have an impressive forty-four per cent lower likelihood of dying – and that's after eliminating every other contributing factor, including physical exercise, gender, habits such as smoking, marital status, and more. Service reduces adolescent depression and suicide risk. It also helps us to forgive ourselves for our own mistakes, which plays a key role in our sense of well-being.[1]

Research by the sociologist Marc Musick of the University of Texas in Austin, along with his colleagues, found that for people age sixty-five and older, volunteering substantially reduced symptoms of depression. When we serve selflessly, it's likely that we turn off the fight-or-flight response. Serving pushes aside the brooding negative emotions that afflict us all, like rage, spite, and envy, all that clearly contribute to stress-induced psychological and physical illness.[2]

To serve others is to give. The truly great have sacrificed their entire lives in the service of others. The most powerful force on the planet is giving. Giving is the one type of love you can rely on since you always choose to give – it is always within your power to do so. It has a direct impact across your entire lifespan. Giving in high school predicts good physical and mental health throughout late adulthood, a time span of more than fifty years. Giving reduces mortality in later life greatly, even if you start late. Giving lowers the incidence of adolescent sadness and suicide. Giving has a greater ability to lower mortality than receiving. Giving to others allows us to forgive ourselves for our own faults, which is essential for the focused life. When we give, we most likely switch off our fight-or-flight reaction. Giving sweeps aside the lingering negative feelings, such as fury, malice, and jealousy, which definitely contribute to stress-related psychological and physical disorders.

Gratitude

We can only truly serve others when we feel a sense of gratitude for humanity at large. I firmly believe that every human, at their very essence, has the ability to feel this universal sense of gratitude. It goes way beyond simply having good manners. Manners are a form of social custom, gratitude is a state of human *being*. To be situated in a state of gratitude is about having an awareness of, and deep appreciation for, all existence and creation. You must have experienced the soothing feeling that you get when you genuinely get to thank someone for doing something for you. We feel great for receiving what we may have received, and we feel greater when we thank them too. And then, they feel appreciated, and they feel great too. And the cycle continues.

Studies show that the most grateful individuals have often been through difficult and challenging experiences in life. Recent research shows that emotions work at lightning speed and often bypass human reasoning, activating more ancient parts of the 'emotional' brain. And so, by cultivating gratitude, we encourage positive emotions that are almost instantaneous. They are more powerful, in their own way, than positive thoughts alone.

According to a recent study on organ donations, the more gratitude a recipient of an organ feels, the faster their recovery. In a 1998 Gallup survey of America teenagers and adults, ninety-five per cent of respondents felt at least somewhat happy when expressing gratitude, and over half felt extremely happy. People who see themselves as grateful – both to others and to creation in general – are healthier, more energetic and optimistic, more empathic, and less vulnerable to clinical depression. Grateful people tend to be less materialistic and so, they are more easily satisfied with what life brings them. If you feel grateful, you are more likely to nurture, care for, and contribute to the welfare of others. You will be more empathetic, forgiving, and helpful.

So how do we begin to practice gratitude in our lives? We often unwittingly climb onto the hedonic treadmill, where we rapidly adapt to good things and begin to take them for granted. Two primal brain regions – the amygdala and the nucleus accumbens – modulate our anticipation of pleasure and reward, and these centres inevitably cause us to crave *new* pleasures. Consciously focusing on gratitude could potentially help us subvert our own insatiability that we discussed earlier. In a study conducted by Philip Watkins and his colleagues, gratitude was strongly linked to a form of emotional intelligence known as mood-repair. Further fascinating evidence of gratitude's power comes from a 2001 study of trauma survivors by the psychologist Russell Kolts of Eastern Washington University. He found that those who scored high on gratitude had significantly lower symptoms of post-traumatic stress disorder. Gratitude should not only be shown to those close to us – or around us – but also to the higher power, to whom we offer our gratitude for being here today. You are more likely to nurture, care for, and contribute to the well-being of others if you are grateful. You'll be more sympathetic, forgiving, and helpful as a result.

Why Serve?
A truly remarkable study emerged from England in 2004 from researchers at the University of Essex. They found that neighbourhoods with the highest levels of volunteerism had less crime, better schools, and happier, healthier residents. This was true of every place studied, from the inner city to the rural village. The researchers looked at 101 localities, mailing questionnaires to around 9,000 individuals and interviewing 3,000 in detail.

According to Doug Oman, "Volunteering is associated with substantial reductions in mortality." Volunteers not only live longer, but they are generally healthier too. One thirty-year long study of 427 women in upstate New York, who were both wives and mothers, found that those who did any kind of volunteering had better physical functioning thirty years later. Volunteer activity significantly reduced symptoms of depression in persons aged 65 and over, according to the research by sociologist Marc Musick which I mentioned earlier.

New research shows that nurturing others may feel good because it is rewarded by spikes in dopamine. A 2005 study in the journal *Molecular Psychiatry* found that a common variation of a gene that regulates the neurotransmitter dopamine was highly linked to altruistic behaviour. In a 2005 study conducted by Alex Harris and Carl

Thoresen of Stanford University, frequent volunteering was strongly linked with delayed mortality in more than 7,500 Americans over the age of seventy, who lived in communities for the elderly. [3]

In a 2018 online poll of 5,000 individuals, when given with the option to play Robin Hood, the majority of both Americans and Germans opted not to take from the affluent in order to transfer money to the poor.

Infants as young as fifteen months are taken aback when crackers are not evenly distributed between two recipients. Toddlers understand that they must share equally with third persons, even if they keep the majority for themselves. Six to eight-year-olds would rather dispose of the odd treat in order to preserve an equal portion when there are an odd number of goodies to be distributed between two receivers. This shows that there is something inherently good about humans, it's not all bad, is it? At eighteen months, children will spontaneously pick up dropped items and open doors or boxes to help an experimenter even when they are not specifically told to do so or given a reward.[4] In fact, some even argue that the basic principle of helping others out of goodwill is what makes us uniquely human.[5]

Great people come to this earth to serve, and not to be served. A candle loses nothing of its light by lighting another candle. We are the candles. By lighting the heart of someone else, we only allow our own hearts to be lit. It's easy to say that we will die for someone. It's much harder to live for them. Love begets love. Shakespeare's Romeo put it nicely: "The more I give to thee, the more I have, for both are infinite."

Satsang: The Cure to Loneliness

The motivational speaker, Jim Rohr, said that we are the average of the five people we spend the most time with. Another well-known saying goes, "Tell me who your friends are, and I will tell you what you are." Who we associate with, who we accompany ourselves with, defines who we are as an individual. Pramukh Swami often used to define the word 'satsang' as keeping the company of those who are true, good, and noble. He used to say that with the company of good people, we are inspired by wholesome thoughts, and thus, we are able to maintain our integrity.

I need not even tell you this, because it is probably obvious. We know that when we are around certain people, their vibes pass on to us. Now, don't get me wrong here, I'm not talking about all the 'energy vibes' stuff here, there's no such 'secret'. But in a very general sense, we know that being around positive people makes us feel more positive and energetic. In Vedic teachings, satsang can be simply understood to mean being in the company of like-minded individuals, who raise our spirits high, who we enjoy being in the presence of, and who also seek the spiritual essence. The company that we keep has a direct impact on our mind and wellbeing.

It's true that so much of our lives are shaped by the people we spend the most time with, and the company that we keep is a common way that we set ourselves up for unhappiness. If you find yourself preoccupied with a certain friendship or relationship that is making you tired, or feeling almost addicted to the idea of being 'less than', or, 'jealous of', you need to gradually phase out of it. You don't need to be rude, abrupt, or even cut anyone out of your life. You do, however, need to understand that the people you spend the most time with will define your future almost irrevocably.

When we hang around those who consistently complain, whine, or have pessimistic views, we know how difficult it can get to a place of positive headspace. We must actively try to stay away from those whose thoughts and minds are limited, and instead hang around those who have a broader mindset. Surround yourself with those who act upon their big ideas, who seriously take action on making a positive change in the world. How you do one thing is how you will do everything.

We all need to belong. We simply cannot be alone. When we are on our own, our health deteriorates and life expectancy is shortened. The average person spends eighty per cent of their waking hours among people, and social time is preferred over alone time. Even those who intentionally seek solitude, such as swamis and monks, are not exceptions to the trend. This helped me answer the long-standing question in my mind of how the swamis at Sarangpur were full of joy and peace – they felt connected. "It is not enough to simply be surrounded by people," one swami told me. "We must also feel a sense of belonging; a united purpose." We need to form emotional relationships with others in order to flourish and sustain the social bonds that are holding us together.

I'm going to take you back to the German story for a moment. After the war, those quick to criticise German citizens accused them of apathy (indifference) because they did nothing to stop the Nazis' persecution. However, there is another point of view that comes from the out-group perspective. Because the individuals targeted were members of society's minorities, the majority did not feel endangered – it was not their concern. Initially, during the pre-war years, the process was gradual, so there did not appear to be a big cause for alarm. People then overlooked what was going on after the ultimate answer was in place.

Of course, as I mentioned earlier, the circumstances that led up to the Holocaust are extremely complicated and there were many contributing factors. We don't want to jump to any judgements or conclusions. It is easy to cast judgement on others in retrospect, but the ease with which people seemed to slip into moral depravity or, at the very least, an unwillingness to help the persecuted is a testament to the power of association. Rather than rejecting an entire nation as indifferent, anti-Semitic, or even evil, it is more sensible to seek reasons that address how people behave once they connect with a group and believe they are different.

The world events today show us that nothing has really changed. History always repeats itself with every ethnic conflict that arises around the globe. One of the most disturbing aspects of our species is that ordinary people will turn on others who they regard as different. British psychologists Steve Reicher and Alex Haslam, who recreated Zimbardo's famous Stanford prison study in 2002, point out, "People do great wrong, not because they are unaware of what they are doing but because they consider it to be right. This is possible because they actively identify with groups whose ideology justifies and condones the oppression and destruction of others."[6]

I don't think I am anyone to conclude whether humans are good or bad, but I do want to share one story. A scorpion and a frog met on a riverbank one day. Because he couldn't swim, the scorpion requested that the frog carry him across the lake on his back. "Hold on," the frog murmured, "How do I know you won't sting me?" "Are you insane?" said the scorpion. "If I sting you, we'll both die." As a result, the frog consented to carry the scorpion across the river on his back. The frog felt a painful, lethal puncture from the scorpion's tail halfway across. "What made you do that? Now we're both doomed," wailed the frog, filled with poison, as they both began to fall into the sea. The scorpion said, "I can't help myself! It's in my blood."

This story of the scorpion and the frog has been retold for thousands of years, it's nothing new. It's a story about how our desires and impulses may take over our actions, even when it's not in our best interests. We want to think we have control, but our biology can occasionally get in the way of what is best for us. We believe that as animals with the ability to reason, we are capable of making educated judgments as we traverse the complexities of life. However, many of the judgments we make are actually influenced by processes that we are not always aware of, or, if we are aware, they appear to be beyond our control. From the Vedic viewpoint, this is considered to be due to the influence of the three gunas that envelope all creation. We all have the capacity to be slaves to our desires and instincts, yet we frequently fail to keep them in check. How many of us have lost our cool behind the wheel of a car, spoken things we should have kept to ourselves, or acted in ways we never thought we could? Scorpions may be rigid and inflexible, but humans have a considerably greater capability to regulate their urges. That onus is on us.

A Disconnection from 'Them'
Today, loneliness lingers over humankind like a thick mist. More people than ever before report feeling lonely. Feeling extremely lonely appears to be as stressful as being punched by a stranger. Those who are lonely are three times more likely to develop the flu than those who have many close relationships with others. When you are alone, almost everything gets more deadly: cancer, heart disease, and respiratory difficulties. It results in depression.

Loneliness comes before depressed symptoms. You become lonely, which is followed by feelings of despair, deep sadness, and depression. And the impact is enormous. Imagine a straight line representing the range of loneliness in our culture. On one end, you are not alone. On the other end of the spectrum, you are completely alone. If you moved from the middle (fifty per cent) to the top (sixty-five per cent), your risk of having depressed symptoms increased eightfold.

We are not made to be alone, we need to live in tribes as bees live in hives. Loneliness seems to no longer be a mere fleeting feeling, but the way most of us are living our lives. People's belief that they live in some form of community, or even have friends that they can count on is falling dramatically.

We eat together as a family much less; we watch TV together as a family much less; and we go on vacation together much less. In the last quarter of the twentieth century, virtually all forms of family togetherness had become less common. We do things together less than any previous generation. Long before the 2008 economic catastrophe, there was a social crash in which we found ourselves alone and lonely significantly more often.

Loneliness isn't simply the absence of other people. It's the feeling that you're not sharing anything important with anyone else. If you have a lot of people around you – perhaps even a husband or wife, a family, or a busy workplace – but you don't share something important with them, you'll still feel lonely.

We've come to assume that doing things alone is the natural state of life and the only way to progress. We've started to think: "I'll take care of myself, and everyone else should take care of themselves as individuals. Nobody else can help you but you. Nobody else can help me except me." These notions have now permeated our culture to the point where we offer them as feel-good chemicals to those who are down, as if it will boost them up.

The Internet arrived, promising us access. But it was born into a world where many people had already lost touch with one another. We live in a culture where people aren't getting the relationships they need to be healthy humans, which is why we can't put down our phones or stand to log off. We will tell ourselves that we spend so much of our time in cyberspace because it connects us - that we are plugged into a swirling party with billions of others. We are designed to connect with one another in a secure, caring way, which is completely absent when it is mediated by a screen. Social media cannot psychologically compensate us for what we have lost – our social lives. Our excessive usage of social media is an attempt to bridge the loneliness gap. "Every status post is just a variation of a single request: 'Would someone please acknowledge me?'" wrote the American comedian Marc Maron.

Becoming 'Free'

For a long time, social scientists have understood that there is a big gap between how we think of ourselves in Western countries and how people throughout most of Asia think of themselves. There are numerous small experiments you may conduct to demonstrate this. For example, present a group of Western friends a photograph of a man addressing a crowd. Request that they describe what they saw. Then approach the next group of Chinese visitors you come across, show them the same image, and ask them to describe it. The Westerners nearly always describe the individual in the front of the group in great detail first, followed by a description of the crowd. For

Asians, it's the opposite way around: they'll describe the crowd first, and then, almost as an afterthought, they'll describe the individual in front of them.

If you want to pursue happiness in the United States or the United Kingdom, you do so for yourself – because you believe that is how it works. You do what most of us do the majority of the time: You get things for yourself, you rack up accomplishments for yourself, and you boost your own ego. But if you seek happiness purposefully in India, Japan, or China, you do something entirely different. You work hard to improve things for your group – for the people around you. That is what you believe happiness to be, therefore it appears obvious to you.

In the West, we have reduced our concept of ourselves to only our ego (or, at most, our family), which has increased our sorrow and decreased our happiness. Just consider the most common and obvious clichés: Be yourself. Be you. We repeat that all the time to one another. We make memes out of it. We say that to encourage folks who are feeling lost or dejected. Because you're worth it, even our shampoo bottles say. But, as I've learned over the years, if you want to stop feeling sad, don't be yourself. Don't make it all about you. Don't obsess over how valuable you are. Thinking about you, you, you is what's contributed to your sadness in the first place. Don't be you. Be us. Become we. Become a member of the group. Make the group's time and effort worthwhile. The true route to happiness comes from tearing down our ego walls of the kingdom – from allowing yourself to flow into other people's stories and allowing their stories to flow into yours; from pooling your identity, from realising that you were never you – alone, heroic, tragic – all along. No, don't be yourself. Be connected with everyone around you. Become a member of the whole. The ego is not the answer. The only solution is to look beyond it. And remember, even if you are in discomfort, you can almost always make someone else feel better.

Back to the topic of satsang, if we look at the definition from a spiritual perspective, Mahant Swami describes true association as four things in the Satsang Diksha: to associate with the ātmā, which is the true essence of our being; to associate with Paramātmā, who is the the true supreme soul, or higher power; to associate with the guru, who is the personification of the highest spiritual state; and to associate with the shāstras, which encompass the true knowledge.

From the bottom of my heart, I can say that I find my inner peace and tranquility through the foundation of satsang in my life. Those that I associate with on a day-to-day basis are aligned with my purpose and values, and that gives me hope, resilience, and faith in life. Choose your company wisely. Check your values. Check those around you. Do they align? Your satsang will determine your outlook on life. Your satsang will define who you become.

Moksha: Eternal Bliss

Hindus, as well as a number of religions flourishing from the roots of India, believe that the ultimate goal of life is to attain moksha, or, ultimate liberation from the cycles of life and death. Moksha is a state of eternal bliss, joy, and happiness derived from God, empty of pain and suffering that accompanies our mundane lives.

The state of param ānanda (eternal bliss) is the state of moksha itself. It is often misunderstood that liberation is reserved only for the life hereafter, but this is not the case. The state of moksha can be experienced here on earth too. To attain moksha it is necessary to live according to dharma, which encourages one to behave in accordance with laws of righteousness and duty, as prescribed by the Vedic scriptures. Truthfulness, devotion, service, charity, restraint, selflessness, family, and non-violence are at the core of dharma.

To attain this state of moksha, all of the 'arts' we've discussed so far are prerequisites to getting a glimpse of this eternal bliss. Once we're regularly taking good care of our bodies, once we understand and have conversations with the mind, and once we begin to establish ourselves in the arts of dharma, knowledge (gnān), detachment (vairāgya), and bhakti, only then can we truly begin living the focused life.

The most important out of these is bhakti. Without bhakti, our life ceases to have true meaning – even with all the knowledge you may imbibe or practice. Without seva and true satsang, it is all futile. It's difficult. The road of the wise is never easy to tread, but it's down to us to take the first step. Then comes the art of ruling.

The Art of Ruling

If the king didn't know the art of ruling, the people would not obey his orders; rather, they would begin to beat him. Then, his country would become desolate, or he himself would behave miserably because no one would obey his rule… Similarly, if the jiva were to attempt to rule the kingdom in the form of the body without understanding the art of ruling, then it would never become happy.
Bhagwan Shri Swaminarayan

This is where all roads meet – in the art of ruling. At the end of the day, we all want to know how we can live a focused life here and now. The questions that crop up within our mind are more to do with ourselves than with other people. And so, it is necessary we rule the kingdom, ministers, and subjects in such a manner.

As we begin to draw this part of our journey to an end, in this final part, I have consolidated my journal thoughts and notes on various topics that I wanted to dive into, but that I didn't want to limit to other parts of this book. You will find that a broad range of areas have been covered, and this by no means is in its full capacity. We will discuss about our own nature, love, trauma, healing, relationships, forgiveness, letting go, success, habits, and a few other topics. Pages are limited, words are limitless. I hope that this part of the book serves not only as an introduction to these various thoughts and truths of human flourishing, but also as a bedrock for the journey to come.

On You

Your life is defined not only by what you think about it, but also by what you think about yourself. Your self-identity is an idea that you've spent your whole life building up. The kingdom and its subjects are near and dear to the ministers and the king. This self-image is often difficult to adjust, partially because the confirmation bias works to affirm our pre-existing beliefs about ourselves.

It's always important to remain humble. Always contemplate on how small we are. We should always stop to think about the reality of our existence. Yes, our presence in this world is integral and necessary, but we should never forget that we are a small speck in the vast cosmos. As much as we may think that life is an illusion, it is also remarkable in, and of, itself. There is a higher power at work that we may try to understand, but we can never fully comprehend. Whenever you feel lost or hopeless, take a step outside, look up into the sky and realise that you have been put on this earth, as a human being, for some reason. You are somewhere where you may never be again. Your actions – every single moment, of every single day – no matter how inconsequential you may think they are, are essential. It also helps to meditate on your mortality; a practice revered by Hindus, Buddhists, and the Stoics alike.

We often think that everyone is thinking about us, judging us, evaluating us, and determining our status in life. But in reality, they aren't. In the digital world, we have all become likened to 'mini-celebrities', at least within our own circles, and so, we become convinced that everyone around us is disproportionately concerned with the smallest of details about our lives. Let me remind you that in a number of decades, you will be gone. The place you call home will be sold to a new group of homo sapiens. Your job will be filled by someone else. Your kids will follow the same pattern. Your work will be done. And you will then pass from this world. I am not saying all of this to depress you. Realising the reality of our existence helps us to align our purpose in life to what we truly want to achieve; it keeps us humble.

Nobody is thinking about us in the way that we think they are thinking about us. Everyone, for the most part, is thinking about themselves. When you feel anxious about your accomplishments or failures, remind yourself that nobody is looking and nobody cares. You may choose to disagree with me, but truthfully, everyone is always focused on themselves. Whether that focus is misaligned, or aligned to a greater purpose, we are all on our own individual journeys. This is true of absolutely everything in life. Nobody is evaluating 'you'. They are taking you at face value. We must stop thinking that we're the at the centre of the universe. This world is not about us. Our lives aren't even all about us. The more we put aside our own spotlight complexes, the more we will be able to live in peace.

Inner peace is the state of being connected to something higher than ourselves. Inner peace is the deep internal feeling that everything is okay and always will be. Why? Because there is a higher power at work. The concept of finding one's 'inner peace' has been central to both spiritual and metaphysical practices for centuries, and it has become even more mainstream with the development of popular psychology. People who live with inner peace are not delusional. They don't believe that they are perfect either. This is not what makes them mentally strong. Instead, they are very well aware of their different strengths and weaknesses. The ability to say to yourself: "I know I am struggling with this, so I am going to take my time and work on it," is one of the most powerful things that you can do. To feel true peace, you must also be willing to be disliked. This doesn't mean that we behave in a malicious or hurtful manner towards others, but it's the understanding that no matter what we do, others will always judge us. Mentally strong people know this. There is no path in life that we can take where we will be free of resistance from others, and so it is necessary that we not only come to terms with being disliked, but also anticipate it and act regardlessly.

The French philosopher and author, Albert Camus said, "In the midst of the winter, I found there was, within me, an invincible summer. And that makes me happy." Pramukh Swami, when asked how we can live in peace, said, "By making others unhappy one cannot gain peace. By making others happy, and helping others benefit, we gain peace and become happy. In the joy of others lies our own. In the happiness of others lies our own. This is an eternal law." The entirety of inner peace is summed up in this. It is the understanding that no matter what is happening around us, there is still a place of total knowing, realisation, and calmness within us. Finding our inner peace is connecting to the deepest truth within us. Inner peace isn't something we create, justify, imagine, conceptualise, or reach for. It's always within us and it's within other people. It's always an option – a choice – that we must simply choose to make.

As much as we also like to think that we are perfect and good, we cannot deny the reality of humanity. Humans *can* be terrible awful, some even to the extent that they feast upon the unhappiness of others, through unpleasant, dangerous, or plan evil actions. I'm sure you can think of some individuals throughout history, as well as those close to you. But what we must also understand is that nobody is really 'wrong'. Nobody is doing anything 'bad' per se. It is simply that no two people think or act alike, and what you might find to be right, may be different for someone else. This isn't delusional thinking or ignorance, this is a liberating truth that will truly set you free. When you begin to see others in a positive light, and begin to notice your own flaws that you need to work on, this is the first step to truly knowing yourself.

Studies have shown that even if people know that something is wrong or harmful, particularly when it comes to their own health, they seem to persist in doing it regardless. Of course, we can say that this is partly due of our brain, because as powerful as they are, they still have their limits. There are many other ways we can destroy ourselves, but one particular way, without a doubt, is the most devastating and damaging of all. It's when we invest all our energy into believing we are not good enough. We fail to love ourselves. I am not particularly fond of positive affirmations as a thing on its own. I believe that to truly grow and develop a resilient mindset, we shouldn't veil our flaws and insecurities, but instead confront them and then work towards eliminating them.

Of course, you are unique, but in the sense that there will never be anyone exactly like you. You have your own way of being in the world, and you have a perspective that is unique to you. You are the only one who thinks your thoughts the way that you do. You are the creator of your own reality, and you live your life according to your own unique values, beliefs, and path. Realising this is the first step.

Don't compare yourself to others. Life isn't a race. Have you ever done something that you're so proud of and feel you've mastered? That is until you see someone else having done a similar thing better than you, and then, in your mind, you feel inferior. Comparison is the fastest way to take the joy out of our life. It's none of your business what others are doing. Live your life focusing on your dharma and purifying your karma.

You must also learn to forgive yourself. Everyone has messed up in the past. You are not alone. Messing up is a part of adversity and growth in human life. Dragging around guilt and self-criticism is unhealthy, pointless, boring, and it will drain you mentally. You don't become better by feeling guilty or sorry for yourself, you just become worse. Guilt, shame, and self-criticism are some of the most destructive forces in our lives. That is why forgiving yourself is one of the most powerful things you can do. This doesn't mean we go repeat the same mistakes again though. We must learn from our errors and mistakes and try our best to stay away from repeated, negative actions.

This sort of thinking may be misinterpreted as deluded, self-centred thinking, and so it is important to draw some distinctions. When taking into account what others say about us, we may choose to ignore certain criticism for our mental peace, and this is fine, but this doesn't mean we should miss out on the opportunity to benefit from all outside criticism. Understand that constructive criticism plays an important role in moulding our life, and we should try to take all criticism positively. The guru of Mahant Swami, Yogiji Maharaj used to say, "If someone points out my flaws, I become happy." What? Yes, you read that right. He loved criticism. He wasn't just saying it, but countless incidents from his life reflect it.

Let's bring it a little closer to home. If different people have been telling you for a while that you're short-tempered, or that they can't be open with you because you instantly disagree with them, how would you react? Here's how we *should* act. First: Could what they are saying be true? At this point, you must be completely honest with yourself and not hide from yourself. Second: Will this information help you better yourself and the lives of others? If the answer is yes, accept and commit to making the changes in yourself; if not, let it go. There's no need to retaliate and react, because where will that get either of you? It is always easier for other people to see in us what we can't see ourselves. This is the very basis of humans fault-finding nature. But, if they can help us connect with our truths, improve ourselves, and live the more focused, authentic life, then it's worth taking criticism on board.

Principles are core to living the focused life as well. A principle is a fundamental truth that we can use to build the foundation of our lives. A principle is not merely an opinion or a belief. The point of having principles is that it shifts us from short-term survival (like other species) to long-term thriving (how we're meant to be). Most things in life are governed by principles. The eastern philosophies encompass it within dharma. The western philosophies incorporate it within virtue.

Stephen Covey explains that principles are a natural law just like gravity. Principles are different to values. Whilst values are subjective, principles are objective. We control our actions, but the consequences that flow from those actions are controlled by principles.

On Others

In the late nineteenth century, one of the founders of sociology, Emile Durkheim, performed a sort-of scholarly miracle. He gathered data from across Europe to study the factors that affect the suicide rate. His findings could be summarised in one word: constraints. No matter how he tried to parse the data, he found that people who had fewer social connections, bonds, and obligations, were more likely to take their own lives. He also found that people living alone were most likely to kill themselves; married people less; married people with children, still less.

A further hundred years of study have actually confirmed the findings of Durkheim. If you want to predict how happy and fulfilled someone is, or how long they will live (putting aside genes or personality), you should look towards their social connections. Having strong social relationships has been shown not only to strengthen the immune system, but also the longevity of life (more than quitting smoking), a speedy recovery after surgery, and reduced the risks of depression and anxiety disorders. Seneca said, "No one can live happily who has regard to himself alone and transforms everything into a question of his own utility." To live a focused life, we need to interact and connect to others; we need to reciprocate; we need to give and take; we need to belong.[1]

It's kind of a paradox though. Despite us probably knowing these facts, we're still lonelier than ever before. We spend less time outdoors than all previous generations. We are more inactive now than at any time in human history. We focus on catering our physical needs of hunger, thirst, and eliminating discomforts, but we forget to tend to our psychological needs. A recent study of 20,000 adults from Western countries found that nearly half of them felt alone. They said that they felt they didn't have meaningful in-person social interactions on a daily basis, and half of them even said they often felt that their relationships weren't meaningful, and also that they felt isolated from others. What's even more shocking is that a fifth of those surveyed said they felt like they had no one to talk to. A large proportions of adults over the age of forty-five suffer from chronic loneliness, whilst younger people (those aged 18 to 38), ironically called the most 'connected' generation in all of human history, are the single loneliest generation in recorded human history. Former Surgeon General Vivek Murthy once said, "During my years caring for patients, the most common pathology I saw was not heart disease or diabetes; it was loneliness."[2] Numerous studies show that it is possible to predict mortality by simply observing the extent to which someone has meaningful connections with others. Isolation damages us profoundly that it can fundamentally change who we are.

In 1951, researchers at McGill University paid a bunch of graduates to confine themselves in small chambers equipped with only a bed and little sensory stimulation (these studies would probably be illegal today). They were allowed to use the bathroom, but that was it. The aim was to observe the students for six weeks. The experiment came to a stop after only seven days when the participants began losing their minds and every single participant dropped out. Almost every participant lost the ability 'to think clearly' whilst several others began to suffer hallucinations. These sort of studies have been reflective of inmates in solitary confinement who become 'actively psychotic and acutely suicidal'.

I'm going to assume you understand what I'm getting at here. Human beings are social animals, and so, we need connections. We need to develop proper alliances with other kings and kingdoms – to flourish together – to flourish as one. Similar to humans, many other animals also form social groups, and in fact, the evidence shows that the more social an animal is, the more intelligent it tends to be. Studies have shown that animals that don't experience social interaction readily develop psychological problems and disturbances. Not only that, studies on monkeys have shown that the brains of monkeys raised in isolation are noticeably different to those raised in company. The point is, sociability is deeply embedded in our very being. The Mahā Upanishad echoes this with its famous verse, 'Vasudhaiva Kutambakam', meaning 'the world is one family'. We are all connected, and we all need each other in order to flourish.

Simply interacting with other people can give us a sense of fulfilment, and this is clear; the mechanism that guides our desire for social interaction is embedded in the same part of the brain that is responsible for the experience of pleasure. EEG (electroencephalogram

– a recording of brain activity) have revealed networks of neurons that display patterns of synchronised activity when two people are interacting. Other studies have revealed that people observing someone smelling something unpleasant will show activity in the areas of their brain that process disgust, and that when our brains read facial expressions the emotion that the expression reveals prompts neurological activity in the areas that process that emotion in ourselves. This is empathy, the ability to understand and share the feelings of others. What I am trying to get at is that a large part of our brain is dedicated to encouraging and facilitating social interactions.

The reverse is true too; social rejection can be dangerous and unpleasant. A study involving a simulation where subjects played a ball game and were gradually rejected by other players showed increased activity in the anterior insular and anterior cingulate cortex, cortical regions that are linked directly to the experience of pain. Social rejection is painful. Even the saying about sticks and stones is completely wrong; being called names *does* hurt. Science shows it. Studies even reveal that we instinctively dislike those who 'blank' us.

Our brains indulge in a process known as 'impression management', where we try to give the best possible impression of ourselves by influencing the perception of others. One study into the neural correlates of this process made subjects present themselves, inaccurately, in positive or negative ways, necessitating a degree of self-deception.[3] The results recorded increased activity in the medial prefrontal cortex and left ventrolateral prefrontal cortex. But what's most interesting is that raised activity was only seen when subjects had to deliberately present themselves negatively. If they had to provide positive representations of themselves, there was no change in activity. Many believe that positive affirmations can change who we become, but these studies could be telling us differently. Whereas, if we have negative thoughts, our brains are influenced greatly. Positive thinking *may* work. Negative thinking *definitely* does.

As we see the humanity of others, we learn to appreciate their suffering. We become less judgmental, more forgiving, more grateful, and less triggered. We develop compassion for others and a passion for serving. Remember, everyone is operating from some wounded state. We must always remember this. All people are suffering to some extent.

The people we relate to and interact with play a huge role in our sense of being – our identity. Scanning studies have revealed that when we contemplate being part of a group or think about those we identify with, we see increased activity in areas like the ventromedial prefrontal cortex and the anterior cingulate cortex. But these areas also show raised activity when we think about our own sense of being. The implication of this is that the groups and communities that we belong to form a key part of our identity. A *Time* magazine poll of over a thousand Americans found that the first four major sources of happiness were all to do with others. For seventy-seven per cent, their children were the major source of happiness. Friendships were a source of happiness for seventy-six per cent. Contributing to the lives of others made seventy-five per cent happy. Their relationship with their partner was a major source for seventy-three per cent.

Helping others is a critical exercise for the heart. We need to help those who aren't part of our inner circle too, and it's good for you, as well as the other person. Our interactions with others are crucial for both our physical and mental well-being.

Everyone is broken in some way. The only answer to a focused life is to love one another. The whole pain of our world today is the pain of barriers. We've had enough with loneliness, independence, and competition. We all need to be united. We all need to thrive together.

Nothing pulls individuals together more than a disaster that forces them to work together in the face of a selfish prejudice. In 2017, the United Kingdom was spared terrorist strikes in London and Manchester. Each of these tragedies exposed the evil side of human nature in the callousness of individuals to inflict pain on innocent others, as well as the majority's readiness to come to the aid of those in need. The general public reacted to these attacks with outpourings of sympathy for the surviving and relatives of the slain. Following the bombing of Ariana Grande's performance, blood donation centres in Manchester received over 1,000 calls per hour. People were moved by the plight of others and wanted to assist in any way they could.

Nurturing others helps those suffering from illness too. Studies on multiple sclerosis sufferers and those living with HIV or AIDS found that when individuals reach out to help others in the same plight, they feel greater mental well-being and have fewer visible symptoms.

In the classic book *Man's Search for Meaning*, the Nazi concentration camp survivor Viktor Frankl writes, "Being human always points, and is directed, to something, or someone, other than oneself – be it a meaning to fulfil or another human being to encounter. The more one forgets himself – by giving himself to a cause or another person to love

– the more human he is..."[4] When we open our hearts to other people and really care about them, it changes not only the way we look at the world, but also the way we act in this world.

When we put this hand-in-hand with seva and satsang, we can truly flourish in life. We enjoy positive interactions, we're compelled to see them, and forming and maintaining social relationships is a reliable source of happiness. We need to conform, we need to belong, so that we can feel safe and secure; so that we can live the focused life.

On Love

The laws of probability state that if you are around the age of twenty, you probably have another 20,000 days or so left before you pass. For the majority of time left in your life, you will spend it with a partner, your children, or your close ones. Disappointingly, despite spending so much time together, too many relationships remain either superficial, tense, or 'dry'.

For the ancient philosophers, the problem with love was obvious. Love is the cause of attachment. Buddha said, "So long as lustful desire, however small, of man for women is not controlled, so long the mind of man is not free, but is bound like a calf tied to a cow." The same applies of women for men. But as we've just explored in the previous section, we need connections, and love is essential to a good life. Whether that be with your partner, your family, or God and guru, love is fundamental to the focused life. But we must learn the distinctions between love and lust; between companionate love and passionate love. We must understand where we will find fulfilment, and where we will not.

The Dangers of Passion

Let's differentiate between passionate love and companionate love to begin with. They are both different. One doesn't turn into the other either. Passionate love and companionate love are two separate things, and they both have different time courses. Passionate love has been shown to diminish over time, as opposed to companionate love which can continue to grow. Passionate love is like a drug. In fact, its symptoms actually overlap with that of heroin (euphoric well-being) and cocaine (euphoria combined with dizziness and energy). But it's no wonder. Passionate love literally alters the chemical activity in several parts of the brain, including parts that are involved in the release of dopamine. Any experience that feels intensely good releases dopamine, and the dopamine link is crucial here because drugs that artificially raise dopamine levels, like heroin and cocaine, put you at risk of addiction. Passionate love gets you high and makes you feel good momentarily, but it also creates as many problems as it may seem to solve (just like heroin and cocaine). Those who think that passionate love is true love end up turning towards fulfilling lust alone. Don't merely go my word, even when you put science aside, take a look at history itself.

The social psychologist Ellen Berschied, at the University of Minnesota, looked into passionate love and concluded that the failure to appreciate the limited half-life of passionate love causes relationships to cripple. She and her colleagues felt that the increase in divorce rates over the past twenty years is partly linked to the increased importance individuals place on intense positive emotional experiences in their lives – experiences involving intimate and romantic love. Relationships are not all about intimate love though. If we are seeking to build a truly satisfying relationship, the best way of bringing this about is to get to know the deeper nature of the individual we are with, and relate to them on that level, instead of merely relying on the basis of superficial characteristics. A sound relationship includes a sense of responsibility and commitment to one another.

Romantic attraction is a pleasure-driven passion that carries its own unique brain chemistry, marked by fevered highs and, at times, wrenching lows. When we 'fall' in love, infatuation propels us to ride a tidal wave of overwhelmingly positive feelings, so that we see our beloved as perfection incarnate. This early bliss helps propagate the species, but it mostly tends to be fleeting. Though falling in love is an experience we all cherish, it isn't the kind of love that does the heavy lifting in life. Staying in love requires many expressions of generous behaviour other than passion and pleasure.

The Harvard psychiatrist George Vaillant, who has followed the lives of Harvard graduates for half a century, gives the example of a judge who met his wife in high school. At age sixty-five, he reported that his love was 'much deeper than at the beginning'. At age seventy-seven, he said, "As life gets shorter, I love Cecily even more."[5]

Mistaking lust for love is a growing problem in society, I need not go into much detail about this. But in our search for love, we often perceive temporary pleasures as love. We've all had the feeling that feels like love, but only to begin with, because then it fades and then we're left unsatisfied, lonely, and sometimes heartbroken. Too often we try to alleviate our pain by indulging in other forms of pleasure, or by hiding away in the corner. Successful relationships and marriages are those based not on passionate love, but on companionate love. True love, the love that is the foundation of strong marriages; the love that is between two hearts, isn't superficial or merely for the sake of social conformity. True love is simply strong companionate love with passion, but in limit, between two people who are firmly committed to one another.

Till Death Do Us Part
We, as a species, need love. When we are young, we take love from our parents, teachers, or carers. As we enter adulthood, we shift to transactional love; we love others often in the exchange for something in return – their love, security, or intimacy. Then there is complete love, where we surrender to loving someone regardless of whether they love us back or not; whether we get anything in return or not. No conditions, no exchange, just a decision to love a person and focus solely on their well-being. Probably one of the most important decisions you will make in your life is who you choose to spend the rest of your life with; who you choose to have kids with; who you choose to create a family with. Who you marry is meaningful; who you have kids with is profound. Building a life with someone who loves you, and who you love back, near guarantees a life of reward interrupted by moments of pure joy. Of course, there are always differences, but when there is true love, we learn to tolerate and let go for each other. One survey found that six in ten Americans who rate their marriage as 'very happy' also rate their life as whole as being 'very happy'. When we are dealing with trying to understand relationship issues, the first stage in the process involves deliberate reflection of the underlying nature and basis of the relationship. When the frequency of your values and beliefs match, the impact on your relationship with another is profound.

Studies show that marriage doesn't only have personal benefits, but it is also economically advantageous.[6] With a partner, you share expenses and responsibilities, you both get to focus on your careers, and it is believed that utilising the wisdom of crowds (couples) generally leads to better decision-making in life. With a partner, there is a streamlining of choices, which lets you allocate your attention on things that will help you grow. Once married, your household worth grows at an average of fourteen per cent a year. Married couples, by their fifties, on average have three times the assets of those who remain single. What's the magic key? Taking marriage seriously, as divorce literally eats into that three per cent. From a scientific perspective, monogamous relationships improve survival odds for offspring, benefitting our species overall.

In any relationship, whether that is true love or transactional, it's human nature to inflate our own contribution to the relationship and minimise the others'. We must decide, especially with our partners, if the relationship as a whole adds joy and comfort to our life, and if it does, then we must commit to always being on the positive side – aim to be generous, and do as much as you can for your partner, as often as possible. Be willing to wipe the slate clean if one or the other makes a mistake, as everyone will at some point. Studies show that forgiveness is a key attribute to sustainable, happy relationships. What often happens in relationships is that people keep score. This creates a dynamic where we never experience the real joy of life. It's all about doing something for someone because we love them and choose their happiness over everything else, full stop. Caregivers are the most important contributors to the human species, and are rewarded with longer lives. Marriage is a promise to give care, every moment of every day. Fifty per cent of marriages end in divorce. Let's make sure we're not in that other fifty per cent.

Today, we find ourselves in a very strange place in history, where we are surrounded by more people than ever before, but we are still lonely. If we lack healthy relationships, we cannot achieve optimal health, peace, or fulfilment in life. Likewise, if our relationships are suffering, we must take active responsibility of them. Loyalty truly demands a huge amount of us – especially at times when our emotions and inclinations run in another direction and love becomes a mere subdued form of duty.

A survey by the National Opinion Research Centre (NORC) at the University of Chicago, published in early 2006 and funded in part by IRUL, found that those in healthy, happy, long-term marriages were highly giving and felt strong love towards others in general. Both married men and women are less likely to die than their single counterparts – and this is especially striking in the case of men. Basically, companionship has positive impacts on well-being. When the eminent psychiatrist George Valliant, followed 456 inner-city men whose lives had begun in extreme difficulty, he found that by their mid-fifties, the nine men leading the happiest lives reported that the single greatest factor in their good fortune was a loving marriage.

In a 2005 study of 147 couples, who had been together for over twenty years, the psychologist David Fenell of the University of Colorado found that lifetime commitment was the most important quality of a happy marriage. Elizabeth Marquardt, who conducted a national survey of 1,500 young adults between the ages of eighteen and thirty-five, found that children in 'low-conflict' marriages did better if their parents made the effort to stay together rather than divorce – even if those marriages were not extremely close or happy.[7]

Men in particular see marriage and children as a package deal, and many who hold their marriages together during difficult or challenging times say that they stuck it out because they didn't want some other man living with their kids. They turn their marriages around for the sake of their kids. Fatherhood is more unstable, culturally, than motherhood.

It's important to remember that in most marriages, good times follow bad. Elizabeth Marquardt notes that even when one spouse says he or she is unhappy at a given point in time, in interviews five years later with those who stayed married, eighty per cent of the previously unhappy souses now reported being happy. We seem to have this perverse idea in our culture that if a relationship is unhappy, it's going downhill fast, and that there's no hope left, so we should just cut it off. But in many cases, people can outlast their problems and togetherness, or loyalty, can help see them through. True love doesn't only change what we do and what we have; it also changes who we are.

Love Despite Conflict
Let's go to the other end of the spectrum for a bit. For those who have never been loved, research shows that the neural networks that allow humans to love will be undeveloped. This has been shown to have major implications in those who have faced trauma, as they may be unable to fully understand and show love. But, given love, the unloved can become loving. Belonging and being loved are at the core of the human experience.

The capacity to love is at the very core of the success of humankind. We love our partners. We love our children. We love our parents. We love our friends. We love God and guru. The prime reason we've survived and thrived on this planet is that we've been able love – emotionally, socially, physically and spirituality. I'd also like to mention that although companionate love is one of life's many bespoke, personal and unique experiences, it never needs to be rushed. How we foster love and build a relationship should also be equally bespoke.

A relationship comes down to these things: how well each person in the relationship accepts responsibility, and the willingness to compromise and create boundaries where needed. People in healthy relationships have strong boundaries, but this is because they take responsibility for their own values and issues, and they don't burden their partner with either. You can confide in another, but you cannot expect them to solve a problem for you. They can hold your hand and walk alongside you in the process, but the walk is still yours alone. You shouldn't expect other people to solve your problems, that won't make them happy, nor does it make you happy. A healthy relationship is when two individuals solve their own problems in order to feel good about the company of each other. Making sacrifices for someone we care about comes from a place of wanting to, as opposed to feeling an obligation or fear of the consequences of not doing so. Love is only love when the actions for it are performed without conditions or expectations.

Emotional engagement and commitment in marriage are both keys to wives' happiness, according to a study of 5,000 by sociologists at the University of Virginia. Wives care about how much quality time they spend with their husbands. They also reported that the happiest wives are those who believe that marriage is a lifetime relationship and should never be ended except in extreme circumstances. If our topmost priority in life is to always make ourselves feel good, or to always try and make our partner feel good, then no one feels good. Our relationships begin to fall apart and we won't even realise it. There is no absence of conflict in a real relationship. Conflict itself exists to show us who is there for us unconditionally and who is just there for benefits. Conflict is not only normal, it's *absolutely necessary* for the maintenance of a healthy relationship. Whoever you choose to spend the rest of your life with, you must love them without expecting anything in return. That is true love. You must respect them without expecting anything in return. That is true respect.

On Healing

Some of us will go through phases of life where we will question things that happen to us. Why me? Why did I suffer? What did I do wrong? I'm sure it's no surprise that these are the wrong questions to ask. Humans *need* adversity. In fact, our minds also need adversity, and that's why they instinctually keep creating problems, even if there aren't any real ones in front of us. The human mind is something called antifragile, a concept that the modern philosopher Nassim Nicholas Taleb goes in-depth about in his book by the same name. It means that our minds, and us too for that matter, get better with adversity. If we deny and reject any kind of real challenges in life, our minds will compensate and create problems to overcome.

Most people are unaware that the sixteenth president of the United States, Abraham Lincoln, battled severe depression throughout his entire life. Known at the time as melancholy, his depression was often debilitating and profound. It nearly drove him to suicide on two separate occasions. Of course, he was known for his jokes and humour (which is what most of us remember him for today), but he actually suffered periods of intense brooding, isolation, and pain. Within, he struggled to manage a heavy burden that felt almost impossible to lift. His life was endured with great difficulty. He grew up in poverty. He lost his mother when he was still a child. He educated himself. He taught himself law. He experienced multiple defeats at the ballot box as he made his way through politics, and, of course, the bouts of depression, which the medical world didn't understand at the time. Lincoln's personal challenges had been so intense that he himself came to believe that they were destined for him in some way. He believed that maybe the depression was a unique experience that prepared him for greater things. He learned to endure all this, articulate it, and find advantage and meaning from it.

If we continue to look throughout history, we will see that those who have been successful and those that have truly grown, have done so through fighting the adversities that they came across. Franklin Roosevelt learnt from adversities faced during The Cold War. Viktor Frankl found meaning through the adversities he faced in the concentration camps. The guru of Pramukh Swami, Shastriji Maharaj, stared adversity in the face and grew through it too. Whether we look at the feeble, or the brave, adversity aids growth. The modern cultural obsession with chasing happiness, shielding oneself from anything triggering, the idea that life is primarily 'good', and that any challenge that we face is a mistake of fate, are what actually cause mental weakness. Shielding the mind from adversity doesn't protect it; it only makes it more vulnerable to anxiety, panic, chaos, and stress.

The Need for Adversity
In the last fifteen odd years, researchers have gone beyond resilience against adversity, and instead chosen to focus on the benefits that severe stress and adversity can have. These benefits are often referred to collectively as 'post-traumatic growth', in direct contrast to post-traumatic stress disorder (PTSD). Researchers have studied people facing a wide range of adversity, including cancer, heart disease, HIV, rape, assault, paralysis, infertility, house fires, plane crashes, and earthquakes. They've studied how people cope with the loss of their strongest attachments; whether that be their children, spouses or partners, or parents. The large body of research shows that although trauma, crisis, and tragedy come in thousands of forms, people benefit in three primary ways.

The first benefit is that rising to a challenge reveals our hidden abilities, and seeing these abilities changes our self-concept. People often say they feel numb, or like they are 'breezing through life', or on autopilot – especially after a terrible loss or trauma. Consciousness is severely altered, yet somehow their body keeps moving. People who have suffered battle in war, rape, concentration camps, or traumatic personal losses often seem to be immune against future stress. Simply put, they recover more quickly, in part because they've learnt to cope with adversity.

The second benefit is strongly linked to relationships. Adversity serves as a filter. We often develop love for those we care for, and we usually feel love and gratitude towards those who cared for us in our time of need. In a large study of bereavement, Susan Nolen-Hoeksema and her colleagues at Stanford University found that one of the most common effects of losing a loved one was that the bereaved had a greater appreciation of, and tolerance for, the other people in their life. One woman in the study, whose partner had died of cancer, said, "[The loss] enhanced my relationship with other people because I realise that time is so important, and you can waste so much effort on small, insignificant events or feelings."

This leads us to the third common benefit. Adversity, whether through trauma or struggle, changes priorities and beliefs towards the present, as well as towards other people. We've all heard grand stories about the wealthy and powerful who at the time of their death (like Alexander), had some form of self-revelatory conversion. Let's look at King Ashoka as an example.

King Ashoka, after assuming control of the Maurya empire (in central India) around 272 BCE, set out to expand his territory by conquest. He was successful. He slaughtered the masses – people and kingdoms. But after a very bloody victory over the Kalinga people, near modern-day Bhubaneswar, he was seized with horror and remorse. He converted to Buddhism, renounced all further conquest by violence, and devoted his life to creating a kingdom based on justice and respect for dharma. He wrote out his vision of a just society and his rules for virtuous behaviour, and had these edicts carved into rock walls throughout his kingdom. He even sent emissaries as far away as Greece to spread his vision of peace, virtue, and religious tolerance. Ashoka's conversion was caused by victory, not adversity, yet people are often traumatised – as modern research on soldiers indicates – by killing as well as by facing the threat of death. Like so many who experience post-traumatic growth, Ashoka too underwent a profound transformation. Adversity is how we grow.

Trauma
I believe that trauma is anything that causes us to suppress a part of our true self and/or make adaptions to our true self. Trauma can also be defined as anything that drives us to believe, subconsciously, that we are not good enough as we are. We often think of trauma in the head, in the metaphorical sense, but it is actually in your body in the literal sense. Trauma is the experience of disconnecting from a fundamental feeling of safety. It is most often associated when one's attachment to their primary caretakers is compromised. But there are actually an infinite number of ways the world can traumatise you, and all to varying degrees. Unless we are able to reestablish a connection, a particularly destructive bias distorts our worldview: We become hypersensitive, which means that we ascribe intent, overthink, overreact, become triggered by harmless stimuli, personalise neutral situations, and remain in a state of mental combat.

Of course, there are many theories about what trauma is and where it originates. Some believe that is passed down physically through our genes. Others believe that it's shared mentally and emotionally through learned patterns of behaviour and observations. Most commonly, trauma is believed to be an interpersonal experience in which one is challenged and then lacks the skills and coping mechanisms to rise to it.

Trauma is a legitimate, physical issue. We store emotions, energies, and patterns at a cellular level in our body and mind. No matter where it may come from, if you have some kind of lingering trauma, it's pretty certain that you will know, because you will feel it physically in your body. You will feel anxious, tense, fearful, full of terror, sadness, or guilt. It will be displaced. It may not even have a clear, direct cause. You will overreact to certain situations and people, and even when a problem is solved, you may still panic. These are all marks of trauma.

In his book *The Body Keeps the Score*, Dutch psychiatrist Bessel van der Kolk goes into great detail about the topic of trauma. He says that after going through a traumatic experience, as much as we try to pretend that nothing's happened and try to get on with our lives as normal, "the part of our brain that is devoted to ensuring our survival, is not very good at denial." Long after a traumatic experience is over, it can be reactivated at even the slightest sign of danger and activate brain circuits and secrete lots of stress hormones. This leads to unpleasant emotions, intense physical sensations, and impulsive and aggressive actions.[8]

After experiencing trauma, your brain rewires itself temporarily to seek out potential threats in anything, which makes it very difficult to both move on from the initial problem, and then to also not develop a victim complex. This is why exposure is so effective as a treatment for fear and anxiety. By gradually reintroducing the stressor into someone's life – and showing them that they can handle it – the brain is able to return to a neutral state because a feeling of control and security is established.

Neurologically, we process stress in three parts of the brain. The first is the amygdala, the second is the hippocampus, and the third is the prefrontal cortex. Individuals suffering from post-traumatic stress disorder (PTSD) have a smaller hippocampus (the centre of emotion and memory), increased amygdala function (the centre of rumination and creativity), and decreased medial prefrontal/anterior cingulate function (the centre that governs complex behaviours like planning and self-development). It then becomes a bit more clearer as to why trauma tends to have a somewhat positive impact on individuals.

- Our brains stop processing memory fully, leaving us with fragments of what happened, which sometimes contributes to the feeling of disassociation.
- Our ability to manage a range of emotions decreases.
- We become stifled and stuck, have trouble planning for the future, and our self-development and actualisation might come to a halt.
- When we enter a state of fight-or-flight, our body literally ceases any advanced function that is not necessary for our survival. The body's main receptors become extremely sensitive and reactive to stimuli.

Stress is a beautiful and essential part of being human that has kept us alive as a species. However, it is not a state that we want to, or is meant to be, sustained for extended periods of time.

Recovery from trauma comes down to something very simple, which is, restoring the feeling of one's safety. However, the most important part of this restoration is that we must establish a feeling of safety in the exact area of life that traumatised us. If we are traumatised by a relationship, we restore the feeling of safety by working on other healthy and safe relationships. If we are traumatised by a job loss, we restore the feeling of safety by having a backup plan. If we are traumatised by being bullied, we restore the feeling of safety by finding new friends.

In the late 1990s, the ACE (Adverse Childhood Experience) Study was published. It took more than 17,000 people who were seeing doctors for routine checkups and asked them about different areas of adverse childhood experiences. They compared the group who experiences what they called 'more ACEs' with the group the experienced none. The results were jaw dropping.[9]

As the number of ACEs a person suffered increased, so did the likelihood the person would suffer from alcoholism as an adult, experience chronic depression, be the perpetrator of more domestic violence, be a smoker, attempt suicide, have an increased chance of teen pregnancy, have serious financial problems, and serious problems performing in their job and, from a health perspective, suffer considerably more health problems including chronic illnesses, be obsessed and, on average, die twenty years younger. A long list, right?

Our childhood experiences definitely shape our later years. But at this point, it's also crucial for me the mention that correlation and causation are not necessarily one and the same, so just because two things happen at the same time, it doesn't necessarily mean one causes the other. The findings of the study, however, had so many correlations that it's difficult to ignore, that we can acknowledge at the same time, life is a complex series of countless events and it is impossible to ever truly separate true causes.

What a lot of people do is try to overcompensate in an area of life that is not the actual problem. For example, if they struggled in a relationship, they begin to hoard money to keep themselves feeling 'safe'. Of course, this is always futile, because the root problem never gets resolved. Healing yourself is returning to your most natural state. And I agree, getting to that place does require a lot. A lot of commitment. A lot of hope.

Healing
Healing requires us to take an honest inventory of our grudges, aggressions, and the reasons behind our longing and fear that we've been ignoring all this time. Healing requires us to go through the full expression of every emotion that we have cut off and buried when we decided we were no longer comfortable with them. We are meant to go through periods of adversity. It is when we must adapt our self-identity to become someone who can handle, if not thrive, in the situation that we are in. Healing is not merely what makes us feel better the fastest. It is building a better version of your life, slowly and over time.

To truly heal, you will have to change the way you think. You are going to have to become very conscious of negative and false beliefs that you might be holding onto, and start shifting your mindset to one that actually serves you. It does not serve us to use endless affirmations to placate our true feelings about where we are in our journey. This is delusional because, when we do this, we start disassociating and get stuck. In an effort to 'love ourselves', we try to validate everything about who we are. This can be damaging. And so the first step in healing anything is to take full accountability. It is no longer being in denial about the honest truth of your life and yourself. It is not okay to be constantly stressed, panicked, and unhappy. Something is wrong, and the longer you try to just 'love yourself' out of realising this, the more delusional you'll become and the longer you will suffer.

When we hold onto fear and pain after something traumatic has passed, we do it as a sort of safety net. We falsely believe that if we constantly remind ourselves of all the terrible things that we didn't see coming, we can avoid them. Not only does this not work, but it also makes us less efficient at responding to them if they do. Fear is not going to protect you. Action will. Worrying is not going to protect you. Preparing will. Overthinking is not going to protect you. Understanding will.

For almost a century, psychologists have assumed that horrible events – such as having a close one die, or becoming the victim of a violent crime – must have a powerful, devastating, and enduring impact on those who experience them. This assumption, that is today, so central to conventional wisdom is in fact wrong. The truth is that the absence of grief is quite much possible, and that rather than being fragile individuals, most people are surprisingly resilient in the face of traumatic and horrible events.

Whilst most bereaved people are quite sad for a while, very few become chronically depressed, and the majority experience relatively low levels of relatively short-lived distress. Although more than fifty per cent of people in the United States will experience a traumatic event such as rape, physical assault, or a natural disaster during their lifetime, only a small fraction will ever develop any post-traumatic pathology or require any professional counselling.

Studies of those who survive major traumas suggests that the vast majority do quite well, and that a significant portion claim that their lives were *enhanced* by the experience. The fact is that negative events do have an impact on us, but they generally don't affect us as much or for as long as we expect them to.

Chronically ill and disabled patients generally rate the value of their lives in a given health state by themselves to be in such states. Healthy people imagine that eighty-three forms of illness would be 'worse than death', and yet, people who actually have those forms of illnesses rarely take their own lives.

Consumers evaluate kitchen appliances more positively after they buy them, job seekers evaluate jobs more positively after they get into them. Our tendency to expose ourselves to information that supports our favoured conclusions is powerful in all areas of life. The human mind loves to exploit ambiguity. We will *always* come our stronger and better. Never forget this.

On Letting Go

Forgiveness is love that can only emerge when the giver has first suffered harm. We will all come to a place, sooner or later, where we must forgive another. Forgiveness frees the giver from bondage to a bitterness that could easily darken his or her view of another, or, of life itself. Dr Fred Luskin, Director of the Stanford University Forgiveness Project writes, "When your thoughts are full of bitterness, fear, self-pity and dreams of revenge, there is little room for love or for the quiet voice of guidance within you." Ironically, although forgiveness is a well-known concept to us all, we sometime misunderstand the act of forgiving others as a sign of weakness. On top of this, forgiving others is often argued as being tough to practice. It is especially difficult to forgive and to ask for forgiveness. At times, we are so caught up in anger, jealousy, resentment, and rage towards others, that we forget towards whom the real damage is inflicted upon.

There is true power and joy in letting go. African Americans in Alabama accepted Governor George Wallace's apology for his racist acts during his 1982 reelection campaign and voted for him in large numbers.[10] Forgiveness is a form of love, but it is a challenging one. When we've been harmed – and sometimes deeply so – it can feel nearly impossible to let go of outrage, anger, and grief. Vengefulness is enticing; there is almost a touch of lust to it. We want to eradicate and get back at those who have transgressed against us, or hurt us. This natural tendency is seductive, but we only end up reliving the original harm a thousand times over in our heads.

I understand that many of us may have been hurt deeply, and we need ways to deal with that hurt. Sometimes, when life pushes us to the brink, there's little else we can do than to be merciful. Not only for others, but for ourselves too. It is easier to forgive if we well and truly face the fact that, were we in another's shoes, we might also make mistakes that seem horrendous in retrospect. We need to recognise our shared humanity; we need to recognise that we are all one.

By forgiving, we restore our own faith in the essential goodness of life and all creation. And yet, the way we choose to do so always remains individual. In the last decade there has literally been an explosion of scientific and popular interest in forgiveness, and there is so much evidence showing the power of forgiveness in enhancing mental and physical health. Psychologists studying forgiveness have now outlined how forgiveness develops, what its benefits could be, and how to create effective forgiveness interventions. Remember, it is *you* that wants a focused life for *yourself*.

According to a 2003 study by Neal Krause, a research professor at the Institute of Gerontology at University of Michigan, forgiving others unconditionally is linked to well-being even more strongly than forgiving others who have earned it through remorse or an apology.[11] Forgiveness also alleviates depression – even in war-torn areas. In one school of around two-hundred children, a hundred were being treated for anxiety and depressive disorders. Those children who learnt forgiveness went from clinical depression to being non-depressed. Combat veterans suffering from PTSD suffer less depression and fewer symptoms of trauma if they are able to forgive themselves and others.[12] When people are in a more forgiving state than normal, they report higher levels of life satisfaction, fewer illness-related symptoms, and they feel they are in a better mood.

A 2005 study by Marina Butovskaya and her colleagues at the Institute of Ethnology and Anthropology in Moscow, Russia, found that reconciliation and peacemaking powered stress hormones in boys aged between seven and eleven.[13] Another study from Robert Enright found that learning to forgive improved blood flow to the heart for veterans who were cardiac patients.[14]

Forgiveness replaces pain with peace and joy. Forgiveness isn't forgetting, condoning, excusing, trusting without reason, forgoing anything, reconciling when in danger, or even forgoing justice. Forgiveness is not a simple act or a onetime gesture; nor is it a pardon in any official sense. Forgiveness is an approach to life, an active act, taken at every moment of every day – it is a work in progress. It brings with it an inner freedom, serenity, and peace that sets the tone for an entire life. Forgiveness sets us free from the burden of guilt and yet, paradoxically, frees us from pain.

One of the most common and mistaken arguments against forgiveness is that when we forgive someone, we are showing them that they can have their way – that they are winning, or have won. People ask why they should give an offender such power? But forgiveness isn't about giving away power. If we're really true to our forgiveness, a deeper excavation has to happen, and that requires courage as well as empathy.

We must also talk about rumination. Ruminating about negative situations is linked to depression, anxiety disorders, and anger. Ruminating sustains the desire for revenge, and recreates the physiological stress of the original harm. It also reinforces the victim role, which is linked with passivity and failure. Forgiving responses actually calm the mind and body. Many feel the need to relive hurt, but in reality this just makes us feel helpless. Empathy, in turn, offers a greater sense of control. We feel the most control when we imagine ways of granting forgiveness to others.

According to research carried out by psychologists Michael McCullough and Giacomo Bono of the University of Miami, "forgiveness is the other side of gratitude."[15] In most simple terms, gratitude is a positive response to benefits, whilst forgiveness is a positive response to harm.

There are four key stages to forgiveness. First is **uncovering**, where we examine the hurt to feel and acknowledge fully what effect it has had on our life. Then there is **deciding**, where we think about what forgiveness is and is not, and what it would mean to us to forgive a particular person who has harmed us. Thirdly, **understanding**. This is the time where we try to understand the person who has hurt us, and what may have motivated that person to do so. What could his or her stressors could have been, and thinking about the positive qualities of that individual, not just the bad. Finally there's **deepening**. During this phase, we may see redemptive meaning in the experience we have had. After all, everything that happens in life is a lesson we can learn from. We may be able to apply our process of being hurt and forgiving to others, offering them some compassion.

Maybe getting angry when somebody has hurt us is natural self-protective. According to the psychologist Kenneth Pargament, professor of psychology at Bowling Green State University, our first response to harm is to protect ourselves, seek safety, and find ways to conserve our well-being. Anger, fear, hurt, and resentment are actually emotional coping techniques that help us do just that.

We've all experienced these feelings, and at first they do indeed help us cope. It's only over time that they begin to erode our sense of well-being. Chronic anger can reinforce a feeling of powerlessness; chronic fear can remind us that terrible things could happen again; and with resentment and hurt comes an underlying feeling of shame and being a victim.

The Medicine of Forgiveness

I recently came across the story of a little five-year-old girl by the name of Kai Leigh Harriot, of Massachusetts, who publicly forgave the man whose bullet had paralysed her when she was only two. In court, this young African-American child with strangely luminous, soulful eyes spoke directly to Anthony Warren, "What you have done to me was wrong ... but I forgive you."[16]

Three years earlier, in 2003, Kai Leigh was sitting on the porch with her older sister when Warren, who had an argument with people living on the first floor, shot three times at the house. He wanted to shoot the person he'd got into a fight with, but he hit Kai Leigh instead. The bullet shattered her spine. In a *Boston Globe* article that followed, reporter Megan Tench noted that when another reporter asked Kai Leigh why she forgave Warren, "she shyly but clearly said, 'I wanted him to tell the world the truth. I know he didn't mean to do it.'"

The article obviously went on to quote others in the Boston area who disagreed with Kai Leigh: "He took her life, now she can't walk forever. Someone should take his life," one man was quoted. But Kai Leigh's mother, Tonya David, was inspired by her daughter. Television footage showed David hugging Warren, twenty-nine, after he apologised for shooting her daughter and just before he was sentenced to around fifteen years in state prison. She only intended on shaking his hand, she said, but he surprised her when he pulled her in for an embrace. Inspired by her daughter's strength, David said she just couldn't let the man go.

Now, I understand that each of us will have our own perspective on how much forgiveness should be granted in this sort of tragedy, but it's clear that Kai Leigh's strength and compassion not only freed her from hate, but also her mother and the man who shot her. They too experienced love rather than hate.

Forgiveness reduces the powerful mixture of anger, hatred, and fear that comes with seeing yourself as a victim of another. We can either always play the victim and wallow in self-pity, or we can forgive and grow. "High forgivers" (those who score high on forgiveness as a trait) show less reactivity in blood pressure and arterial pressure. One 2001 study found that the impact of forgiveness was truly global: from age eighteen onwards, the extent to which people reported the tendency to be forgiving strongly protected them against psychological stress.

Truly Moving On...
It may sound cliche, and you've probably heard it a hundred times but, forgiveness starts with you. The moment you decide to forgive yourself and let go of your negative feelings, you begin treading the road of freedom. Even when it comes to other people, forgiveness is about taking care of yourself, not them. It's about putting the desire for peace, before the desire to be right and superior. It's about taking responsibility for your own happiness, instead of pretending that it is in someone else's hands.

Forgiving others is uniquely and positively associated with life satisfaction after age forty-five. For older adults, as the end of life becomes a more palpable reality, the concerns of life shift to meaning, purpose, and loving others. About eighty per cent of adults are more invested in relationships than in competition or achievement.

If you find yourself ruminating over a hurt and are not ready to forgive, you can always shift to gratitude. Think about all that is good in your own life and all that you appreciate. Remember, forgiveness is a positive response to harm. By focusing on the good, you move anger and hurt away from yourself. And I have to throw this in, as the new-age cliché goes, energy flows where attention goes.

Apologies also help too. It is, in fact, the single largest predictor of forgiveness. To offer and accept an apology is really one of the most potent and poignant human interactions. More than anything, a sincere apology can truly help to restore a relationship. Studies show that someone who imagines an offender offering a strong apology feels more positive and experiences decline in heart rate and other physiological measures of stress. In other words, apology heals the recipient. If an apology seems warranted, offer it with sincerity. Apologising is not just a social nicety, it is a sign of courage and humility. Saying "I am sorry," or, "I was wrong" is an important act to bind relationships. They also help the other person trust you and feel safe around you. But most importantly, there is an unquestionable sense of freedom experienced when you apologise. Unconsciously, you release a heavy burden from your heart.

Holding onto any form of resentment is like taking a slow poison – it will slowly destroy you from within. If you're having issues with someone close to you, then it is your responsibility to explain how you feel without shifting the blame onto them, and *regardless of the result*, forgive them. At the end of the day, if you want to be free, you have to learn to let it go. If the anger or resentment you feel is to someone you really don't care about, then why hold on? Free yourself and let it go. Why do we care if they understand what they have done or not – what good does it do us? And let's not even pretend for a second that it is to make them 'improve', or, 'become a better person'. That isn't your responsibility, nor is it mine; that is there's alone. Stop seeking apologies or acknowledgement of your corrections. Get over it and let it go. The longer we remain attached to resentment, the longer negativity will linger within our minds. Once you feel that you've truly forgiven someone, wipe the slate clean. What often happens is that we form judgements about people and then, we hold onto them, and no matter what they do, we always perceive them through the lens of that judgement. This really means we haven't forgiven them; we haven't truly let go. We must release all expectations, clean the slate, and start over (if we need to, that is). What you choose to focus on, is what you will create more of, and that is what will fill your life.

We are meant for change. We are designed to evolve. Our bodies show us this as we eliminate and replace cells to the point that some believe we are essentially completely made 'new' again every seven years. Our mental and emotional growth follow a similar process, but it occurs much more often. When it comes to letting go – whether that be of a person, situation, or a result – we cannot force ourselves to do it, no matter how much we want to. We are not going to let go the moment someone tells us, 'why don't you just move on', or, 'just let it go'. We start to let go the moment we decide to take one step towards building a new life. We start to let go the moment we realise that we cannot continue to revolve around a missing gap in our life. We can only move on when we start to build something new. Too often we become mentally trapped in these places from which we still crave the experience. When we unhealthily attach ourselves to something in the past, our perspective of it is often distorted.

In reality, acceptance is simply the act of allowing yourself to move on to the next thing in life. There is nothing that will release you from your thoughts, other than having new, positive thoughts to fill your mind. It's only when we look back and say, "Hold on, I may not be okay with the fact that this happened, and I may not even ever get over it, but there are new things I must focus on in my mind and heart, and that is exactly what I'm going to do." Learn to accept the new things that come into your life, and if there aren't, put new things in your life. To let go, we must change our inner monologue. We must stop telling ourselves stories of what was and what could have been. It isn't here now, so accept it. Don't pick and choose what parts of a person or situation you want to let go of either. Let go fully. It's an all-or-nothing deal. Accept that moving on is a choice that is only in your hands. Understand that this is not a unique situation just for you, and that virtually everybody has dealt with this to a greater or lesser extent than you have.

At some point in your life, you come to understand that if you continue to protect yourself, you will never truly be free. It's that simple. We are scared, and so we lock ourselves in the palace within our minds, closing all the windows and blinds shut. In the darkness, we cannot feel the sunlight. We are trapped. Most of us go day-to-day protecting the commander within and trying to make sure nothing goes too wrong. Instead of realising this later in life, isn't it time to understand now?

> **How to Let Go**
> 1. Change your inner chatter.
> 2. Don't pick and choose what parts of the situation or individual you want to let go. Let it all go.
> 3. Change your plans.
> 4. Accept that at least for now, even if you do feel emotions towards them or the situation, you are choosing to move on anyway.
> 5. Understand that this is not a unique situation and that virtually everybody has experienced something similar to this to some extent.

How to Emotionally Detox
I'm not saying it's easy. Letting go and true forgiveness are some of life's hardest challenges. Somewhere deep down within us, there is a bank of accumulated emotions, some of which may be old and negative. Pain, regret, guilt, anger, fear, loneliness, grief, hate, worry … the list could be endless. Not only can harbouring negative thoughts and emotions hold us back from our life's full potential, but it can have a major impact on our health too. Finding ways to numb these emotions won't resolve any issues in the long-term, even though it may seem like it in the short-term. Contrary to traditional belief, crying to let your emotions out is not a sign of weakness, it is a physical form of expression of the deep-seated emotions, which creates space to let go. We must try to detach from what is going on around us, and learn to give ourselves space to reflect and feel. Many find distractions as a

means to fill up emptiness in their life, but that is exactly what they are – distractions from addressing what is truly going on within you. If you need some time out, turn off your phone, log out of social media, take a break and go for a walk. Minimise non-essential activities as much as you can so that you can focus on emotional healing and your spiritual connection to the higher power.

Physically allow yourself to increase oxygen, hydration, exercise, and rest as a way to connect to your emotional (mental) body. Be gentle and kind to yourself. Keeping a journal is a great way to start. By keeping a journal, it can help you identify negative emotions and where they might stem from, in a safe and confidential space. Journaling helps us to be really honest with ourselves – we don't need to hide, and once it is written down, it is literally out of our minds.

We Are What We Own?
Letting go also applies to the physical possessions that we hold so dearly. It is the reluctance to let go of our goods that reveals one of the most interesting aspects of human life. There are currently more self-storage facilities in the United States than McDonald's locations, despite the fact that sixty-five per cent of storage customers also have garages (most filled with hoarded items, not cars).

As soon as we get our hands on anything, we overvalue it. The 'endowment effect', as this bias is known, is one of the most robust occurrences in behavioural economics. In summary, we anticipate to receive more money when we sell an item than we would be prepared to spend to acquire the identical item. Despite popular belief, the endowment effect is not ubiquitous. When researchers began looking at different civilizations and cultures, they noticed something remarkable: the individualist-collectivist component affected the magnitude of the endowment effect.

When you think about it, we spend far more time seeking pleasures than we do consuming them. We go out to acquire more things in a never-ending, and ultimately futile attempt to improve who we are. This may make us feel more successful, but the paradox is that as we accumulate more things, we become less content. Many readers would undoubtedly disagree with the assertion that materialistic aims are unsatisfactory. In reality, people may dismiss this book's underlying warning message as irrelevant to them. Many people are persuaded that possessing more than they need would satisfy them, and their whole drive in life is based on this notion. But I have a question for you: If we were satisfied with ownership and what we possess, why don't we stop collecting more stuff?

If we value ownership just for the sake of the goods we have collected, we are validating behaviour that is ultimately damaging to others. We should live simpler, less cluttered, and less competitive lifestyles. Unfortunately, most of us do not realise this until we are towards the end of our lives. Arthur Schopenhauer warned, "Whoever attaches a lot of value to the opinions of others, pay them too much honour." And yet, who is immune to the opinions of others? Learn to let go of your ego. Let go of attachments. Let go of who you think you should be, who others think you should be. There is a surrender to what is – to the moment.

"Are you going to tell me? Or is that a secret?" He replied jokingly.
"No! Of course it's not a secret. We spoke about so much. The mind, body, and the soul. We spoke about letting go, detachment, happiness, self-discipline, spirituality, and so much more. I had so many questions, and I still do. But I can't keep bugging him."
"You know you're fortunate to have had such time with him, and I'm sure all your questions will be answered with time."
"I hope so," I responded.
"You know what? You should share these conversations with others… I mean if you want… I'm sure they'd help many other people. I know I'd love to hear about it."
"It'll give too much of a boost to my ego. I don't know if I could do that." I said lightheartedly. Deep down, I still felt this.
"Why would it? If you keep God and guru at the forefront of what you do, your ego will be silenced. After all, it is they who inspire us to do whatever we do, right?"
"I guess…"
"Then," he asked. "When will we hear these conversations?"
The clock struck, and the bell rang, as countless swamis and devotees hurriedly made their way up the grand stairs of the majestic temple. I looked up at the marvellous architecture. It almost felt like I was in a divine abode. I *was* in a divine abode. Maybe this swami, who'd sacrificed his entire life to God, guru, and society was right. Maybe there was something to what he was asking of me. After all, I was in the direct presence of Keshav. I had just had a conversation with Keshav…

Flourishing the Kingdom

> The remaining faults of the mind should be eradicated
> by contemplating 'I am the atma, separate from desires.
> In fact, I am completely blissful.'
> *Bhagwan Shri Swaminarayan*

The journey has only just begun. We've had a good discussion; a lengthy one too. The world we live in today may a difficult one, but we must accept that. We must take care of the vessel in the form of this body. We must learn to train the commander and the monkey. We must practice the arts of flourishing the soul. One step at a time.

In the Pāndava-Gitā of the Mahābhārat, Duryodhana says, "I know what is right but I am not able to practice it. I know what is wrong but I am not able to keep away from it." Duryodhana was a prince. He would have become the king. But, he failed to control his mind, realise his true self, and ultimately, he failed to maintain faith in Keshav. Our king is already within us. Keshav is always within us. We must ignite that spark and start living 'The Keshav Way; today. It's time to tread the path of the focused life.

The ubiquity and importance of modern social media platforms like Facebook and Instagram have increased our need of approval and validation from others. We know, deep down, that when we compare our accomplishments and achievements to those of others, we experience emotions of inadequacy. "Every time a friend succeeds, I die a little," novelist Gore Vidal remarked. We are continually reminded that others appear to be doing better and living more fulfilling lives than we are. We validate the worth of other people's posts by 'liking' them. We retweet their thoughts. We experience FOMO (fear of missing out), and believe that we are being overlooked whilst everyone else is being invited to the best parties.

We, like false prophets, anxiously seek followers to validate our worth. We are human meerkats, always on the lookout for potential threats in order to protect ourselves, and our groups. But instead of surveying the area for potential hazards in order to protect the group, we are socially peacocking in an effort to be recognised – desperately seeking approval.

The hedonic treadmill of social comparison, on the other hand, is a never-ending perpetual motion machine. There is also something fundamentally flawed in the notion that we must always be happy. Today's marketing and self-help industries make us feel terrible if we are unhappy, and as a result, we become progressively dissatisfied, seeking methods to improve ourselves through our purchases. To feel unhappy is normal – it's part of the human condition. Never put yourself down, or see yourself as worthless, especially when you're stuck in a deep hole. You will grow. You will emerge stronger. Have patience and faith in the God, guru, and yourself.

Real inner growth is completely dependent upon the realisation that the only way to find peace and contentment in life is to stop thinking about yourself. You grow when you let go of the 'I' inside your head. We evolve when we diminish our ego completely. When we do everything tailored around 'me', we experience dissatisfaction, discontent, and disconnection. The only way to experience inner peace is by realising this.

We live on a planet with breathtaking mountains, oceans, art, music, food, and connections, yet we've grown so accustomed to it all that we've lost sight of the wonder right in front of us. Every day, we should be thankful for the fact that we are alive. Except that the majority of us aren't. Instead, we're in agony because the outside world isn't behaving as we'd like. We have a preconceived notion of how life should be and believe that in order for us to be happy, the world must look a specific way. And when it doesn't bend to our plans and aspirations, we're disappointed and can't seem to get over it.

There are 7.7 billion other people on the planet who have their own ideas about how the world should be. Every person's tastes are moulded by the experiences and concepts they were taught as children, at school, through friends or societal norms, and whatever and whoever else has shaped their perspectives on life. Nobody is the same, and everyone has a different point of view. So, expecting this huge, cosmic work of art – something so complicated it's nearly beyond comprehension – to manifest in a unique way for each of us doesn't make much sense, does it?

Life is simply a series of moments. When we cling to a moment, believing that everything must remain exactly as it is for us to be happy, we are disappointed when it does not last forever. And when we reject the natural flow of life, we push it away. We reject moments, we push the natural flow of life away, and we don't allow ourselves to observe the higher power at work.

We simply have to surrender to Keshav. We must believe that life is constantly attempting to teach and guide us so that we can maximise our human experience and showcase our true talents. Most misery occurs because we are fixated on how life is 'supposed' to be. Despite our futile attempts, we are not the centre of the universe. We're merely visitors on this planet, passing by. Life happened before we arrived, and it will continue after we leave. Ninety-three per cent of all humans who have ever lived are no longer alive. Congratulations on being one of the eight per cent of people who are still alive despite all odds.

Your life is precious. Your life is valuable. Your existence is magnificent. Regardless of what it may seem like, this is the time to be alive. Janak woke up from his dream, and now, it is time for us to wake up too. Realise that you are distinct from your body, but take care of it. Learn to have conversations with the commander and the monkey. Limit your desires and diminish your ego – completely. See the world as one family. Live life according to dharma and righteous conduct. Find your purpose. Be compassionate. Know that world is full of suffering and pain, and only God, guru, and the ātmā are the highest truths. Detach from the results of outcomes and learn to let go. What is destined for you will always find its way to you. Serve others selflessly, dive into the world of satsang, and experience eternal bliss here and now.

Being human is the ultimate gift.

It's high time you start living it that way.

There is no greater attainment than the human birth.

There is no greater attainment than Keshav.

A Final Message

I hope this book inspires you to embark on your journey with confidence, knowing that life will unfold for you. You have an amazing opportunity to uncover your own breakthroughs and new views. I encourage you to forge your own path in order to discover the amazement and wonder that awaits you. There will never be a time when you are completely 'ready'. Take the risk anyway. If you're ready to put in the effort, you can live a lovely life of healing and participation. I'm here to encourage you, and if you ever want to talk, I'm at @the.keshav.way on Instagram, or you can contact me via my website vinaysutaria.com. I try my best to answer every message.

With my humble prayers and wishes, whilst recalling Dhruvji's prayer, I hope that you can begin living the focused life. I hope that you too can truly discover and connect to Keshav.

Vinay Sutaria
16 November 2021
Sarangpur, India

Acknowledgements

I would like offer my sincere gratitude and heartfelt prayers to His Holiness Pramukh Swami Maharaj (1921-2016), whose life and teachings have been the foundation of how I aim to live my life. My spiritual guru, His Holiness Mahant Swami Maharaj (b. 1933), who has been a constant inspiration and example in living a life of humility, integrity, divinity, and perfected character. Without their blessings, love, support and guidance, this book would never have been possible. I am eternally grateful to my gurus.

I'd also like to extend special thanks to Swamis of Neasden Temple, as well as the various swamis and Sanskrit scholars of BAPS, for their continuous insights, guidance, and support in ensuring clarity and authenticity, and for providing guidance in my times of need. Special thanks to Stuti Patel for the illustrative diagrams and drawings for this piece of work. Thanks to all the silent editors and proofreaders, who came forward and offered to read the manuscript, on top of dealing with my own endless stream of edits, reviews and changes to the text. A shoutout to Prime Graphics for the cover design and formatting.

Finally, I express my gratitude to you for the love, support, and blessings that you haven given me. To every one of my readers, family, friends, well-wishers, and supporters online. It is because of your enthusiasm and love that I even had the opportunity to put my thoughts onto paper. I hope that you enjoy my humble attempt to pass on the practical wisdom that I have shared with you.

About the Author

Vinay Sutaria is a young, budding IT professional by day, and an avid reader and writer by night. He graduated with a degree in Computer Science from the University of Leicester. Born and raised in the UK, Vinay is a well-versed speaker and is known for his powerful and inspirational oratory skills. He refers to himself as a lifelong learner, who loves to share his ideas with others. Vinay is also a member of the BABCP (British Association for Behavioural and Cognitive Psychotherapies). He regularly travels to India, where he gains new experiences and insights into philosophy, science and life. Vinay is also the author of The Keshav Way.

Connect with Vinay on Instagram:
@the.keshav.way

Vinay's Books:
The Keshav Way: An Intuitive Approach to Transform your Life
Keshav: Ancient Wisdom for Focused Living

Vinay's Website:
www.vinaysutaria.com

Notes

The Kingdom of the Soul

1. Swaminarayan's teachings are collated in a scripture known as the Vachanāmrut. This metaphor in particular is detailed in Vachanāmrut Gadhadā II-12 (The Art of Ruling). Available at anirdesh.com/vachanamrut.
2. The three bodies doctrine is referred to over twenty times in the Vachanāmrut. The first instance is in Vachanāmrut Gadhadā I-7.

Exiting the Matrix

1. Mahābhārat, Vana Parva 313.116
2. Ware, B. (2012). *The top five regrets of the dying: A life transformed by the dearly departing.* Hay House, Inc.
3. Barlett, D. L., & Steele, J. B. (2004). *Howard Hughes: His Life & Madness.* WW Norton & Company.

Prāna - The Life Force

1. Harvold, E. P., Tomer, B. S., Vargervik, K., & Chierici, G. (1981). Primate experiments on oral respiration. *American journal of orthodontics, 79*(4), 359-372.
2. Burhenne, M. (2015). *The 8-Hour Sleep Paradox.* Mark Burhenne, DDS.
3. Ashley, F., Kannel, W. B., Sorlie, P. D., & Masson, R. (1975). Pulmonary function: relation to aging, cigarette habit, and mortality: the Framingham Study. *Annals of Internal Medicine, 82*(6), 739-745.

Architecting the Kingdom

1. Williamson, A. M., & Feyer, A. M. (2000). Moderate sleep deprivation produces impairments in cognitive and motor performance equivalent to legally prescribed levels of alcohol intoxication. *Occupational and environmental medicine, 57*(10), 649-655.
2. Nota, J. A., Hermanson, J. V., & Coles, M. E. (2021). Sleep disturbance is associated with less emotional reactivity in individuals with heightened repetitive negative thinking. *Current Psychology,* 1-9.
3. Mitler, M. M., Carskadon, M. A., Czeisier, C. A., Dement, W. C., Dinges, D. F., & Graeber, R. C. (1988). Catastrophes, sleep, and public policy: consensus report. *Sleep, 11*(1), 100-109.
4. Malik, S. W., & Kaplan, J. (2005). Sleep deprivation. *Primary care: Clinics in office practice, 32*(2), 475-490.
5. Colbert, A., Yee, N., & George, G. (2016). The digital workforce and the workplace of the future.

⁶ Nederkoorn, C., Vancleef, L., Wilkenhöner, A., Claes, L., & Havermans, R. C. (2016). Self-inflicted pain out of boredom. *Psychiatry research, 237,* 127-132.

⁷ Guthold, R., Stevens, G. A., Riley, L. M., & Bull, F. C. (2018). Worldwide trends in insufficient physical activity from 2001 to 2016: a pooled analysis of 358 population-based surveys with 1· 9 million participants. *The lancet global health,* 6(10), e1077-e1086.

⁸ Pasiakos, S. M., Margolis, L. M., Murphy, N. E., McClung, H. L., Martini, S., Gundersen, Y., ... & McClung, J. P. (2016). Effects of exercise mode, energy, and macronutrient interventions on inflammation during military training. *Physiological reports,* 4(11), e12820.

⁹ Owen, N., Healy, G. N., Matthews, C. E., & Dunstan, D. W. (2010). Too much sitting: the population-health science of sedentary behavior. *Exercise and sport sciences reviews,* 38(3), 105.

¹⁰ Baddeley, B., Sornalingam, S., & Cooper, M. (2016). Sitting is the new smoking: where do we stand?. *British Journal of General Practice,* 66(646), 258-258.

¹¹ *Research shows walking increases blood flow in the brain.* New Mexico Highlands University. (2017, April 24). Retrieved September 18, 2021, from https://www.nmhu.edu/research-shows-walking-increases-blood-flow-brain/

¹² University, S. (2014, April 24). *Stanford study finds walking improves creativity.* Stanford News. Retrieved September 18, 2021, from https://news.stanford.edu/2014/04/24/walking-vs-sitting-042414/

¹³ Khatri, P., Blumenthal, J. A., Babyak, M. A., Craighead, W. E., Herman, S., Baldewicz, T., ... & Krishnan, K. R. (2001). Effects of exercise training on cognitive functioning among depressed older men and women. *Journal of aging and physical activity,* 9(1), 43-57.

The Commander and His Monkey

¹ Milton, J. (2018). *Paradise lost* (pp. 163-178). ARC, Amsterdam University Press.

² Bhagavad Gita 6.6

³ Swamini Vato (English Edition), 5/130

⁴ Katha Upanishad 1.3.3

⁵ Daniel Kahneman gives the idea System 1 (Thinker – the commander) and System 2 (Feeler – the monkey) in his book, (2011) *Thinking, Fast and Slow.*

⁶ Haidt, J. (2006). *The happiness hypothesis: Finding modern truth in ancient wisdom.* Basic books.

Ego: It's All About Me

1. Menon, M. K., & Sharland, A. (2011). Narcissism, exploitative attitudes, and academic dishonesty: An exploratory investigation of reality versus myth. *Journal of Education for Business, 86*(1), 50-55.
2. Chidester, D. (1991). *Salvation and Suicide: Jim Jones, the Peoples Temple, and Jonestown.* Indiana University Press.
3. Sassoon, J. (2019). State of repression: Iraq under Saddam Hussein, by Lisa Blaydes.
4. Ballard, R. D., & Crean, P. (1988). *Exploring the Titanic* (p. 64). New York: Scholastic.
5. Purushottam Bolya Prite (English Edition), pg. 359
6. Twenge, J. M., & Foster, J. D. (2010). Birth cohort increases in narcissistic personality traits among American college students, 1982–2009. *Social Psychological and Personality Science, 1*(1), 99-106.
7. Mathews, J. (2006). For math students, self-esteem might not equal high scores. *Washington Post, 18.*
8. Csikszentmihalyi, M., & Csikszentmihaly, M. (1990). *Flow: The psychology of optimal experience* (Vol. 1990). New York: Harper & Row.
9. Bloom, P. (2013). *Just babies: The origins of good and evil.* Broadway Books.
10. Engelmann, J. M., Herrmann, E., & Tomasello, M. (2012). Five-year olds, but not chimpanzees, attempt to manage their reputations. *PLoS One, 7*(10), e48433.
11. Greene, J. D. (2013). *Moral tribes: Emotion, reason, and the gap between us and them.* Penguin.
12. Gazzaniga, M. S. (2000). Human-The Science Behind What Makes Us Unique.
13. Anderson, E., Siegel, E. H., Bliss-Moreau, E., & Barrett, L. F. (2011). The visual impact of gossip. *Science, 332*(6036), 1446-1448.
14. Bloom, P. (2005). *Descartes' baby: How the science of child development explains what makes us human.* Random House.
15. Tappin, B. M., & McKay, R. T. (2017). The illusion of moral superiority. Social Psychological and Personality Science, 8 (6), 623–631.
16. Epley, N. (2015). *Mindwise: Why we misunderstand what others think, believe, feel, and want.* Vintage.
17. Ledford, H. (2014). We dislike being alone with our thoughts. *Nature: International Weekly Journal of Science, 3.*
18. Sapolsky, R. M. (2017). *Behave: The biology of humans at our best and worst.* Penguin.
19. Mehta, K., Kramer, H., Durazo-Arvizu, R., Cao, G., Tong, L., & Rao, M. (2015). Depression in the US population during the time periods surrounding the great recession. *The Journal of clinical psychiatry, 76*(4), 0-0.
20. Barr, B., Taylor-Robinson, D., Scott-Samuel, A., McKee, M., & Stuckler, D. (2012). Suicides associated with the 2008-10 economic recession in England: time trend analysis. *Bmj, 345,* e5142.
21. Reeves, A., McKee, M., & Stuckler, D. (2014). Economic suicides in the

great recession in Europe and North America. *The British Journal of Psychiatry, 205*(3), 246-247.
22. Dixon, J. C. (2020). Understanding perceived worker insecurity in Europe, 2002–2016: economic freedom and neoliberalism as alternative theories?. *Sociological Perspectives, 63*(1), 5-28.
23. Young-Eisendrath, P. (2008). *The self-esteem trap: Raising confident and compassionate kids in an age of self-importance*. Hachette+ ORM.
24. Moran, L. (2012). Desire for Fame: Scale Development. *Psychology and Marketing, 29*(9), 680-689.
25. Johnson, A. M., & McSmith, A. (2006). Children say being famous is best thing in the world. *The Independent*.
26. Gazzaniga, M. S. (1998). The split brain revisited. *Scientific American, 279*(1), 50-55.
27. Gazzaniga, M. S., & LeDoux, J. E. (2013). *The integrated mind*. Springer Science & Business Media.
28. Tappin, B. M., & McKay, R. T. (2017). The illusion of moral superiority. Social Psychological and Personality Science, 8 (6), 623–631.
29. Croyle, R. T., Loftus, E. F., Barger, S. D., Sun, Y. C., Hart, M., & Gettig, J. (2006). How well do people recall risk factor test results? Accuracy and bias among cholesterol screening participants. *Health Psychology, 25*(3), 425.
30. Brock, T. C., & Balloun, J. L. (1967). Behavioral receptivity to dissonant information. *Journal of personality and social psychology, 6*(4p1), 413.
31. Van der Velde, F. W., Van der Pligt, J., & Hooykaas, C. (1994). Perceiving AIDS-related risk: Accuracy as a function of differences in actual risk. *Health Psychology, 13*(1), 25.
32. Dawson, E., Savitsky, K., & Dunning, D. (2006). Don't Tell Me. *I Don't Want to Know*.
33. Alicke, M. D., & Govorun, O. (2005). The better-than-average effect. *The self in social judgment, 1*, 85-106.
34. Isaacson, W. (2015). Steve Jobs (London. *Abacus*.)
35. Hood, B. (2012). *The self illusion: How the social brain creates identity*. Oxford University Press.
36. Petrus, G. M., Lewis, D., & Maas, C. S. (2007). Anatomic considerations for treatment with botulinum toxin. *Facial Plastic Surgery Clinics, 15*(1), 1-9.
37. Demand for Botox boomed during the pandemic. Here's how to know if it's right for you. Retrieved 19 September 2021, from https://www.insider.com/what-is-botox-why-is-it-popular-cosmetic-procedure-wrinkles-2021-4
38. Consumer Resources - News and Trends - New Study Suggests Young Adults More Approving of Cosmetic Surgery. Retrieved 19 September 2021, from https://www.surgery.org/consumers/consumer-resources/news-and-trends/new-study-suggests-young-adults-more-approving-of-cosmetic-surgery
39. Skin Cancer Facts & Statistics - The Skin Cancer Foundation. Retrieved 19 September 2021, from https://www.skincancer.org/skin-cancer-

40. information/skin-cancer-facts/
41. Lemaitre, B. (2016). Connecting the obesity and the narcissism epidemics. *Medical hypotheses, 95*, 10-19.
42. Cole, D. A. (1989). Psychopathology of adolescent suicide: Hopelessness, coping beliefs, and depression. *Journal of abnormal psychology, 98*(3), 248.
43. Watts, A. (1951). *The wisdom of insecurity: A message for an age of anxiety.* Vintage.
44. Collins, J. C., & Collins, J. (2009). *How the mighty fall: And why some companies never give in.* Random House.
45. Neff, K. D., & Vonk, R. (2009). Self-compassion versus global self-esteem: Two different ways of relating to oneself. *Journal of personality, 77*(1), 23-50.
46. Vachanāmrut (English Edition), Gadhadā I-20

Desire: The Source of Suffering

1. Vālmiki Rāmāyan 9.9.13
2. De Graaf, J. (2002). Affluenza: The all-consuming epidemic. *Environmental Management and Health.*
3. Gen Nexters Say Getting Rich is Their Generation's Top Goal. Retrieved 19 September 2021, from https://www.pewresearch.org/fact-tank/2007/01/23/gen-nexters-say-getting-rich-is-their-generations-top-goal
4. For India's Newly Rich Farmers, Limos Won't Do (Published 2010). Retrieved 19 September 2021, from https://www.nytimes.com/2010/03/19/world/asia/19india.html
5. Jaikumar, S., & Sarin, A. (2015). Conspicuous consumption and income inequality in an emerging economy: evidence from India. *Marketing Letters, 26*(3), 279-292.
6. Trump knew a 'scary' amount about Bill Gates' daughter's looks, says Microsoft founder. Retrieved 19 September 2021, from https://www.independent.co.uk/news/world/americas/donald-trump-bill-gates-hiv-hpv-daughter-jennifer-looks-helicopter-a8357141.html
7. Kasser, T. (2002). *The high price of materialism.* MIT press.
8. Kasser, T. (2002). *The high price of materialism.* MIT press.
9. Villiger, L., Schwander, M., Schürch, L., Stanisic, L., & Brönnimann, S. (2017). The" Royal Charter" Storm of 1859.
10. Oh, D., Shafir, E., & Todorov, A. (2020). Economic status cues from clothes affect perceived competence from faces. *Nature human behaviour, 4*(3), 287-293.
11. Isoda, M. (2021). Socially relative reward valuation in the primate brain. *Current Opinion in Neurobiology, 68*, 15-22.
12. Douglas, J. E., & Olshaker, M. (1998). *Mindhunter: Inside the FBI's elite serial crime unit.* Simon and Schuster.
13. Chesler, P. (2015). When women commit honor killings. *Middle East Quarterly.*
14. Instagram Rich List 2020 hopperhq.com

[15] Tiptoeing on Social Media's Tightrope. Retrieved 19 September 2021, from https://www.washingtonpost.com/graphics/2019/entertainment/lele-pons/
[16] Sapolsky, R. M. (2017). *Behave: The biology of humans at our best and worst.* Penguin.
[17] Buss, D. M. (2019). *Evolutionary psychology: The new science of the mind.* Routledge.
[18] Evans, R. J. (2015). *The Third Reich in history and memory.* Oxford University Press, USA.
[19] Evans, R. J. (2005). *The coming of the Third Reich* (Vol. 1). Penguin.
[20] Kershaw, I. (2001). *The" Hitler Myth": Image and Reality in the Third Reich.* Oxford University Press, USA.
[21] Evans, R. J. (2006). *The third Reich in power* (Vol. 2). Penguin.
[22] Lindner, E. (2006). *Making enemies: Humiliation and international conflict.* Greenwood Publishing Group.
[23] Hansen, G. C. (1965). Alexander und die Brahmanen. *Klio, 43*(1), 351-380.
[24] Vachanāmrut (English Edition), Loya 10
[25] Mahābhārat Shānti Parva 205.6
[26] Frederick, S., & Loewenstein, G. Hedonic Adaption. *Well-Being: The Foundations of Hedonic Psychology,* 302-29.
[27] Paraphrased from Vachanāmrut (English Edition), Gadhadā II-47
[28] Lieberman, D. Z., & Long, M. E. (2018). *The Molecule of More: How a Single Chemical in Your Brain Drives Love, Sex, and Creativity—and Will Determine the Fate of the Human Race.* BenBella Books.
[29] Katha Upanishad 2.3.14

Anger: A Brief Insanity

[1] Lavergne, G. M. (1997). *A sniper in the tower: The Charles Whitman murders.* University of North Texas Press.

The Fault of Fault-Finding

[1] Wright, R. (2010). *The moral animal: Why we are, the way we are: The new science of evolutionary psychology.* Vintage.
[2] Heine, S. J., & Lehman, D. R. (1999). Culture, self-discrepancies, and self-satisfaction. *Personality and Social Psychology Bulletin, 25*(8), 915-925.
[3] Dunning, D., Meyerowitz, J. A., & Holzberg, A. D. (1989). Ambiguity and self-evaluation: The role of idiosyncratic trait definitions in self-serving assessments of ability. *Journal of personality and social psychology, 57*(6), 1082.
[4] Pronin, E., Lin, D. Y., & Ross, L. (2002). The bias blind spot: Perception of bias in self and others. *Personality and Social Psychology Bulletin, 28*(3), 369-381.
[5] Baumeister, R. F. (1999). *Evil: Inside human violence and cruelty.* Macmillan.
[6] Glover, J. (2012). *Humanity: A moral history of the twentieth century.* Yale University Press.

The Modern Battles

1. Americans Check Their Phones 96 Times a Day - Asurion. Retrieved 19 September 2021, from https://www.asurion.com/about/press-releases/americans-check-their-phones-96-times-a-day
2. RootMetrics. Retrieved 19 September 2021, from https://rootmetrics.com/en-US/content/rootmetrics-survey-results-are-in-mobile-consumer-lifestyles
3. Helft, M. (2011). The class that built apps, and fortunes. *The New York Times*, 7.
4. Fogg, B. J. (2009, April). A behavior model for persuasive design. In *Proceedings of the 4th international Conference on Persuasive Technology* (pp. 1-7).
5. Teen social media use may increase risk of mental health problems. Retrieved 19 September 2021, from https://hub.jhu.edu/2019/09/11/social-media-teen-mental-health
6. Holt-Lunstad, J., Smith, T. B., Baker, M., Harris, T., & Stephenson, D. (2015). Loneliness and social isolation as risk factors for mortality: a meta-analytic review. *Perspectives on psychological science*, 10(2), 227-237.
7. Stratton, J. (2020). Death and the spectacle in television and social media. *Television & New Media*, 21(1), 3-24.

Training the Monkey Mind

1. Bhagavad Gītā 8.15
2. Isaacson, W. (2015). Steve Jobs. Abacus
3. Robinson, P. (2005). *The CNN effect: The myth of news, foreign policy and intervention*. Routledge.
4. Aurelius, M. (2013). *Marcus Aurelius: Meditations, Books 1-6*. Oxford University Press.
5. Hanh, T. N. (2002). *Anger: Wisdom for cooling the flames*. Penguin.
6. Folger, J. P., Poole, M. S., & Stutman, R. K. (2021). *Working through conflict: Strategies for relationships, groups, and organizations*. Routledge.
7. Frank, A. (2010). *Anne Frank: The diary of a young girl*. New York.
8. Müller, M. (2013). *Anne Frank: The Biography*. A&C Black.
9. Vachanāmrut (English Edition), Gadhadā I-38: In this talk, Swaminarayan stresses upon the need to daily reflect on ones actions in order to continuously improve on the personal and spiritual path.
10. Popova, M. Celebrated Writers on the Creative Benefits of Keeping a Diary. Retrieved 19 September 2021, from https://bit.ly/keshav-famous-journalists
11. Power, B. Dear Diary... The surprising health benefits of journaling. Retrieved 19 September 2021, from https://bit.ly/keshav-journal
12. Bhagavad Gītā 2.47
13. Del Maestro, R. F. (1998). Leonardo da Vinci: the search for the soul.

Journal of neurosurgery, 89(5), 874-887.
14   Yajur Veda
15   Eagleman, D. (2015). *The brain: The story of you.* Canongate Books.
16   Oakley, B., Sejnowski, T., & McConville, A. (2018). *Learning how to learn: How to succeed in school without spending all your time studying; a guide for kids and teens.* Penguin.
17   Baumeister, R. F., & Vohs, K. D. (2003). Willpower, choice, and self-control.
18   Newport, C. (2016). *Deep work: Rules for focused success in a distracted world.* Hachette UK.
19   Lazar, S. W., Kerr, C. E., Wasserman, R. H., Gray, J. R., Greve, D. N., Treadway, M. T., ... & Fischl, B. (2005). Meditation experience is associated with increased cortical thickness. *Neuroreport, 16*(17), 1893.

The Art of Dharma

1   Olivelle, P. (2008). 6. Semantic History of Dharma: The Middle and Late Vedic Periods. 6. *Semantic History of Dharma*, 1000-1018.
2   In the Shikshāpatri, Swaminarayan writes: *Dharma Gneyo Sadachar (Righteous conduct is dharma).* This is also echoed throughout Hindu scripture, including the Mahābhārat Moksha Dharma and Yajnavalkya Smruti.
3   Bhagavad Gitā 3.35
4   Ware, B. (2012). *The top five regrets of the dying: A life transformed by the dearly departing.* Hay House, Inc.
5   Amid Cheers, a Message: 'They Will Be Caught' (Published 2011). Retrieved 19 September 2021, from https://www.nytimes.com/2011/05/02/nyregion/amid-cheers-a-message-they-will-be-caught.html
6   Davies, W. (2015). *The happiness industry: How the government and big business sold us well-being.* Verso Books.
7   Fleming, P. (2015). *The mythology of work.* University of Chicago Press Economics Books; Pink, D. H. (2011). *Drive: The surprising truth about what motivates us.* Penguin.
8   Dittmar, H., Bond, R., Hurst, M., & Kasser, T. (2014). The relationship between materialism and personal well-being: A meta-analysis. *Journal of personality and social psychology, 107*(5), 879.
9   Marshall, C. W. (2003). *Shattering the glass slipper.* M Power Resources.
10 Bhāgavata-Purāna 8.7.44
11 Srinivasan, A. V. (1984). *A Hindu Primer: Yaksha Prashna.* Periplus Line LLC.
12 White, R. C. (2009). *A. Lincoln: a biography.* Random House.
13 Singer, T., & Bolz, M. (2013). *Compassion: Bridging practice and science.* Max Planck Institute for Human Cognitive and Brain Sciences.
14 Greene, J. D. (2013). *Moral tribes: Emotion, reason, and the gap between us and them.* Penguin.

The Art of Knowledge

1. Benedict, J., & Keteyian, A. (2018). *Tiger Woods*. Simon and Schuster.
2. Good news: The world is getting better. Bad news: You were wrong about how things have changed. Retrieved 19 September 2021, from https://www.weforum.org/agenda/2018/08/good-news-the-world-is-getting-better-bad-news-you-were-wrong-about-how-things-have-changed/
3. Rosling, H. (2019). *Factfulness*. Flammarion; Pinker, S. (2018). *Enlightenment now: The case for reason, science, humanism, and progress*. Penguin.
4. Roser, M., & Ortiz-Ospina, E. (2017). Global rise of education. *Our World in Data*.
5. Pinker, S. (2011). *The better angels of our nature: The decline of violence in history and its causes*. Penguin UK.
6. Pinker, S. (2018). *Enlightenment now: The case for reason, science, humanism, and progress*. Penguin. p. 214-32
7. Ibid., p. 199–213.
8. Internet Users in the World by Regions, June 30, 2018, pie chart, InternetWorldStats.com, https://www.internetworldstats.com/stats.htm.
9. Extreme poverty is falling: How is poverty changing for higher poverty lines?. Retrieved 19 September 2021, from https://ourworldindata.org/poverty-at-higher-poverty-lines
10. Pinker, S. (2011). *The better angels of our nature: The decline of violence in history and its causes*. Penguin UK. p. 249–67.
11. Pinker, S. (2018). *Enlightenment now: The case for reason, science, humanism, and progress*. Penguin. p. 53–61.
12. Ibid., pp. 79–96.
13. Orenstein, W. A., & Ahmed, R. (2017). Simply put: Vaccination saves lives.
14. Klerman, G. L., & Weissman, M. M. (1989). Increasing rates of depression. *Jama*, 261(15), 2229-2235.
15. Weissman, M. M., Wickramaratne, P., Greenwald, S., Hsu, H., Ouellette, R., Robins, L. N., ... & Hallmayer, J. (1992). The changing rate of major depression: Cross-national comparisons. *JAMA*, 268(21), 3098-3105.
16. Herbst, C. M. (2011). 'Paradoxical'decline? Another look at the relative reduction in female happiness. *Journal of Economic Psychology*, 32(5), 773-788.
17. Cohen, S., & Janicki-Deverts, D. E. N. I. S. E. (2012). Who's stressed? Distributions of psychological stress in the United States in probability samples from 1983, 2006, and 2009 1. *Journal of applied social psychology*, 42(6), 1320-1334.
18. Newswire, M. New Cigna Study Reveals Loneliness at Epidemic Levels in America. Retrieved 19 September 2021, from https://www.multivu.com/players/English/8294451-cigna-us-loneliness-survey/
19. The Edelman Trust Index finds a continued decline in social trust across most of the developed world. See "The 2018 World Trust Barometer: World Report," Retrieved 19 September 2021, from https://www.edelman.com/sites/g/files/aatuss191/files/

2018-10/2018_Edelman_Trust_Barometer_Global_Report_FEB.pdf
20 McPherson, M., Smith-Lovin, L., & Brashears, M. E. (2006). Social isolation in America: Changes in core discussion networks over two decades. *American sociological review*, 71(3), 353-375.
21 Mandela, N. (2008). *Long walk to freedom: The autobiography of Nelson Mandela*. Hachette UK.
22 Retrieved 19 September 2021, from https://wjh-www.harvard.edu/~dtg/LEVARI2018COMPLETE.pdf
23 Durkheim, E. (2014). *The rules of sociological method: and selected texts on sociology and its method*. Simon and Schuster.
24 Bhāgavata-Purāna 1.2.11
25 Shwetashvatara Upanishad 6.21
26 Shwetashvatara Upanishad 4.10
27 Hume, D. (2003). *A treatise of human nature*. Courier Corporation. Hume writes that "all knowledge degenerates into probability; and this probability is greater or less, according to our experience of the veracity or deceitfulness of our understanding, and according to the simplicity or intricacy of the question" (1739, part 4, section 1).
28 Mundaka Upanishad 1.2.12
29 Bhāgavata-Purāna 11.3.21
30 Bhagavad-Gītā 4.34
31 Bhāgavata-Purāna 9.4.68
32 Bhāgavata-Purāna 11.9.29

The Art of Detachment

1 Bhagavad-Gītā 2.47
2 Bhagavad-Gītā 2.71
3 Josephson, M. (2019). *Edison: A biography*. Plunkett Lake Press.
4 Blundell, J. (2008). *Margaret Thatcher: a portrait of the Iron Lady*. Algora Publishing.

The Art of Bhakti

1 Oman, D., Thoresen, C. E., & McMahon, K. (1999). Volunteerism and mortality among the community-dwelling elderly. *Journal of health psychology*, 4(3), 301-316.
2 Wilson, J., & Musick, M. (1999). The effects of volunteering on the volunteer. *Law and contemporary problems*, 62(4), 141-168.
3 Harris, A. H., & Thoresen, C. E. (2005). Volunteering is associated with delayed mortality in older people: analysis of the longitudinal study of aging. *Journal of Health Psychology*, 10(6), 739-752.
4 Warneken, F., & Tomasello, M. (2006). Altruistic helping in human infants and young chimpanzees. *science*, 311(5765), 1301-1303.
5 Tomasello, M. (2009). *Why we cooperate: Based on the 2008 Tanner lectures on human values at Stanford*. A Boston review book.

⁶ Smith, J. R., & Haslam, A. (Eds.). (2017). *Social psychology: Revisiting the classic studies*. Sage.

The Art of Ruling

¹ Baumeister, R. F., & Leary, M. R. (1995). The need to belong: desire for interpersonal attachments as a fundamental human motivation. *Psychological bulletin, 117*(3), 497.

² Murthy, V. H., & Murthy, V. H. (2020). *Together*. Harper Collins Publishers.

³ Farrow, T. F., Burgess, J., Wilkinson, I. D., & Hunter, M. D. (2015). Neural correlates of self-deception and impression-management. *Neuropsychologia, 67*, 159-174.

⁴ Frankl, V. E. (1985). *Man's search for meaning*. Simon and Schuster.

⁵ Vaillant, C. O., & Vaillant, G. E. (1993). Is the U-curve of marital satisfaction an illusion? A 40-year study of marriage. *Journal of Marriage and the Family*, 230-239.

⁶ Zissimopoulos, J. M., Karney, B. R., & Rauer, A. J. (2015). Marriage and economic well being at older ages. *Review of Economics of the Household, 13*(1), 1-35.

⁷ Fenell, D. L. (1993). Characteristics of long-term first marriages. *Journal of Mental Health Counseling*.

⁸ Van der Kolk, B. (2014). *The body keeps the score: Mind, brain and body in the transformation of trauma*. Penguin UK.

⁹ Carlson, J. S., Yohannan, J., Darr, C. L., Turley, M. R., Larez, N. A., & Perfect, M. M. (2020). Prevalence of adverse childhood experiences in school-aged youth: A systematic review (1990–2015). *International Journal of School & Educational Psychology, 8*(sup1), 2-23.

¹⁰ Battistella, E. L. (2014). *Sorry about that: The language of public apology*. OUP Us.

¹¹ Krause, N., & Ellison, C. G. (2003). Forgiveness by God, forgiveness of others, and psychological well–being in late life. *Journal for the scientific study of religion, 42*(1), 77-93.

¹² Karaırmak, Ö., & Güloğlu, B. (2014). Forgiveness and PTSD among veterans: The mediating role of anger and negative affect. *Psychiatry research, 219*(3), 536-542.

¹³ Butovskaya, M. L., Boyko, E. Y., Selverova, N. B., & Ermakova, I. V. (2005). The hormonal basis of reconciliation in humans. *Journal of physiological anthropology and applied human science, 24*(4), 333-337.

¹⁴ Waltman, M. A., Russell, D. C., Coyle, C. T., Enright, R. D., Holter, A. C., & M. Swoboda, C. (2009). The effects of a forgiveness intervention on patients with coronary artery disease. *Psychology and Health, 24*(1), 11-27.

¹⁵ Bono, G., Emmons, R. A., & McCullough, M. E. (2004). Gratitude in practice and the practice of gratitude. *Positive psychology in practice*, 464-481.

¹⁶ Hurd, H. M. (2006). The morality of mercy. *Ohio St. J. Crim. L., 4*, 389.

www.ingramcontent.com/pod-product-compliance
Lightning Source LLC
Chambersburg PA
CBHW021429080526
44588CB00009B/474